PIAGET AND KNOWING

PIAGET AND KNOWING
Studies in Genetic Epistemology

edited by
BERYL A. GEBER

ROUTLEDGE & KEGAN PAUL
London, Henley and Boston

First published in 1977
by Routledge & Kegan Paul Ltd
39 Store Street,
London WC1E 7DD,
Broadway House,
Newtown Road,
Henley-on-Thames,
Oxon RG9 1EN and
9 Park Street,
Boston, Mass. 02108, USA
Printed in Great Britain
by Unwin Brothers Limited,
The Gresham Press, Old Woking, Surrey
A Member of the Staples Printing Group

ISBN 0 7100 8500 1

CONTENTS

PREFACE viii

INTRODUCTION: ON KNOWING
Beryl A. Geber 1

Part one COGNITION AND EPISTEMOLOGY 13

1 EMPIRICISM AND PSYCHOANALYSIS:
A PIAGETIAN RESOLUTION
Roger Holmes 16

Part two DEVELOPMENTAL CHANGES IN UNDERSTANDING 49

2 LOGICAL INFERENCES AND DEVELOPMENT
Peter E. Bryant 53

3 THE OPERATIVE AND FIGURATIVE ASPECTS OF
KNOWLEDGE IN PIAGET'S THEORY
Hans G. Furth 65

4 OPERATIVITY, LANGUAGE AND MEMORY IN
YOUNG CHILDREN
Eric A. Lunzer 82

Part three EXAMINATIONS OF PIAGET'S THEORIES 115

5 THE THEORY OF FORMAL OPERATIONS -
A CRITIQUE
Peter C. Wason 119

v

6   AN EXAMINATION OF PIAGET'S THEORY OF
PERCEPTION
W.H.N. Hotopf   136

Part four   INTERACTION IN THE DEVELOPMENT OF
COGNITIONS   175

7   TIME CONCEPTS AND TENSE FORMS IN
CHILDREN'S SPEECH
Gisela Szagun   179

8   TOWARDS A DEVELOPMENTAL SOCIAL
PSYCHOLOGY
Beryl A. Geber   208

INDEX   250

CONTRIBUTORS

PETER BRYANT is Lecturer in Psychology at the Institute of Experimental Psychology, University of Oxford

HANS FURTH is Professor of Psychology at Catholic University, Washington D.C.

BERYL A. GEBER is Lecturer in Social Psychology, London School of Economics and Political Science, University of London.

ROGER HOLMES is Senior Lecturer in Industrial and Social Psychology, London School of Economics and Political Science, University of London.

W.H.N. HOTOPF is Professor of Psychology at London School of Economics and Political Science, University of London.

ERIC A. LUNZER is Professor of Education at the University of Nottingham.

GISELA SZAGUN was formerly a student in the Department of Social Psychology, London School of Economics and Political Science, University of London.

PETER C. WASON is Reader is Psycholinguistics, University College, London.

PREFACE

There is an interesting progression to the student's
contact with psychology.   When the young man or woman
first decides that psychology is really what he most
wishes to study he is quite certain about the nature
and possibilities of the discipline.   Year after year
interviewing prospective students one learns that
psychology is the study of behaviour - hopefully human,
but not necessarily so - and that it helps one to
understand people.   It is all so simple, so straight-
forward, so total.   This is stage one: an understanding of psychology through a glorious global, head-on
attack.

This stage does not survive long into the first years
of undergraduate life.   In the face of the frontal
attack psychology fragments, its spurious simplicity
and coherence fractured.   Like a distracted traveller
the student is led into by-ways and narrow alleys,
losing the certainty of following a single main route.
The side roads are interesting, even fascinating, but
it is not always easy, in this stage of the student's
contact with psychology, to bring together these separate ways into a clear topography of psychology.
Increasing distinctions between the paths as they are
travelled frequently produce a sense of loss, of
bewilderment; there is a need to reconstruct the
separate ways into a 'true' representation of the
'reality' which has been lost.   And so from the dis-
tractions of stage two to the synthesis which marks
stage three.

Attempts at synthesis do on occasion give new
insights into psychological processes.   But they
commonly serve a more important function - they allow
the student to feel the master of his subject, to
attain a sense of competence and of operative under-

standing. Synthesis also marks the gaps, inconsistencies and the inadequacies in current theory and
research which may not appear until it is clear that
the parts do not fit together into an acceptable
facsimile of the conceived whole. It is from these
discrepancies, discovered in attempts at synthesis,
that new research can arise.

The fourth stage in the student's contact with psychology marks a return from synthesis to fragmentation.
A discrepancy, a problem of some sort, is now dissected,
its minutiae examined, its structure and mode of
functioning put under the intellectual microscope.
The focus is narrow, penetrating. It is this stage
that characterises empirical psychology.

Quite often the student, his headlong assault on
psychology leaving him holding but a segment of the
whole, finds the process of synthesis almost impossible.
And the researcher and teacher, absorbed in the challen-
ging details of their researches, are not always able
to help put the parts together again. For the research
psychologist too, working along a fairly narrow problem-
bounded part of psychology, what is happening outside
his immediate area of interest is often unknown, and
the relation of his work to other developments in psychology is not always clear.

It was these twin problems - helping students synthesise separate aspects of psychology and, as research
workers, familiarising each other with our own thinking
- that prompted the series of seminars on which this
volume is based. It represents an integration of a
number of separate researches all of which are concerned, in one way or another, with the basic problem
of how we know. This book, like its associated
seminars, represents not only the interests of the
authors but also the needs of students, both undergraduate and graduate, for whom it has been prepared.

The seminars were held in the Psychology Department
at the London School of Economics and Political
Science, and drew upon only a portion of those psychologists who were working in this, and related areas.
Its aim was to focus on synthesis through examination
of the relevance of the theories of Jean Piaget to
particular research areas in psychology.

This is not the first volume to owe its existence to
the impetus given to psychology by Piaget. It will
certainly not be the last, nor the most comprehensive.
What it aims to do is to present an integration of some
of the research problems that are current by showing
how each is concerned with the problem of knowing and

understanding and how together they throw light on some
of the issues raised by Piaget.

The London School of Economics was a particularly
appropriate venue for these seminars concerned as it is
with the social sciencies.   It is these disciplines
that reflect our conception of the workings of society,
be the context political, economic, geographical or
sociological.   What the seminars aimed to do was to
investigate some of the psychological processes involved in the development of our conceptual system.
As we shall later argue, one of the major implications
of psychological studies of cognition after Piaget is
that the way we conceive of our world, particularly the
causal relationships we imply, reflects closely the
current status of our view of the development of knowledge.

The preparation of this book has involved many
people.   Each of the contributors has been aided by
research assistants or associates and many of the papers
reflect comments and criticisms made during their presentation at the seminar series.   As editor I have been
encouraged by the patience and forebearance of all my
co-authors.   I have been particularly fortunate in
being able to call on Professor Norman Hotopf, who
organised the initial seminar series and whose brain-
child this volume is, for help and advice.   Dr Peter
Wason, whose kindness resulted in him being especially
consulted, is owed particular gratitude.   I should like
also to thank Routledge & Kegan Paul for permission to
publish in slightly altered form Roger Holmes's paper
from 'Legitimacy and the Politics of the Knowable',
London, Routledge & Kegan Paul, 1976.

My colleagues in the Department of Social Psychology
at the London School of Economics have shown considerable interest in this volume and have been encouraging
when the inevitable crises occurred.   To all of them,
to the secretaries who have prepared the manuscripts,
and to Michael, Jan and Nicholas who were always around,
my thanks.

BERYL A. GEBER
London School of Economics

INTRODUCTION: ON KNOWING
Beryl A. Geber

This is a volume concerned with the question of knowing, with how we realise and understand the world around us, both physical and social, concrete and abstract. The immediacy of many of our transactions with the world, and indeed with each other, masks the complexity of the process by which these transactions occur. Whether tinkering with motor-car engines, or working out new recipes in the kitchen, budgeting our expenditure to fit our income or reading a novel, we are engaged in making assumptions on the basis of our knowledge and adjusting our expectations in the light of what actually, or even potentially, happens. Even in less obviously intellectual pursuits, such as recognising objects or trying to catch the eye of a busy shop assistant, the observed action is based on sets of relatively complex, interlocking expectations. The speed of many judgments and decisions belies the complexity that goes into their making.

In a similar fashion the certainty with which we decide on a course of action or with which we assign labels to objects and assign objects to categories belies the changing nature of the assumptions on which they are founded. We are all aware of the charm and humour of the child's errors in thinking: that water poured from one beaker into another taller and thinner is now *more* water, that the sun is called 'sun' because it *is* the sun and shines. We expect these oddities in childhood, we expect them to disappear in adulthood. These are clear alterations in the structure of the concepts on which we base our assumptions. Yet even as adults the forms of our thought are not static, and certainly historically thought and knowledge, in its content, has undergone change as remarkable as that of child to adult.

1

How we achieve knowledge and the nature of the corpus acquired have been matters of concern to philosophers and scientists throughout time. This is not the place to summarise the history of their speculations and conjectures, nor to describe the methods devised for their testing. What is worth noting, however, is that the psychologist, studying the process of knowing - both the acquisition and the use of knowledge - does so against a long and honourable tradition.

The concern with knowing, with the process of cognition, is central to psychology. It is central not simply because we need to understand the operation of this process within the context of the subjects of our discipline, but also because understanding the growth of knowledge and the process by which we know reflects back onto the status of the discipline of psychology itself. Whether it is unique in this regard is a matter of speculation, but certainly the study of knowing has a reflexive function for psychology. The status of our own data, of our own speculations and research, is affected by the evidence that we accumulate about the development of knowledge in the individual.

The idea that understanding the process by which the individual acquires knowledge can illuminate the more general epistemological process is an important one, and one that reflects the debt that we owe to Jean Piaget. For Piaget the study of the development of knowledge in the individual through his life space is an important method for investigating the more extensive issue of the development of our epistemological system - 'the problem of knowledge, the so-called epistemological problem, cannot be considered separately from the problem of the development of intelligence' (Piaget, 1970, p. 704).

The relevance of studies of cognition for psychological theory is therefore twofold - it describes and explains the processing of information by the individual and his development and utilisation of knowledge and reflexively illuminates the processes by which psychological knowledge is constructed. There are implications for the body of psychology in the models we build of cognitive functioning. And, of course, the opposite also applies. The concern of psychologists for a science based on observable public data leads not only to suspicion of the mental and mentalistic, but also to a model of behaviour and of cognition which is distinctly mechanistic. A mechanistic predictive discipline describes mechanistic predictable responses.

There are inherent limitations in the mechanistic model, even in the area where it has traditionally had strong support, namely learning. Recent evidence from learning studies strains considerably the assumptions on which this model is based (see Sameroff 1971, for a discussion of this), and certainly in describing the development of knowledge the model is not of great value. And yet, discarding the model may well mean altering our ideas about the nature of psychology itself. If we are to support a transactional, or even a dialectical model, where the subject and the object define each other and can alter their nature in the process thereof, what does this imply for the nature of psychology?

We are only now beginning to understand the full impact on our scientific assumptions of a general system's theory such as that of Van Bertalanffy. And of a perspective such as that of Piaget's: 'the limit between subject and object is in no way determined beforehand and what is more important, is not stable' (Piaget, 1970, p. 704). This perspective, which implies that objectivity is in no way an initial property, demands the notion of knowledge being constructed out of the interaction between subject and object. The structures so constructed are not given in the objects, nor in the subjects, but in the interactions between them. What students of cognition now have to do is to explicate the process by which structures are built, understand the organisation of such structures, and account for both their stability and change.

Mechanistic models, tied to the observable, suspicious of the mentalistic, can only aim for descriptive representations of the psychological visible. To use a term of Piaget's (Piaget, 1970, p. 717), they are indices, signifiers that are not differentiated from their significants and imply a relatively static view of knowledge. What these cannot do is account for change - knowledge, both personal and psychological, is seen as a fact, not as a process.

Throughout his exceptionally productive career Piaget has charted the development in the child of particular types of intellectual structures, concentrating on the dynamic processes by which these come about. The process is anchored on the one hand to the biological evolutionary history of the species and on the other to the historical and cultural milieu within which life occurs. This duality, looking both to biology and to society, permits his theory

great explanatory range.   It can be of relevance to
the student of perception, of memory and of learning
as much as to the student of language development, of
education and of social behaviour.   Piaget's
writings serve admirably as a structure on which one
may attempt to synthesise and integrate separate
strands of development in psychology itself.   The
theories have value not only in themselves, not only
in their reflexive impact on psychology but also as
a bond between separate strands of psychological
endeavour.   The chapters which follow will reflect
this commonality.

The tributes to the work of Piaget are to be found
not.only in the volumes analysing his theory and presenting supporting research, but also in the number
of simplified descriptions of his theoretical position
provided for teachers, social workers, laymen and
even psychologists.   A further description in the
context of this book seems redundant.   Individual
authors will be drawing attention to specific aspects
of the theory relevant to their own research.   There
are, however, certain assumptions about the development of knowledge which Piaget makes, which should be
discussed in order to provide a frame for the separate
papers.   It is also important to emphasise that the
theory of Piaget is constantly being modified.
Piaget has referred, quite rightly, to himself as
'one of the chief "revisionists of Piaget"' (Piaget,
1970, p. 703).   It is one of the excitements of
working in this area that there is a fluidity, a
sense of movement and of change, in the relationship
between the theory and the research.

Piaget's theory assumes that the same explanation
is involved in three processes: the adaptation of
the organism to its environment during growth, the
adaptation of intelligence in the course of the construction of its own structures, and finally the
establishment of epistemological or cognitive relations.   All of these involve sets of structures constructed and continuously reconstructed in interaction
between the subject and the external world.   The
central concept of the theory is that in order to
know something one must act upon it and therefore
transform it;   and related to this, that structures
are the result of construction.   'The living organism
is not a mere mirror image of the properties of its
environment.   It evolves a structure which is constructed step by step in the course of epigenesis ...'
(Piaget, 1970, p. 705).

Piaget has described the development of structures, through the processes of assimilation and accommodation. Assimilation is the integration of external elements or input into existing structures.   All behaviour, in his system, is grafted onto existing structures, and therefore involves assimilation.   If however only assimilation were involved we could not account for change or development: for Piaget there can be no assimilation of input to existing structures without these structures being modified thereby.   This counterpart to assimilation is accommodation and refers to the modification of a structure by the elements it assimilates.   Cognitive adaptation consists of an equilibrium between assimilation and accommodation. The ratio of accommodation to assimilation in any activity may vary 'but as long as assimilation and accommodation are in equilibrium ... we are back in the proper domain of intelligence' (Piaget, 1970, p. 709).

The fundamental equilibrium between accommodation and assimilation is attained with greater or lesser difficulty depending on the level of development reached and the nature of the problems encountered. The theory describes the process of stages of development necessary for the attainment of true or proper intelligence.   Research by Piaget and his associates has traced the developmental stages or principal periods of development, in the construction of knowledge of space, time, movement, number, cause and so on.   Integrated into the general theory are the processes of language, play, imitation, perception, memory and representation, so that the theory, although frequently variously interpreted by others, presents the potential for linking many different lines of psychological endeavour.

It is worth mentioning a distinction that Piaget makes between two types of knowledge - operative and figurative.   The operative aspect of knowledge refers to those activities that attempt to transform reality whereas the figurative only attempt to represent reality as it appears.   The first embodies what Piaget calls the 'knowledge-as-assimilation' hypothesis (Piaget and Inhelder, 1971, p. 384), the second is 'knowledge-as-copy'.   For Piaget's theoretical system the distinction between these two aspects of knowledge is critical, and although both theses (knowledge-as-assimilation and knowledge-as-copy) share the hypothesis that the object exists, they differ in the way they regard our acquisition of knowledge

of that object.   If one accepts the knowledge-as-copy
view then the perception of, and image induced by, the
object are sufficient to provide knowledge and all that
action does is to smooth out the errors which might
occur;   the epistemological problem is that of matching
the phenomenon and its image.

The operative aspect of knowledge, however, assumes
that one knows the object by acting upon it in order
to transform it, and that one discovers its properties
through these transformation.   Cognition is not based
simply on the object but on the interaction between
the subject and the object 'resulting from the action
and reaction of the two' (Piaget and Inhelder, 1971,
p. 387).   It refers to two types of acquisition, one
relating to the interconnections between properties of
the object, the other to the co-ordination of the
actions themselves, which need to be structured - 'the
laws of the object are only discovered and established
through the instrumentality of the operational structures, since they alone make possible the processes of
relating or corresponding ...' (Piaget and Inhelder,
1971, pp. 387-8).

Both these aspects of knowledge, the figurative and
the operative, are involved in cognition, but imply
different things and emphasise different elements.
They do, however, interact in so far as the operative
function serves in the structuring of the figurative
aspects, and for Piaget knowledge always presupposes
the intervention of action;   knowledge is not a passive
copy of external reality, but transcends and transforms
it.

We therefore have a theory of knowledge which
emphasises the active construction of knowledge, the
interaction of the subject and object.   Knowledge
develops, it is a dynamic process, influenced both by
the social environment and the process of maturation.
The process of development is an invariant sequence of
stages, with each stage necessary for the formation of
the next;   the basic processes of assimilation and
accommodation would demand this much.

This dependence of the stage on the antecedent ones
emphasises the advantages of a developmental, onto-
genetic approach to cognitive functioning.   The
understanding of what occurs at one moment in time is
enhanced by what came before and what follows, and
indeed it is conceivable that only by putting a
behaviour into a time context can it be fully understood.   Because psychological processes are complex
and multi-determined it is always tempting in trying

to understand them to separate them from their time-
space context.   Indeed, it is tempting too, to
separate processes from each other, perception from
memory, memory from language and so on.   This time-
space isolation is perfectly legitimate but unless
one recognises that this separation has occurred it
is possible to misinterpret one's observations.

Many actions which are taken to indicate deep-
seated, constant personality traits, may be more
appropriately explained by reference to the social
context;   it is shown in studies judging emotion from
photographs that accuracy is increased by knowing the
situation in which the photograph was taken, and by
knowing the preceding condition of the subject.
Errors of interpretation can be minimised by increasing
the contextual information against which judgment is
made.   This is not to deny value to studies which
ignore contextual issues, only to point to their
limitations.

In a similar fashion it is possible to examine psychological functioning without reference to a time
dimension: there are however insights which are best
afforded by the use of an extended time period and an
examination of development and change during that
time.   There is nothing discreditable in ignoring the
developmental perspective, but it remains true that
certain questions are best answered by reference to
this perspective.   Take, as an example, the vexed
question of the relationship between language and
thought.

It is certainly clear from the literature that many
of the major theses about the question of linguistic
determinism or of cognitive independence from the
mould of language were posed without recourse to observation of children, and answered similarly.   However, it is also equally apparent from the recent
exciting advances in studies of language and thought
that utilising a developmental perspective provides a
dimension which considerably sharpens the evidence on
which to base one's eventual conclusion.   Similarly,
social psychologists have asked and answered questions
about the relationship of the individual and his group
without examining changes in this relationship over
time, particularly over the individual's life span.
This is not to say that they have ignored children,
but rather that they have regarded children as adults
manqués.   And very often children have been studied
simply because they were available and not for any
theoretical reason.   They never questioned whether

groups of children were equivalent to groups of adults and whether the dynamic processes within these groups are similar. Even though the evidence may indeed support the view that groups of children are not really different from groups of adults, what is important is that the idea of a developmental relativity was not even raised. Concern with outcome rather than with process, is often associated with a mechanistic model even though lip-service may be paid to the dynamic processes within the group. And it is not only social psychology that can be faulted: many other studies of children do not adopt a long timescale, allowing for a truly developmental perspective. The implications of their observations for psychological theory are therefore often obscure.

The link between social psychology and development has been forged on two levels. The first refers to anthropological literature and makes assumptions about societal change and economic development: McClelland and Atkinson's work on the historical and social correlates of achievement motivation is one such example. Making cross-cultural reference or examining developments within one social group over a period of time demands the adoption of a dynamic framework of analysis, and this implies that we can specify antecedent and consequent conditions. It is sometimes easier to do this if one assumes that these sets of conditions are themselves fixed and unchanging: indeed we frequently in our socialisation prepare children for yesterday or today, rather than for an as yet unknown future. This idea that development is the process of movement between two fixed points may allow for a spurious dynamism within a closed system, but not for the uncertainty of change and growth within an open one.

The second link between development and social psychology is forged through the individual, though concern with the mechanisms and processes of socialisation. Traditionally socialisation theory espoused a model of the passive child moulded by the active society, a mechanistic rather than a dialectic approach: it was essentially an environmentalist view of growth. Recent research has moved the nature-nurture pendulum back to the nature end of the continuum, and the evidence both of the competence of the infant and the orderliness of development have demanded a change in the assumption of the inertness of the infant. The overall, orderly pattern of development reported by Piaget has, as Kelvin (1970) has shown, important

implications for the social psychologist's interpretation of socialisation. Kelvin suggests that whereas
socialisation, that is adjustment to, and adoption of,
group behaviours and attitudes, continues throughout
life it takes different forms in childhood from
adulthood - 'the child becomes socialised by accepting
norms of behaviour; the adult becomes socialised by
accepting norms concerning values' (Kelvin, 1970,
p. 271).

The transition between these two types of socialisation may well be better understood by reference to
Piaget, more particularly to the change from specific
concrete and action-related relationships which
characterise early thought to thought which is more
general, abstract and transcends immediate environmental constraints. The implication of this change,
as Kelvin indicates, is that 'The child has ... to
learn *what* to do before he has the capacity to reason
out fully *why* to do it' (Kelvin, 1970, p. 272), and
further

he has to start to cope with the demands of the
social environment long before he can fully understand the reasons for these demands ... he has to
learn to act as if he accepted the values of his
community or culture, long before he can have any
notion of these often highly abstract values (ibid.).

The implication of this developmental change for
social behaviour and social cognition is only now
slowly being understood. It raises a number of
questions about social control, about responsibility
and about the conception of the social reality. It
also raises points about social behaviour and social
norms; answering these questions would propel us
forward in our conceptualisation of social man.

Whenever we have had to consider questions about
the nature of man it has proved necessary to look at
the very earliest behaviours available to us. There
is no value in looking at an ancient, much experienced,
well-lived, old gentleman to resolve the issue of the
relative contribution of heredity and environment to
behaviour: nor is there much value in examining only
one such case. It has been shown necessary to look
at the responses of new-born infants in many situations
and contexts in order to begin to establish the limitations and flexibility of the infants' capacities.
Similarly, we can only gain a limited insight into
the social nature of man - whether he is unquestion-
ably social or has to learn to become so; whether he
is 'naturally' selfish and aggressive or whether

society makes him so - by ignoring developmental
changes.   The choice between viewing man as did
Rousseau or as did Hobbes can be debated and argued
with reference to personal ideology: it can only be
sustained by observation of the developing human.
In arguing for the use of an historical perspective
in understanding the family and the relationship
between parents and children, Philippe Ariès (1962)
writes

> I can tell the particular nature of a period in the
> past from the degree to which it fails to resemble
> our present.   This dialectic of past and present
> can be fairly safely neglected by historians of
> 'short periods' but it must be used in the study of
> manners and feelings whose variations extend over
> a 'long period' (p. 9).

It can justifiably be argued that understanding man
demands a similarly time-related study.

The implication of all of this for psychology shows
our indebtedness to Piaget.   Piaget is certainly not
unique in calling for studies of change over the
individual's life-span, nor even in suggesting that a
developmental perspective is essential for understanding intelligence and epistemology.   Werner and Bruner
amongst others lay stress on describing the pattern
of development and explaining the ontogenesis of relatively mature cognition.   Where Piaget makes his
particular contribution is in the range of problems
and the variety of areas to which his articulated
theory can be applied.   We are indebted to him in
bringing to our attention the potential for relating
a number of separate psychological processes and
domains of content directly, as well as through a
developmental perspective.

Understanding cognition, discovering the stages
involved in getting to know the world in which we live
and understanding ourselves as well, examining the
historical and the life-space context of change and
of growth, these are some of the benefits Piaget's
writings have brought.   But theories adjust to information and to criticism in a manner analogous to that
of the accommodation of schema.   The theory, like
all scientific theories, must be amenable to testing,
to change, to falsification.   In the papers that
follow a number of such examinations are presented;
they are presented in an order which reflects the
matters raised in this chapter.

REFERENCES

ARIES, P. (1962), 'The History of Childhood', New York: Vintage Books.

KELVIN, P. (1970), 'The Bases of Social Behavior', London: Holt, Rinehart & Winston.

PIAGET, J. (1970), Piaget's Theory, in P. Mussen (ed.), 'Carmichael's Manual of Child Psychology', vol. 1, New York: Wiley.

PIAGET, J. (1972), 'Psychology and Epistemology: Towards a Theory of Knowledge', Harmondsworth: Penguin Books.

PIAGET, J. and INHELDER, B. (1971), 'Mental Imagery in the Child.   A study of the development of imaginal representation', London: Routledge & Kegan Paul.

SAMEROFF, A.J. (1971), Can Conditioned Responses be Established in the New-born Infant?, 'Devel. Psychol.', vol. 5, pp. 1-12.

Part one

COGNITION AND EPISTEMOLOGY

Piaget raises the question of the relations of epistemology to the ontogeny of intelligence: he suggests
that by understanding the growth of intelligence within
the developing individual we will reflect the processes
which occur in the development of epistemological
systems. His particular dialectical constructivist
approach to knowing is however only one way in which
the process can be construed. The empiricist tradition for instance embodies the notion that fact and
reality are 'out there', waiting to be found and
examined by tools which are independent of the examiner.
The object and the subject can be separately described.
This empiricist tradition is an attractive one for
science and certainly continues to inform a great
deal of research, but it has implications which are
different from those of Piaget's constructivist structuralism. And certainly the empirical tradition
differs from one whose basis is subjective exploration,
the psychoanalytic. For psychoanalysis, the influence
of which is implicit in a wide range of psychological
explanation, reality is subjective and resides within
the perceiver. Searching the external world for that
which is 'real' does not necessarily reveal answers.

Psychology has been divided between these opposing
views of the source of knowledge and of the associated
models of man. The paper by Roger Holmes which constitutes this section of the book examines the conflict
between empiricism and psychoanalysis and proposes a
resolution of this conflict in terms of Piaget's
theoretical system. Holmes describes the apparent
basis for conflict between the systems and demonstrates
the fallacious basis for this conflict. It is concerned with the derivation of knowledge and illustrates
the use to which Piaget's theory can be put beyond the
description of individual development.

15

Chapter 1

EMPIRICISM AND PSYCHOANALYSIS: A Piagetian resolution

Roger Holmes

Psychoanalysts and experimental psychologists are not always mutually at ease. They may not read each other's paper, attend each other's conferences, or even try to see the other's point of view. In this paper I shall argue that such a situation is no simple consequence of specialised concern - those with common interests coming together to discuss - but the result of something more important. For each side feels, not just that the other side rejects it (though of course it does to some extent) but also that such rejection is in some way desirable; desirable - for the other could be a threat.

In this paper I shall attempt first to point out the nature of this conflict; second, to account for its occlusion, and last to show how an acceptance of Piaget's approach could modify this divisive state of things. Piaget, it will be argued, can show how all of us - empiricists and psychoanalysts alike - can come to terms with what the other has to say.

First, the nature of the conflict between the two approaches. This may, perhaps, be illustrated in terms of the 'present' and the 'past'. Any statement made at any time can be seen in two different ways: we can either see it as reflecting what is actually 'there' or, on the other hand, as showing us how someone feels. The first of these, what someone sees - the contribution from the outside world - will be called the 'present'; the second, what someone 'feels' - a contribution from the inside - the 'past'. The pure case of the 'present' would be something visually wholly unambiguous, like Nelson's Column in Trafalgar Square, the pure case of the 'past' would be a dream.

Now the conflict between psychoanalysis and the rest can be summed up by saying that, whereas the empiricist concerns himself with the 'present', that which reflects not the observer but the observed, the psychoanalyst concerns himself with the 'past' - not with the observed but with the observer.

Perhaps as good a point as any to talk about the beginning of empiricism is the invention of Galileo's telescope. Anyone, provided that they were adequately sighted, looking down the telescope would see Jupiter's moons. So successful was this telescope, indeed, that the only way an observer could preserve his 'past' virginity was to refuse to look down it at all. The empiricist learned his lesson. Wherever possible he has preferred data that speak with their own voice, particularly those immediate data known as sensory 'facts'. Somewhat lower in the empiricist's scheme of things come those constructions known as 'theories', because theories are more open to personal choice; quite excluded has been the rampant subjectivity of wanton 'phantasy'.

Very different is the psychoanalyst. He is not interested in what is actually 'there'. Indeed, if everyone saw what was actually 'there', the psychoanalyst would not be in business at all. He is interested in the past, the idiosyncratic history we all have had. And he is interested in the past in the particular way - not just as a subject of public discourse, but as a locus of a particular, 'private' cause. 'Private' in that it reflects not the behaviour but the feelings of those concerned - feelings that hold their own validity. The experienced motive, the wish, what will here loosely be called 'the Will' - even if unconscious - is held to be the key.

So there's our conflict: on the one hand the 'public present', on the other, the 'private past'. The conflict does not end there, it expands with its very elaboration. With every advance in their respective disciplines, the two orders are driven further and further apart. For the empiricist, any 'cause' (that is, identifiable, lawful antecedent) is not only many-sided but also something apart, alien and distant from that which he explains. The fear of the empiricist is always that he should be accused of that twentieth-century form of scientific heresy - 'circularity' - explaining something by recourse to itself. This is just what the psychoanalyst does - for him causality is inward and unique: he appeals to a limited set of forces that lie 'within'. For him the relevant cause is in the motive of the person

concerned, a motive defined in the experience of that
very person - that which is to be explained enfolding
its own point of origin.   The stress on the unconscious nature of psychoanalytic causation has obscured
the circularity of this position and given the notion
of psychoanalytic cause a spurious independence.
That psychoanalysts prefer unconscious motives is
neither here nor there - for even if unconscious they
remain the feelings of the person that is to be
explained, feelings that, it is hoped, psychotherapy
will bring to his awareness.   Far more truly unconscious are the empiricist's own causes - no one can
possibly have a clue as to how the injection of certain
drugs can, say, make him feel differently.

It will be the thesis of this paper that this self-
perpetuating division between the 'public present' and
the 'private past' is illegitimate, that it impov-
erishes our notion of what is 'there'.

Neither side, when they come down to it - whatever
their philosophical sophistications - subscribe to
the view that 'reality' can only be a reality as
stated or observed by someone.   Reality is taken to
be 'there' by empiricist and psychoanalyst alike.
Not 'as seen by someone', just 'there'.   The result
is that both sides believe that there can be a final
separation of the knower from the known.   Thus each
can remain distinct - the one personal and intimate,
the other impersonal and blind.

This duality brings great advantages.   For since
they are distinct, one can declare irrelevant what
cannot be absorbed.   One can write off the subjective
(or the objective) as of no concern.   The two can be
considered, quite literally, different 'universes of
discourse', that do not impinge.   And is not this
course justified?   Without a separate 'self' would we
exist at all?   And without a separate 'outside',
would we not be totally alone?

Certainly our partisans - both empiricist and
psychoanalyst alike - would seem to think so.   They
both agree that they themselves and the outside world
are both 'really there' in some ontologically primary
sort of way.   Not only do they assert it, but, having
done so they then declare as 'pathological' anyone who
does not agree.   In this they have good precedent:
the notion of the 'pathological' (or the 'deviant',
the 'heretical', or the 'revisionist') has been the
necessary escape clause for every self-sufficient
moral, political or epistemological system there ever
was.

This time however it is doing rather better. The notion of the 'pathological', with its concomitant assumption of unquestioned 'health', performs the unlikely feat of making it possible for two conflicting approaches to exist at once. And is, in consequence, welcomed by them both.

The psychoanalyst welcomes it with open arms. As much as any empiricist, the psychoanalyst takes the notion of the external reality for granted - it is the touchstone of mental health, no less. He does so for two reasons - it gives him a professional identity, and it preserves his explanatory assumptions intact. It gives him a professional identity since he is one of the ones who specialise in these 'pathological cases'. The 'pathological' is his concern. And just as well too, for if his subject-matter were not special, he would find himself alongside other psychologists - and so in danger of being absorbed.

He can preserve his explanatory assumptions intact since it allows him to lose interest in that which would, to say the least of it, put a severe strain upon his system of explanation. For how could psychoanalysis - that which stresses the inner, private past - ever account for the apparent non-existence of that private past? How can those who specialise in distortion - and explain distortion in terms of ever earlier distortion - escape the closed explanatory world that the notion of 'distortion' implies? They do not escape or even see the need to do so, for they feel no trap. That people grow up and achieve objectivity is not seen as a problem, as of course it should be. Psychoanalysis resorts to the empirically self-evident to save it from its greatest theoretical difficulty of all -`how it can, *in its own terms* account for its later non-existence.

The empiricist can certainly account for that. By definition - his whole system of explanation is based on the assumption that the 'public present' can override the 'private past'. Not only this, but the empiricist will then go ahead and proscribe - as 'unreliable' or 'subjective' - any awareness that does not have this conclusive force. Only facts can count.

But facts are self-defining - or rather defined by the very fact that they can be observed. And this is their great weakness. For that which is accepted without question cannot be absorbed into any wider context. 'Facts' in consequence are epistemologically alone, quite as much as the psychoanalyst's

'will'.   For how can they be integrated with non-facts?
- for instance, theories?   How, furthermore, can they
be integrated with a prioris of a different kind?   Not
just the 'will', just mentioned, but also, for instance
numbers.   That two plus two equals four is declared
equally absolute and secure, but granted this, what
then is the relationship between facts and numbers?
Both of these are seen as quite distinct, and, being
distinct, need not be related.   That which is self-
evident need have no past.

And thus it is the world is divided into a trinity
of primitive existences - facts, feelings and taut-
ologies (the old distinction of the Vienna Circle)
each solitary in its inviolable sphere.

But what happens when the observer does not oblige?
When someone looks down the telescope and does not see
Jupiter's moons?   When someone insists that two plus
two equals five?   This, of course, is where the
psychoanalyst comes in and since people always have a
motive, whatever its causal status may be, the psychoanalyst can always find something to say.   But what
can the empiricist do?   He cannot resort, as can the
psychoanalyst, to the inner experiential wish - his
whole approach stresses the message and not the
listener, the enduring 'public' not the vagrant 'past'.

What he can do is - just like the psychoanalyst -
bring in the idea of 'health' to save the day.   Just
as the psychoanalysts can use the 'obviousness' of
that which does not interest him - the public present -
to preserve the inviolability of his private past, so
too can the empiricist, in a very similar way, invoke
the private past (or something very like it) to preserve the inviolability of his public present.
Thanks to the convenient notion of 'pathology', those
who do not see are written off as witnesses;   their
testimony is used as reflecting what they 'are' and
not what is 'there'.   The suspected observer, being
'pathological', becomes an object of study in a
special way.   Something must be wrong with him:
subject becomes object and the empiricist violates
one of the prime articles of his scientific approach
and renders that approach invulnerable.

And so something must be done - and that something
is none less than the abandonment of our idea both of
the public present and also of that which gives the
public present its human aid and comfort, our idea of
'health'.   We must abandon that there is but one
'present' that all 'right-minded' men subscribe to.
That people should agree at all must be seen as the

problem to be resolved, not the base line on which to build.

This suggested re-phrasing of the problem of the known is drastic indeed, far more drastic than appears at first sight.   It can be shown that it not only presents us as a problem that which erstwhile justi- fied itself - the public present - it does something a good deal more unnerving than that - it sets us the task of accounting for how we ever come to agree on anything at all: how we ever come to the awareness that areas of circumstances can be called 'the same'.

And that in turn has consequences - namely, how we ever can define.

This last consequence is perhaps the most far- reaching of them all.   Begging the question - taking definition for granted - is the price we pay for in- telligibility.   And not just intelligibility in the ordinary sense, but any identity, any yardstick what- soever.   An approach that destroys our public and then our private present, would reduce us to self- defeating relativity - a relativity where, in the last event, neither we ourselves, nor 'truth' in any independent form, could ever be.   And by the same token - for 'we' ourselves would not exist as we feel we do (the distinction we make, for instance, between subjectivity and objectivity - 'I will' and 'I can't help' - being now but problem area, not ground on which to build) and 'truth', even scientific truth, arrived at after discipline and research, would be but conclusions that we - as all else in causal flux - would be bound to reach, and so would have the same status as any other conclusions whatsoever.   The Nobel prizewinner and the gormless idiot who does not want to know being but brothers beneath the causal skin.

And that is where we shall begin - stripped of identity, criteria or 'truth'.   All these must be seen as consequence - consequence of that which is necessarily before the known.   And how can that be done?   Certainly not by studying 'objectivity' on its own terms, for that, too, implies distinctiveness. And all distinctiveness, whether between subject and object, between movement and rest, between necessary logic and random fact, between random fact and under- lying law - all this must be seen as consequence. Consequence of that which everyone (when he has finally been defined) achieves alone.

We are indeed reduced to formless 'subjectivity' - to taking as base line what will later patronisingly

be written off as 'subjectivity'. This does not mean
that we can assume any personal identity beforehand -
that, too, must be derived - but rather that we must
plot the emergence of that distinctiveness that allows
us to define - to recognise 'the same' - and so finally
agree.

And someone has done just that. And that person
is Jean Piaget.

We will now have a brief look at Piaget and see how
his contribution (or rather, one of his contributions,
for he is an infinitely fertile man) can help us with
the problems we have so far met - namely the derivation
of distinctiveness, or articulation, of 'the same' -
of the public present that is so manifestly 'there'.

Piaget, as he never tires of telling us, is a 'genetic
epistemologist', that is, he is concerned with the relationship between genes and epistemology, and the central
point of this relationship, the link between the genes
and what is known, has been the equilibrium.

An equilibrium is a state of affairs that reverses
the normal course of time. With an equilibrium it is
easier to predict the future than to describe the
present. Whatever may be the state of agitation of
water in a cup - and that state may well tax the most
detailed account - one can be assured that, sooner or
later it will revert to its predictable, 'equilibrated'
calm.

Piaget has seized upon the equilibrium as the necessary precondition for the awareness of similarity. As
a biologist he cannot but accept that the organism is
'active' (i.e. exists) at all times; but this poses
certain problems. If the organism does exist (i.e.
contributes to awareness), how can its contribution be
neutralised? The answer is an equilibrium. It is an
equilibrium that allows the active organism to achieve
the passive awareness of continuity, for with an equilibrium the activity of the organism resolves itself into
apparent rest, and from apparent need of explanation.
Piaget has tackled the most interesting question of them
all: under what circumstances do we see no problem in
what - and that - we know.

In tackling this question Piaget has elaborated an
exhaustive account of the entire process of intellectual development. In one span he has covered the
(sensory) empirical, the theoretical and the tautolo-
gical (as in number and logic). Almost everything,
indeed, except for the psychoanalytic. But that's to
come.

Piaget is concerned with the development of intelligence, the way that awareness elaborates itself and
so allows of a more sophisticated conditionality - an
awareness that so obviously reflects what is 'really
there' that it, then, needs no explanation in individual terms.

Take the most elementary awareness of them all -
the ability to 'identify' - to achieve the awareness
of enduring, recognisable stabilities and so to see
'what's there'.   This, with Piaget, needs explanation.

Nothing could be more certain to us as adults than
that the world is full of 'objects', entities with
some measure of invariance that can be referred to as
somehow existing in themselves, independent of changes
in their surround.   Thus, if I see a cup before me,
I see a cup - and that is all there is to it (as the
positivists might say).   Not so with Piaget.   Seeing
a cup is an achievement we may not attain until seven-
teen months or so.   Furthermore, seeing a cup has
the properties of an equilibrium.

Because we do not see a cup.   We see bits of a cup.
We see it from below or from above or from some other
angle.   Each of these viewpoints, though, become for
us the 'same whole cup'.   Fragmentary perspectives
are resolved into an emergent 'whole'.   An emergent
whole that has the properties of an equilibrium.   The
'past' - the angle, the particular viewpoint that
meets the eye - may vary if we or it should move.
Not so our 'present' awareness, that does not change.

And so we say we cannot help but see.   This is an
achieved passivity and self-evidence, wholly dependent
on our active powers.   It is inference and extra-
polation - even at the basic level of what we see -
that makes possible order and continuity in our lives.
Without this ability to equilibrate, to restore the
passing to that which then endures, we would never
escape kaleidoscopic flux - a flux wherein movement
itself could not be recognised, for movement depends
upon the continued identification of that which moves.
But we do have the powers, and they convince so completely that it is only with effort that we come to
realise how much activity must underlie the stabilities
that frame our lives.

Two terms can here be introduced.   They are not
Piaget's but will serve.   These terms are those of
'content' and 'criterion'. (1)   The 'content' of an
awareness is the particular perspective or viewpoint
that actually impinges on the eye.   If one is looking
at a cup from below, for instance, it only comprises

that part that can actually be seen.   On their own,
as already stressed, these 'contents' would lack
coherence.   But they are not on their own.   Somehow
they equilibrate into 'criteria'.   'Criterion' is
the term being used for the 'whole', stable cup we
actually feel we see.   With equilibrium, time has
had a stop - and that resting-place is a 'criterion'.
   But we need not stop at the immediately visual.
Mental development with Piaget, is the elaboration of
ever more abstract 'criteria' that emancipate themselves from the 'contents' on which they rest.   Three
examples will be given, those of classification,
measurement and the manipulating of mutually defining
symbols (numbers and logic).   These examples will
not attempt to give any detailed idea at all of the
steps by which the development is achieved, rather,
all three will show how the establishment of 'criteria'
goes hand-in-hand with our growing notion of what we
call 'the same'.
   The growing notion of 'the same' is manifest with
classification.   Classification allows us to group
together and in grouping together to ignore the idiosyncratic.   This is achieved through greater abstraction - an abstraction that permits the possibility of
wider-ranging equilibria.   If a child learns of
'cups in general', then each separate cup can now be
'subsumed' and so no longer be seen as different and
apart.   There is now more similarity and less uniqueness in his life.
   There is nothing new in this.   The move from
'content', 'single cup', to 'criterion', 'cups in
general', is no different from the move from 'content'
of particular perspective to 'criterion' of 'seen
whole cup'.   There, too, was a loss of uniqueness.
Before the cup was conserved (i.e. the 'criterion'
was derived) each separate perspective must have
spoken with insistent poetic force.
   The next example - measurement - is very similar
to classification.   Indeed a measure is but a puri-
fied, monothematic 'class'.   Most classifications
make various demands - thus a cup must have a handle,
be something you can drink out of, but not more than
a certain size, and so on.   Some classifications are
simpler, so simple, indeed, that they have but one
base.   When such 'criteria' can be varied along the
quality (called 'dimension') that defines them, we
have a 'measure'.
   It is presumably a task of supererogation to point
out that measures allow us to see 'the same' where

erstwhile uniqueness stood.   A thermometer allows
even the queen's ante- and the queen's bed-chamber to
be in certain respects the same.   They both have
warmth in varying degrees.   Indeed, with a measure
there cannot be differences at all unless they be of
the same dimension.   Measurement is but another and
more searching form of recognition - the ability on
which all classification rests - a recognition that
allows of graded awareness of similarity.

Finally we come to symbols - logic and the use of
numbers.   Here 'criteria' take the final giant step
to total independence.   For symbols now can define
each other and so achieve an equilibrium apparently
quite separate from lesser happenings in space and
time.   At least Pythagoras and Plato thought so;
they considered such free-standing 'criteria' were
so obviously 'really there' that they could not be
accounted for in content earthly terms.

Yet, numbers, too, are based on past experience.
They are but abstractions from past situations that
can be variously re-combined to the extent that they
do not belong in their implications to specific situations.   They are the interplay of 'criteria' dependent on each other for the equilibrations in which
their implications permit them to participate (i.e.
three equals two plus one, equals one plus one plus
one, etc.).

All this is very abstract.   The only really important point though, is Piaget's contention that such
'criteria' - 'criteria' that now define each other
and so appear autonomous and outside time - are themselves awarenesses achieved in time and are but the
last example of the whole process of development.
This development has, arguably, biological roots and
witnesses the consequence of activity upon the contents we all have met.

So much for a Piagetian account, taken at something
like blitzkrieg rate.   How, one might ask, can such
a very abstract, rarified - and compressed - account
as this help us with the problems we have met?
Indeed, are not the issues raised by this recital so
difficult and so abstract that we were better off
before it began?   At least we were bewildered in a
fairly uncomplicated way.

The liberty to choose one's own shortcomings is
(or should be) a basic civil right and so will not be
questioned here.   However, for those inclined, it
might be pointed out that Piaget with his account of
development has shown us in principle how the public

present can be the inheritor of the private past, how
the individual can become aware of that which will be
seen as being 'the same' - and so become a base line
that apparently can define itself. Without the idea
of equilibrium and of emergent 'criteria' it is
difficult to see how this feat could have been
achieved. It is equilibria that underlie the similarities of classification and of measurement. It
is equilibria that manifestly underlie those mutually
defining definitions we call numbers. With numbers,
to repeat, 'contents' and 'criteria' are interchange-
able and the free-standing equilibrium has been
achieved.

So far this has only referred to the individual on
his own, the solitary development we all experience
in growing up. By an identical extension of the
argument, we can see how a public, not private,
present can be achieved and how the individual 'agree-
ing with himself' through his privately derived
'criteria' can come to accept stabilities that others
share. This is not just because others may have the
same genetic equipment as ourselves so that unless
there is a fairly drastic difference in environment
we shall come to the same conclusion as others do,
but, of more interest and moment, because more
abstract and elusive agreements can be considered in
the same terms. A discussion that results in 'agreement' is but another example of the emergence of a
superordinate 'criterion' that then subsumes the
'contents' of the various individuals' contributions
on which it rests. We all chip in our 'content
point of view' and 'consensus', or whatever it is,
emerges. Note, further, that by this account, those
of different abilities will not achieve similar
agreements and so will not live 'in the same world'.
This, of course, is manifestly the case.

This point - that of the derivation of a possibly
idiosyncratic public present - may be as good a point
as any on which to consider some of the implications
of the Piagetian approach for the thesis argued here.
The most obvious is that it undermines empiricism -
at least as here described. Empiricism that, it was
argued, depended for its whole force upon the separation of the public present from the private past, is
now held to be the consequence of that very private
past! Empiricism prided itself on its 'obviousness' -
that was why 'facts' were 'facts' - but this 'obviousness' is now argued to have a conditional inferential
base. Indeed public 'facts' are no longer qualitatively

different from those private 'hypotheses' that were
once put below the salt.   Worse still, they are no
longer finally distinct from those wanton 'phantasies'
that were quite excluded from the feast.   For what
is a phantasy but an awareness that has not yet
achieved articulation? giving us thereby an insight
into the unequilibrated ground?

But, it could be argued, equilibration involves
disciplined interaction with the world around.   As
such it must clearly be superior to impulsive
phantasy.   This is true, but a 'fact', disciplined
though it may be, need not necessarily be veridical
for that reason.   This is not just for the practical
reason that people may not agree, but because of the
logical reason that the whole idea of a 'criterion'
before the event is undermined.   Once that happens,
there is no abiding timeless on which to rest, and
nothing can be assumed with final confidence.   Not
even the existence of 'objectivity' itself, let alone
'subjectivity', 'logical necessity' or 'health'.   All
we are left with is the constant re-confirmation of
a past assumption.   All standards before the event
imply an escape from that arbitrary, conditional and
to some extent predictable sequence we call 'time',
and, by his notion of an equilibrium, Piaget has shown
us how the timeless 'criterion' can be achieved.

Is all over then bar the shouting?   In one sense,
yes.   Once one has admitted that the present is consequence - and taken the statement seriously and not
considered it as something too abstract and academic
to warrant weight - then everything that has been
said should presumably follow.

Should.   But this is really but a glimpse of the
promised land.   What has not so far been tackled at
all is 'how'.   And once we look at this, difficulties arise.

For two forms of 'knowing' can be inferred from
Piaget, both of which can be argued to have disastrous consequences - the second form of knowing even
more disastrous than the first.   These two forms of
knowing are the psychological - that learning follows
the 'reconstruction' of the 'anticipation' - and the
biological - that learning results from the 'accommodation' of the organism to 'unassimilated' contingency.

First, the psychological form of learning - that
learning results from the 'reconstruction' of an
'anticipation'.   It is a feedback formulation since
it argues that the organism must be active in order
to learn - there must be an 'anticipation' before

there can be a 'reconstruction'. (2)   FB formulations
are, of course, very common (cf. 'set', 'expectancy',
besides 'anticipation') and can be argued to be
'necessary' in that they embody the fairly elementary
assumption that we participate in all we know - and
do so by virtue of being alive at all.   After all,
we don't learn everything, see everything, or want
everything.   Being alive at all argues a continuing
identity - and hence selectivity - in our ability to
react.

But now the difficulties start, for although necessary, it is not compatible with elementary awareness
since elementary awareness can manifestly give us
experiences that are not dependent on any antecedent
anticipation, expectation or hypothesis whatsoever.
This brings us back to Galileo's telescope and the
apparent 'existence in itself' independent of the
observer that the empiricist stressed.   If we do
accept that learning does consist of anticipations
and reconstructions how can we ever arrive at the
awareness of a world wherein objects can exist in
themselves?   Any account that starts from an FO-FB,
anticipation-reconstruction basis must not only account
for the emergence of a world that impinges itself
willy-nilly, but must also account for how the
'criterion' can be moved from observer to observed.

The difficulty of shedding the FO 'criterion before
the event' and achieving the FB 'criterion in the perceived' is none other than the difficulty the very
different approach adopted by the psychoanalysts
encountered.   These have been excluded for a while
and although we shall not return to them until later,
still we can see that they were taxed on this very
point - that of not accounting how 'psychic reality'
(which has affinities with the FO 'criterion before
the event') could ever, on its own terms, account for
its subsequent non-existence.   Both cases present
clear parallels: how can the knower ever become
irrelevant to what he knows?

But the difficulties we have found ourselves with
our psychological account pale into insignificance
when we come to the second, biological approach.   As
befits a genetic epistemologist with a background in
biology, Piaget sees knowing as the outcome of process,
a process that is biological at its roots and reflects
the unceasing rhythms and regulations of organic
life, rhythms and regulations that are necessary for
the maintenance of the separate identity of the
organism in question.   In order to maintain the

processes that permit continued self-regulation, the
organism must rhythmically transact with the world
around - take in, transmute and then exude. We must
take in food, digest and then excrete. In doing so,
the organism affects not just itself but the environment as well - wheat once fed upon becomes manure.
Indeed, organism and environment are, in this scheme
of things, interdependent - the influence of one must
act upon the other and so in due course react upon
its source. If people stopped breathing they would
stop exhaling and this latter would affect the oxygen
in the air. Conversely a change in climate can
influence the resources available to the organism, in
turn affecting the organism and this in turn affecting
the organism's contribution to that environment.

An organism that has achieved stability and balance
with the environment is said by Piaget to be 'adapted'.
Adaptation is the point of repose in which transactions of a particular form can reciprocally maintain
their interaction.

It is in this setting that we can look upon the
known. Knowledge like all else is but a commodity
that can be transacted, only in this case the trans-
action takes on a more complex form - for what the
organism takes in is awareness and what the organism
releases is activity.

In a sense, of course, all output from the organism can be seen in terms of activity - excretion and
exhalation, after all, are acts - and similarly all
input can be seen in terms of knowledge, breathing
involves some filtering by the organism of what is
breathed. With knowledge though this reciprocal
effect of assessment upon activity is vastly increased. An organism that was only capable of
reflexes would have no need to know in the sense
that we commonly use the word at all.

The process of knowing may resemble the process of
breathing in certain critical respects but one central
respect it differs. For knowledge and activity can
enrich each other: indeed knowledge can elaborate
itself in its very activity. When presented with a
problem of breathing, for instance - perhaps because
we are at too high a height - we can breathe faster,
but that is about all the accommodating we can do.
With 'knowing', though, in an unknown dangerous place,
we can not only look around more carefully (the
analogue of breathing faster) we can actually - under
certain limited conditions - change the structure of
the way we know.

If 'to look around more carefully' is similar to breathing faster, altering the 'structure of the way we know' would need as its equivalent something like changing the way we breathe - such as by growing gills if we found ourselves under water.   Of course, over the aeons of evolution this has happened to lungs. Evolution, too, permits of structural adaptation - or 'learning'.   For 'learning' is the ability to alter the way that we react, an ability, in consequence, justified - from the organism's point of view - by the success of that adaptation.

The forms that such learning can take and the conditions necessary for it to take place is Piaget's principal concern.   This will not be pursued here. What will be mentioned, though, is how, in principle, this process of adaptation - or rather re-adaptation - can occur at all.

It can occur when the organism can notice changes in the environment and then do something about it. At this point two Piagetian terms must be introduced, those of 'accommodation' and 'assimilation'.   'Accommodation' occurs when the organism modified its response to meet an environmental change - growing gills is a major structural accommodation; hurrying to catch a train when you suddenly realise you have less time than you thought is a minor behavioural form of accommodation.   Assimilation, the companion term, determines the form that the accommodation will take. We can't grow wings on realising we are late, we have to go on using the legs we've got.   The environment is assimilated by being absorbed into the resident processes of the organism - we humans assimilate through lungs, fish through gills.

Adaptation in Piaget's terms is an equilibrium between accommodation and assimilation.   An organism is adapted when it has come to terms with an environment (has accommodated to it) and so been able to absorb that environment into its patterns of response (i.e. assimilate the environment).   Threats to adaptation can come from two sources, the environment and the organism itself.   The environment may change and the organism may have to come to terms with that change.   Of more interest is disequilibration coming from within.   The intellectual development of an organism as it grows up can be looked upon as a series of internally determined disequilibrations imposed upon the organism through its greater capacity to 'notice'.   The disequilibrations are then accommodated to through the elaboration of existing assimilatory

processes - we become more aware of the complexities
of the world around us and come to terms with them by
adapting the forms of awareness we have already
achieved.   This assimilatory development can be in-
definitely extended but, however elaborate it may
become, it has its roots in what is virtually a here-
ditarily determined biological response to the world
·around - a response anchored at all times in the
structure of the organism that makes it possible -
and is enriched by it.

Which is, of course, why certain species can 'learn'
more than others.

So much for the bones of the biological, process
form of knowing.   Why, it might be asked, should its
consequences be 'even more disastrous' in its implications than those of the psychological, FO-FB form of
knowing?

Because, in brief, not only does it suffer from
the same disadvantages in an even more acute form,
but, in addition to that, it presents us with a whole
new panoply of meaninglessness - a meaninglessness
where, it must be admitted, minor matters like 'disadvantages' are of but passing concern.

First, 'the same disadvantages in an even more
acute form' - 'assimilation', that steers the activity
of the organism, bears a clear resemblance to FO (and,
come to that, to the psychoanalyst's 'will' as well),
just as 'accommodation' bears a clear resemblance to
the earlier FB.   Now not only will 'assimilation'
have all the same difficulties in accounting for the
apparent existence of the world around us as did the
earlier form of knowing, but this very activity of
the organism - the FO and 'anticipation' on which all
depends - is thereupon itself downgraded to being but
part of the wider process of 'adaptation'.   And such
'anticipation' is quite as influenced by 'reconstruction' as 'reconstruction' is by 'anticipation'.
Indeed the process form of knowing, when successful,
quite undermines both FO and FB - the bases of both
psychoanalysis and empiricism!   Both these terms
are now descriptive conveniences carrying no final
causal weight.   One can no more have an anticipation
(or FO) without some form of response (or FB) - or
conversely - than one can breathe in without breathing
out - or conversely.   A factor that cannot be avoided
is never decisive in itself.   Only a factor that
cannot be, can have an unambiguous effect.

However, to do justice to the 'process' form of
knowing - and to catch a glimpse of a 'whole new

panoply of meaninglessness' - it must be admitted
that it is not interested in the 'truth', 'objectivity' or anything that implies that what we know
is 'really there'.   It is not interested, for knowing
is now a practical affair, not concerned with 'truth'
but something quite different - our ability to
survive.

The way we know is but part and parcel of the
equipment that we possess.   As such it should be
judged - and has been by evolutionary history - not
as being 'right' or 'wrong' but as being helpful or
unhelpful, quite a different matter.   This is not
to say that knowledge cannot be 'right' or 'wrong'
but rather that the fact that we as a species think
something is 'right' or 'wrong' need have no conclusive force: it merely suits us from the point of
view of our survival to think the way we do.
Different species survive in different ways and so
no doubt 'know' different things.   This goes for
ourselves as well: the sights, sounds, colours and
poetry we all recognise are those that enable us to
live.   It is insufferable arrogance to assume that
they should be more.   We may as a species have transformed the world; in another sense we may have been
incapable of asking ourselves questions that we were
unable to answer.   The spirit of an age is seen in
the questions that are not asked.

The thesis can be simply stated: despite its
'utter meaninglessness', the biological, process
assumptions will be given pride of place.   The psychological assumptions and the psychoanalytic 'will'
assumptions that we all recognise in our daily lives
will be considered but maladaptive, disequilibrated
variants of the process assumptions.   The growth of
articulated awarenesses - the conservations and constancies that end up by our attaining what we call
the public present - will be seen as a form of re-
equilibration.   Awareness of the public present,
then, the starting point for the empiricist and end
point for Piaget, is re-adapted biology.

As the organism becomes re-adapted, so does it
become aware of the causal forces that operate upon
it.   An organism that is totally non-adapted would
have no idea - from its own feelings - of what were
the causal agencies at work.

A few words about earliest feelings may not be out
of place here, for such feelings, it will be argued,
provide the ground and backdrop of any articulation
we can achieve.

These early feelings are almost certainly those of
'omnipotence' - the belief that there is no distinction between FO and FB, between 'must' and 'is',
between 'will' and reality.   How could we believe
anything else before we had become aware of outside
regularities that could refute?   But, of course, this
would not mean that omnipotence for one moment should
be believed on its own terms as carrying causal
weight.   'Causality' refers to necessary antecedents,
not FO insistence.   FO insisting on its own explanatory self-sufficiency is, indeed, itself but another
example of that illusory self-sufficiency summed up
by 'omnipotence'.

Refutation - the loss of 'omnipotence' - comes from
accommodation - of meeting the world on its own terms,
not ours.   Three main headings will be taken to show
how adaptation could ensue, these three will be those
of 'visual objects' (and will subsume the constancies
and conservations that end up with the public present),
the adaptation implicit in the grasping of logical
relations (logic and numbers) and finally, briefly,
'structures'.

Imagine a child lying in a pram with some rattles
tied across the pram in front of him on a string;
however that rattle is hit - whatever the nature of
the FO - the rattle will rattle and after a while
stop - FB will be the same, unflinchable in its
inevitability.   FO 'omnipotence' will have been dis-
abused.

Where FB can be independent of any one FO, there
can FB attain its own identity and no longer be assimilated to ignorant FO 'omnipotence'.   The greater
the range of FOs, the more this will be the case.
The child, a bit older, may seize, suck, bang, throw
and drop the rattle - go through a whole repertoire
of initiating activities.   The more ways in which
he 'explores' the rattle or whatever it is he is
interested in, the greater identity that rattle can
have.

And so an equilibrium is established and the inner
'will', to that extent is curbed.   And by the same
token it cannot be wished into something that is not
itself.   And that will occur when the outside is to
some extent equilibrated.   A child playing with a
pair of scales can become aware that the weights he
puts upon them can cancel each other out, and, in
cancelling each other, reflect their indifference to
his 'will'.

From this kernel, the 'factual' world and eventually

the public present itself, can be derived.   This
learning by accommodation to equilibria allows underlying causal 'process' to resolve itself into the
empiricist's spiritual base - namely the present.

For the empiricist there is only the present.   The
'here and now' is the only final real.   It is only
because a fact is wholly 'present' (pun) that it is
trustworthy at all.   To set off, like Piaget does,
to define the present in terms of the past, is to
enter a quagmire of infinite regresses from which no
articulation could escape.

And yet the 'present' seen in these terms is, of
course, outside time.   It is only because events
abide and do not change - i.e. allow time to flow past
them - that the empiricist can speak with confidence
at all.   Time is the great diluter.   Plato was quite
right to place his defining ideas in heaven.   The gods
do not age.

Hence the power of talking in terms of equilibria -
whether of the knower or of the known.   With equilibria, the flux can articulate itself.   If there
were no equilibria, all would be changing flux, if
there were nothing but equilibria, nothing would ever
change.   Equilibria allow us to calibrate that which
is not itself.

They also allow us to define mutually defining
relationships, logic and number (though only number
will be commented on here).   This whole area has
always been peculiarly intractable to the empiricist.
By his own book, as we have seen, he can only talk in
terms of the 'present' - and numbers, are not
'present'.   Or rather they are everywhere and nowhere at the same time, necessarily true and yet
invisible.   As a result they have always been dealt
with with a kind of respectful disdain.

There are no such problems in the Piagetian scheme
of things.   Since all awareness depends on the
memory of past activities, and there never is a
clear-cut 'present' that speaks with unambiguous
voice, there is no base line that can exclude.
Numbers are but the consequence of another form of
equilibration.

A re-equilibration not due to failure - or, at
least, not immediate failure.   So far we have considered the derivation of the '+0' world of the self-
evident 'fact'.   That derivation was based four-
square on failure - variation of FO was neutralised
by consistent FB response (however the rattles were
hit, they always settled down again after a while).

But we do not always meet consistent responses in our exploring of the world. To a fairly considerable extent the world we live in (and the infant's world) is within our control - that is, determined by the organism's FO initiative (clearly cognate with the active '+-' way of knowing) and not the environment's FB response. Thus the child can put paid to his rattle on a string (and their 'inevitable' FO reducing re-equilibration) by breaking the rattle or the string. A bit later he can turn a piece of plasticine into all sorts of wonderful realities, or again he can cry out, express hunger and pain and so bring about (he hopes - this is no doubt critical for mental health) his mother's presence. In all these ways, the child does not have to accommodate unilaterally. In the contrary, he can bend reality to his will.

This creative, emergent aspect of the reality that surrounds us - the houses we have built, the very life we have carved out for ourselves upon this planet - has almost been totally ignored by the empiricist and left, in consequence, to those who derive from Marx and Hegel (such as Sartre and Laing) to explore. And no wonder. The empiricist is concerned with the enduring - that which cannot be wished away - not the magical. And our sense of control - and successful control at that - over the daily realities we have to deal with is magical by any standards that do not beg the question. And it is magic - creativity aware of its own achievements - that underlies our grasp of numbers.

Which 'magic' we must now explore.

Before we explore this, a certain number of pre-fatory definitions are in order. This is not just that numbers themselves must be defined more closely but so too must 'identity', for numbers exemplify in its purest form a new kind of identity. Namely 'identity-in-context'.

So far, we have only considered 'identity-in-itself' (these terms are not Piaget's by the way). Identity-in-itself - the identity we have considered - is that which, by definition, resists context. The supreme form of an identity-in-itself is the visual object. A visual object is only identifiable at all to the extent that it resists the context that surrounds it, it has always been the bedrock of the empiricist's approach. Each of Galileo's moons, for instance, went on being 'there', resisting con-text in a bloody-minded way in spite of all the oaths, prayers, conjurations and dismissals that were brought to bear on it.

But of course lots of the environment is less principled and bends with outer persuasion.   It behaves 'lawfully'.   This brings us to the new form of identity - identity-in-context.   Identity-in-context is quite different from identity-in-itself. Entities are now defined not in the way they resist external changes but in the way that they conform to them.

Thus we can have the 'class' of metals that respond to magnetism and the 'class' of metals that do not. This kind of identity is different from the earlier identity-in-itself in that it is not an absolute. Thus, not only can this identity be a matter of degree (some metals needing more magnetism than others) but can also be a matter of conditionality - two objects being the 'same' if one considers their reaction to condition X, but different if we consider their reaction to condition Y - water and oil are both liquid but they respond differently to fire.

Thus the whole notion of 'identity' becomes diluted into a matrix of possible consequences, what something 'is' being but the residual unaccounted for, the timeless Platonic defining ideal.

At this point, an important and quite new idea must come in, that of 'reversibility'.   Reversible is an adjective given to those changes that can be undone.   Thus water freezing is 'reversible' since water that is frozen can return to its non-frozen state - and vice versa - without affecting in any permanent way its identity-in-context.   But compare the process of freezing to that of burning!   Burning really is a goal of no returns.   Once burned, burned. This does not mean that that which is burned achieves an identity in itself, just that the original pre-burning state cannot be recaptured.   Time has moved on.

Now reversibility (or rather irreversibility) has a complex, asymmetrical relationship with identity. Put baldly, irreversibility has the wider span, for, although all irreversibles do not have identity-in-itself, anything that has identity-in-itself is irreversible.

Ashes have been irreversibly transmuted; but ashes have no immutable identity-in-itself.   Ashes can be used in the garden to help in the eternal cycle of change.   But, although the irreversible need not have identity-in-itself, the objects that have identity-in-itself must be irreversible - visual objects (our prototype of that which has identity-in-

itself) for instance, are all irreversible and cannot
be changed to what they are not.   Hence, of course,
their hypnotic power and the weight put upon them by
the empiricists.

'Fact' - the obtrusive 'self-evident' - has been
argued to be never pure, but always admixed (at least
in any articulated form) with the knower's powers of
integration.   But facts, for all that, retained some
alien FB base - some input from the outside world we
were not adapted to.   With numbers, though, we go
one further and the activity of the observer - present
in all we see and know - achieves its own equilibration.   Numbers (as such) exist only in the minds of
men.

Or so it would appear.   Numbers, after all, are
entirely self-defining and are suspended in mid-air.
What is '2'?   1 + 1.   And what is '1'?   2 - 1.
The circle is complete.   And furthermore quite
detached from anything else.   Each number has zero
identity-in-itself, but numbers as a whole, taken as
a package deal, have an invincible meta-identity-in-
itself. (3)

And how is this derived?   The empiricist, as we
have seen, has no answer.   If we were honest he
would be a Platonist.   For Piaget, though, the
problem does not exist.   For numbers, like all else,
are the result of activity - only this time activities
that are spread in time, not anchored (as with our
last example of the visual object) in the here and
now.   Numbers are but a form of ordered memory.
And memories have a curious immortality.

Numbers are spread in time (hence their odd quality, already referred to, of being everywhere and
nowhere, of being necessarily true, and yet quite
invisible) and that which is spread in time can also
achieve an equilibration (only, of course, at the
cost of losing immediate identity-in-itself).   This
equilibration too can be irreversible - numbers,
once achieved, need not then turn into anything else.

Thus, in order to understand numbers we must
understand how people learn them.   The awareness of
numbers is achieved through abstraction, as indeed
with Piaget, are all awarenesses.   Abstraction of a
particular kind - not that of 'objects' but of 'acts'.
Numbers summarise the implications of what we have
done.

Numbers are based on the 'magical' abilities of
the doer - on the child's ability to control and
manipulate his environment.   This activity allows him

some measure of escape from the intrinsic qualities
of the present (since he can change the present) but
does not (since the child's control is but limited
control) enable him to escape some, at least, of the
consequences of those acts.   Time, which gives way
to our initiative, all too often catches up with us
and shows us the consequence of what we have done.

Numbers summarise some of the delayed consequences
of creative acts - those that can be ordered in
degree.   And, more particularly, can be undone.
Activities, too, can sometimes be 'reversed'.

Not always, of course.   So far, the great weight
has been on 'irreversibles' - that 'done' that cannot
be 'undone'.   The perception of visual objects, for
instance, has this quality - 'contents' merge into
'criteria' and there lock - what is seen cannot be
unseen.   (Hence, indeed, its resilient identity-in-
itself.)   But the same does not go for all forms of
activity.   Some activity is cyclical - like breathing - some activity has a wider inevitability - like
that of maturing and eventual decay - and some
activity can be undone.

The child can build a tower of bricks and knock it
down.   We can all of us come home again at night,
get divorced, even commit suicide.   All these re-
versals are a way of bringing back the past - to the
time when there was no tower, had not left home, been
married or been born.   It is out of such bringing
back that we can escape the self-justifying flow of
process, and learn to compare the consequences of
our acts.

If we are children, we can do more than knock down
towers.   We can collect our marbles in a pile and
then scatter them over the room again.   We can bring
together and then separate.   We can add and then
subtract.

It is out of such activity - of taking together
and then spreading apart - that numbers are born.
Even number one, basic identity, can be thought of as
that which cannot be taken apart.   We learn that
'two' - 'one' + 'one', the result of an act of bringing together - has features in common with the
results of other such acts of bringing together -
whether such acts concern such empirically different
contents as bricks, sweets or teddy-bears' legs.   In
every case, where two has been realised, another one
can give us three - and three is different from two
in that three cannot be split into two.

And so on.   Very soon a different form of rever-

sibility emerges - not what might be called the 'voluntary reversibility' of knocking down bricks but the
'imposed reversibility' implicit in the degree of
articulation already achieved.   Voluntary 'reversibility' refers to what is done, 'imposed reversibility', to what is necessarily learned.

'Imposed reversibility' can be seen as ground
determining its own figure.   If we know that there
are thirteen cards in a suit at bridge, for instance,
then we know that if we can account for ten of that
suit in three hands, that the three remaining cards
must be in the unknown hand.   A child will learn
that, if he has four and takes one away, he will be
left with that set of implications we call 'three' -
and need not look, after a while, to confirm.   Thus
does framework slowly assert its own autonomy.
Indeed it ends triumphant and dictates a form of
reality, quite unachievable by direct empirical
approach.   The allusion is to the number 'nought' -
an absolute consequence of a logical necessity, a
necessity itself based on experience.

This grasping of necessity is greatly accelerated
by the ability to 'internalise' our acts.   We need
no longer actually eat our cakes and knock over our
towers, now we can begin to imagine what would happen
if we did.   'Flout 'em and scout 'em', say Shakes-
peare's underlings in 'The Tempest' (and we are all
Time's underlings), 'thought is free'.   With this
freedom we can envisage the timeless consequence of
acts that could not be done.   Consequences that
could themselves be starting points and so contribute
in turn to the wider framework that defines, and is
defined by, those relationships we call 'number'. (4)

And thus does 'adaptation' once more return.   Only
in a very curious way.   Not, as with visual objects,
where FO and FB equilibrate, but rather where FB,
bending back upon itself in time (through the good
offices of memory) defines itself quite independently
of any FO supposition.   With numbers it does not
matter where you look.   And so the psychological
world of anticipation and reconstruction - and
activity, such as knocking down towers - is quite
left behind.

Only to be revealed again by those who study not
the nature but the genesis of our awarenesses.   And
those who study that (and look at children like Piaget
has done) will realise that these two - 'nature' and
'genesis' - cannot be kept apart.

So far we have had examples that have either been

very concrete or very abstract.   The 'very concrete'
equilibrium was, of course, that of the visual 'conservation', the 'abstract' equilibrium, the one we have
just discussed, that of 'number'.   The question to
which we can now briefly address ourselves is whether
there could be a form of equilibrium in between - that
was neither as concrete as the one nor as abstract as
the other, but just as 'equilibrated', just as
'necessary' as what we see or how we add.

   The answer to this question is a modified 'yes'.
'Structures' can emerge whenever the initial observations can themselves be modified by the conclusions
that they have made possible.   Put in the terms used
above, whenever the visual hard datum of the identity-
in-itself leads to the development of assumptions that
then modify our view of that datum.   This, of course,
happens all the time - the identity-in-itself of
water, is seen also to possess the identity-in-context
of being changeable to steam or ice; this, in turn,
leads to the meta-identity-in-itself of 'ice-water-
steam'.   This meta-identity-in-itself can be argued
to a 'structure' since we now see that what we first
started with - the 'necessary' fact of the existence
of 'water', with all its context-resisting identity,
is now 'really' (or 'usefully to be considered but' -
or whatever other form of triumph or apology we use
to gloss over the miracle) but part of a wider
identity.

   Structuralism is the consequence of definitions
becoming consequences.   Whenever this happens - and
it is constantly happening - we are put in an
impossible dilemma from which there is no escape.
Except, of course, evasion - the usual resort before
the extremely high status of some of the advocates of
the structurist position (such as Piaget himself)
made it impracticable.

   The consequences of definitions becoming consequences is very serious since it means that the time-
bound datum (identity-in-itself) becomes absorbed by
the time-free (because always enduring) assumption
(the meta-identity-in-itself) that it has made
possible.   And it is not just the identity-in-itself,
but also identity-in-context that is absorbed.   The
'event' of water turning into ice, for instance
(water exhibiting its identity-in-context) is but
part of a process (water turning into ice and steam)
that has always happened and always will.

   Thus are the hard data of science trivialised by
the assumptions they make possible - assumptions that

constantly grow as science progresses.   As the present
of the identity-in-itself is progressively absorbed by
the reciprocally defining - and hence, enduring, meta-
identity-in-itself - the natural sciences tend to
become as emancipated from the here and now as numbers.
Numbers, of course - implications wholly shorn of the
adventitiousness of the identity of itself - are the
limiting case to which all structures tend.   Parmen-
ides - who argued that there could be no change -
laughs again.

Not least, because the arguments for this progression cannot be refuted.   Not, that is, from the
Piagetian perspective - subsuming the identity-in-
itself into the meta-identity-in-itself is no different
from subsuming a 'content' into a 'criterion' (a meta-
identity-in-itself is clearly a 'criterion' writ large)
and so necessary for the awareness of any articulated
sensory datum whatsoever.   The object must be conserved before it can be observed.

'Structures' are but another example of equilibration - of data reciprocally defining each other and
so escaping their several parts.   The only escape
from structuralism is a Platonism that insists that
the identity-in-itself cannot be reduced.   It may or
may not give the empiricist consolation to note that
his staunchest ally in this matter - equally adamant
about not being 'reduced' - is the psychoanalyst.

Structuralist knowledge has all the necessary
strengths and practical weaknesses of knowledge after
the event.   It may be able to swallow its own tail
and then suspend itself in mid-air - but only after
someone has put it there.   Piaget, structuralist
though he is, and stressing the necessary self-
equilibrating quality of an equilibrium once arrived
at, though he does, is also a child psychologist who
plots the painstaking steps by which this subsequent
emancipation is achieved.   To deny the logical force
of the structuralist position (unless, of course, one
becomes a clear-headed idealist of some kind) is
silly, but to adopt a superior attitude towards those
that are still earthbound is perhaps sillier still.
Certainly it is more sterile - kicking away the ladder
that has enabled one to get up to where one has, is
condemning oneself to never getting any higher.

Anyway we may not be interested in those lofty
altitudes.   There is, after all, plenty to talk
about besides the absolute.   Our lives may be lived
at a very low level of discourse and of no interest in
the wider scheme of things, but, for all that, they

are the only lives we are likely to get.   There may
be only fifty-two cards in the pack and every hand we
get may be a sampling of those fifty-two, nevertheless
our particular hand (i.e. 'life') may present us with
problems enough - as well as an identity which,
limited in our horizons as we are, we tend to cherish.

Now, at long last, the relevance of the above con-
tentions to the psychoanalytic approach.   It might,
at first blush, be thought that the psychoanalyst
would welcome the Piagetian thesis.   Has it not undermined the psychoanalyst's arch-enemy, the empiricist?
And has it not done so by insisting - just as the
psychoanalysts do - on the explanatory primacy of the
'private past'?

The answer to this question is, of course, 'yes',
but this is a 'yes' that brings but little cheer to
the psychoanalyst.   Little cheer since the 'private
past' is not necessarily the inner 'will'.   Indeed,
the whole Piagetian progression is one of emancipation
from, not continued thraldom to, the inner will.   In
other words we start riddled with egocentric phantasies - but we end up at the end of the day, contem-
plating those impulse- and random-free awarenesses we
call 'structures'.

Unless something goes wrong.   What now requires
explaining and what should be attempted is not, as
the psychoanalysts contend, the persistence of primitive impulses in later life (adult neurotics being
described in terms of early impulses) but rather the
loss of these very impulses.   We should not ask why
neurotics are still crippled by their past, but how
it is possible that any of us ever can escape.

As we do.   For the psychoanalyst to turn his back
on the developments we make and to insist that the
area he is left with - those that do not develop as
others do - can be treated on its own, with its own
set of laws (the 'will', etc.) that are quite enough
in themselves, is to behave like an old, blind
emperor still claiming total power, not 'recognising'
the provinces he has lost.

Just as the empiricist loses the explanatory
primacy of the 'fact', so too does the psychoanalyst
lose the explanatory primacy of the 'will'.   Both
'fact' and 'will' are now but staging posts in a process of adaptation - the latter ('will') primitive
and deluding in its explanatory force, the former
('fact') equilibrated and deluding in its explanatory
self-sufficiency.   Once we adopt a 'meaningless'
biological approach we can no longer escape facing up

to the more important question: how it is possible
that we should even escape the immature - shed our
imagined feedback of 'phantasy' and adopt instead
sophisticated awareness.

A pitifully small attempt to answer this question
has been made in this paper (in the assumption that
equilibration is the consequence of constant FB to
varying FO, the child playing with its rattle) and no
more will be done here. It may be worth noting
before moving on, though, that there is no reason in
principle why the answer - when we do get it - should
be anything like we expect it to be. It is quite
possible that we have wrongly defined the problem -
with the result that we would not recognise the
answer if we saw it.

So far, the process approach has been hostile to
psychoanalytic assumption. That, however, is not
the end of the story. Although it has been critical
of explaining people in their own terms, it can help
elucidate the psychoanalyst's own problems.

Perhaps the best example here is that of the derivation of the ego - surely one of the psychoanalyst's
great weaknesses. The ego can now be seen to be an
equilibration, that is a resolution of disparate
tensions, not a unitary concept in its own right; an
equilibration, furthermore, that marches *pari passu*
with our other equilibrations. Just as we learn to
'conserve' objects outside ourselves and see them
whole, so we learn to 'conserve' impulses inside ourselves and feel them whole. The two are almost
certainly mutually dependent - were there no stabilities outside we would surely be hard put to it to
integrate our inner conflicts.

An ego can be looked upon as derived and the
Piagetian approach can give us a form (that of equilibration) by which the derivation could be achieved.
This again helps us in the phrasing of psychoanalytic
problems since it suggests that processes such as
'projection' and 'introjection' are not, as their
names suggest, based upon the existence of the antecedent ego but rather processes that precede the
development of the mature ego. From this point of
view, residual projection and introjection in later
life can be looked upon as islands cut off from
wider experience by the rising tide of equilibration.

Equilibration, like all articulation, implies
delimitation. Before equilibration has been
achieved, all must have seemed an absolute - absolute
desirability, absolute despair. Hence the ruthlessness

of the very small child.   Hence, also, his guilt - for
guilt is based on the assumption of irreversibility.
'Reversing' has to be learned - first practically and
then in thought.   Before such ability has been
achieved, each impulse and act must have a final consequence.   But we do grow - emotionally as well as
mentally and physically - and an acknowledgment that
this process somehow or other occurs makes possible a
quite new (and more optimistic) view of mental illness.

Freud, for instance, noticing the great difficulty
people had in free associating argued that this drift
to coherence was in fact a defence - the underlying
pain thereby being repressed.   But from the Piagetian
point of view, it is perfectly possible to look on
this excessive coherence in a different way - not
negatively, as arguing a move away from underlying
motive, but positively, as arguing a move towards
maturing structure.

Once granted that the move towards structure is
'natural' like growing up, then, to say that people do
not free associate because they 'will' not to do so
(since they are anxious to avoid pain), is like saying
of someone who is physically but not mentally mature,
that his physical maturity - which is after all all
the poor man has - is a 'defence' against his mental
backwardness.

In other words, painful feelings are not necessarily
'repressed' but can also be left behind, relics of a
failure in normal development.   Once more, what has
to be explained is not the persistence of the old but
the emergence of the new.   The new can no longer be
taken for granted - as it was all too much, for
instance, with the ego.

And the new cannot be explained by what is already
(experientially) 'there'.   The new is explained by
what is not yet (experientially) 'there'.   There is
no reason why we should experience the causes that
bring about our maturation any more than we can
experience the causes that are responsible for our
eventual senescence.

The psychoanalyst has been content to leave these
questions unanswered because of his insistence on the
surprising relevance of the 'will'.   Even passively
experienced awarenesses - like being the innocent
victim in a car crash - can, it is stressed, be
illuminated (and the patient relieved) by a reference
to an active, not passive will.   From this it has
been assumed that the active feeling must have been the
cause.   Even if the active impulse is 'there', buried

in the unconscious, this need not urge that the impulse
is primary.   Indeed the impulse could itself be perfectly well the consequence of the crash.   After all,
it had to come from somewhere.

If the psychoanalyst dislikes this analysis, he may
take comfort from the thought that a directly analogous suggestion was made for the empiricist.   He,
too, had his absolute - not FO of the inner 'will' but
the FB of the outer 'fact'.   This 'fact' stood
alone - quite as alone as the psychoanalyst's 'will'.
For both psychoanalyst and empiricist, though, it is
being suggested that FO is itself influenced by that
very FB over which it had had such varying fortunes.
In both cases, it is being suggested, some form of
equilibration ensues.   In the latter case, though, it
must be admitted, in a rather primitive way: for the
FO to assume 'responsibility' and, hence, guilt where
it itself was but passive victim, argues an as yet
imperfect grasp of external relevance.

Masking all this, and rendering confusion worse confounded, has been the great red herring of the unconscious.   The unconscious, being remote, reeks of
primitive 'cause' and so endows, as said at the very
beginning of this paper, its findings with a quite
spurious finality.   That the unconscious should thus
be considered as some sort of a First Cause is but a
comment on the psychology of the psychoanalyst - or,
perhaps, his patient.   Perhaps, at the end of the
day, the psychoanalyst pays the price of talking a
language his patient can understand.

A far greater moment than the distinction between
conscious and unconscious is that between FO neutralised into equilibration and FO as yet unequilibrated
and 'free'.   FO neutralised is witnessed in our
learned articulations - the constancies of vision,
the conservations of intelligence, the abstract equilibria of numbers and the necessary equilibria of wider
structures; the FO as yet unequilibrated is seen in
the impulse and willed desire that has not yet run its
course; it is seen in 'purpose' and in the insistence
that precedes reason.   The relevance of psychoanalysis
is that it gives us an insight into the nature of the
unequilibrated will.

 A will - if its own insistence can be credited -
that totally misleads; but, for all that, is inevitable and the basis of our conscious lives.   It misleads because - according to this biological, process
approach - it only exists as a separate entity at all
under conditions where it cannot be believed.   It is

only when the organism ceases to be adapted that FO
and FB break apart, no longer fused in mutual definition; FO then, severed from the equilibrating
restraint of FB, can dream its own dreams of what
reality should be.

And this happens to us all at birth - that violent
disruption that reduces us to awareness and to need.
But then, bit by bit, equilibration is restored; FO
is once more modified by FB and, its illusions being
lost, acknowledges what is 'there'.

Equilibration is where psychic reality stops.
There is no 'purpose' in the way we see (Galileo's
inquisitors saw the moons despite all inner 'will'),
there is no longer any motive in our awareness that
one plus one equals two (and it took Piaget to show
that once there had been), and once we achieve wider
structures - well, then there is no observer (and so
no illusion) left at all - all being subsumed in
wider, necessarily equilibrated, constancy.

The way we see, the way we count, the way we disappear in structure - all this was impulse once. An
equilibrium is cause cancelling itself out; and, in
this case, that cause (in its psychological form) is
the inner 'will'.

But, of course, this 'will' - equilibrated in large
part though it be - does not retire. It cannot,
since the relationship between FO and FB is not sym-
metrical. FO precedes FB - it has to because the
organism is 'alive'. However elaborated in structure
it may become, underlying FO is necessarily antecedent
- and so 'there'.

Forever being equilibrated, forever being renewed.
We recognise this FO as 'free will' - that inheritor
of our infantile omnipotence - as insistent to us
(however jaundiced, apathetic or intellectually con-
vinced to the contrary we may be) as pain. This
free will does not express itself in random terms (as
it should if it were really 'free') but (with adults)
fuses with those relatively structured courses of
action we call 'purposes'.

Purposes - disciplined but still assertive 'will' -
informs all but the most adapted of our acts - leaving
behind as legacy those summaries of our aspirations
and successes we call 'definitions'. It is hardly
possible to define at all without reference to past
uses - or past hopes. A 'cup', as we have already
seen, is 'something we drink from' (that is, 'something we have managed to drink from'), a 'paper' (such
as this one) is 'something that has been written', a
'church' is a place where people 'pray' to God.

It is virtually impossible to exaggerate the importance of this form of definition.   After all, it
forms the basis of that extension of the non-animistic
we call 'science'.   'Science' is but the articulated
outcome of men's enterprise - an enterprise that sees
the 'control' of 'independent' (sic) variables, the
establishment of 'functional' relationships and,
frequently, indeed, seeks to establish 'cause'.

The purposive base of science is all too readily
forgotten.   We are both pushed and pulled towards
presumptions of anonymity.   We are pushed because
purpose is in our blood and creeps all too readily into
what we know.   We have none of us wholly escaped our
self-centred past - so self-centred, indeed, that it
was unaware of its own relevance.

But there is a pull as well as a push.   There is
the lure of anonymity for those who would presume they
do not count - for only thus can they insist that
others must agree.   A devastating blow, indeed, to
many a scientist's pride would be to suggest that his
observations are but a reflection of his point of
view.   The high priest of that twentieth-century
version of the Holy Ghost - 'objectivity' - would be
revealed as guilty of the twentieth-century version
of mortal sin - 'subjectivity'.

This need not happen of course - a grotesquely
patronising remark in a paper like this which, after
all, is parasitic on what others have established -
but it well can.   Scientists are human too, and all
of us, unless we are alert to the motivational dimension of what we see as 'there', are all too prone to
be seduced into assumptions of personal irrelevance.

The psychoanalyst, by giving us some insight into
the motivational and pre-articulate base of what we
later take as 'there' can provide an admirable correc-
tive to our presumptions of personal impotence.

To throw away the insights of psychoanalysis
because they are not fully equilibrated - where
nothing else, by definition, at that primitive stage
of development can ever be attained - is like commit-
ting suicide because we have no hope of being
immortal.

Or, rather, pretending that we are not alive.

NOTES

1 I hope it will become clear that the use of the
   word 'criterion' is not quite as misleading as

      might at first appear; however, to keep its some-
what specialised meaning clear, the tedious resort
of inverted commas will be used - as it also will
be for the term 'content'.

2 The term 'anticipation' and 'reconstruction' will
not here be used, but 'feed out' and 'feedback',
written FO and FB for short.

3 Meta-identity-in-itself is a higher order identity
in itself. It is a criterion of a set of criteria,
which criteria thereby become contents themselves.

4 For those interested, this can be rephrased in
'content' and 'criterion' terms. Each number can
be looked on as a 'criterion' (or equilibrium) that
subsumes its varying 'contents' - 'contents' that
are themselves 'criteria' of varying 'contents'.
Thus 'six' is a 'criterion' (or equilibrium) subsuming 'content' five plus one and 'content' four
plus two, etc., and five is a 'criterion' (or
equilibrium) subsuming various 'contents', one of
which is six minus one. Where 'content' and
'criterion' are thus mutually defining, the circle
is closed and equilibration is complete.

Part two

DEVELOPMENTAL CHANGES IN UNDERSTANDING

Piaget's theory traces changes in the intellectual or cognitive processes of the child over time. Particular interest has centred on the change from pre-operational functioning to concrete operational functioning. This change marks the growth of the child's capacity to understand certain conservations, to decenter his attention, to combine information or items into classes and then to operate on the classes that have been formed.

The three papers in this section report experimental studies examining the nature of the child's thinking during this period of middle childhood, but each study has focused on a different aspect of development. Bryant has centered on the development of logical inferences, particularly inferences of a transitive nature. If the child is presented with a number of separate items of information of the form A > B; B > C and so on, what inferences can he draw from these, for instance, about the relationship of A to C? Piaget's theory and research has predicted that young children, in the pre-operational period, should not be able to relate the discreet pieces of information so as to form a series and therefore should not understand the relative position of each item in the series. Bryant's experiments have shown that in certain circumstances the child can draw logical inferences from a transitive series, and his paper reports work in this area.

Much debate has been generated since Bryant reported his first experimental findings, and the debate is reflected in this section. Professor Furth's paper describes research into memory changes in children over time, changes which reflect the child's growing understanding of the properties of the environment, an

understanding which is more than a figurative representation but implies operative, or transformational knowledge.   Professor Furth provides a clear and succinct
statement of the two aspects of knowledge embodied in
Piaget's theory - the figurative and the operative.
And during the course of his argument he suggests that
Bryant's experimental paradigm has probed only the
figurative aspect of knowledge.

The relation of operativity, memory and language is
reported by Professor Lunzer.   The research he refers
to was specifically designed to test the relation of
Piaget's theories of operativity to work which derives
from the main body of psychological thinking and
research.   And the results he reports on the relation
of operativity to memory necessitate some caution in
interpreting the role of operativity in recall in the
Furth experiments.

Popper has written that
objectivity is closely bound up with the *social
aspects of scientific method,* with the fact that
science and scientific objectivity do not (and cannot) result from the attempts of an individual
scientist to be 'objective', but from the *friendly
- hostile co-operation of many scientists*
(Popper, 1966, p. 217).

These three papers examining separate but related
aspects of the development of cognition allow one an
insight into the testing of hypotheses and the generation of discourse which is the stimulus to scientific
psychology.

REFERENCES

POPPER, K. (1966), 'The Open Society and Its Enemies',
vol. 2, London: Routledge & Kegan Paul.

Chapter 2

LOGICAL INFERENCES AND DEVELOPMENT

Peter E. Bryant

What do we mean by logical development?   It really has
two possible senses.   The first and weaker sense is
that children will get better at solving logical problems as they grow older.   But if this is all that
logical development means, it cannot be very important.
For it would be amazing if it were not so.   We should
be enormously surprised if we gave children a series
of problems involving various logical moves and did not
find that the younger children failed more often than
their elders.   In fact we already know from intelligence tests, from Piaget's work and from many other
sources that the expected thing happens.   Children do
get better at this sort of task as they grow older.
  But there are a number of reasons why this obvious
'development' should happen, and this is because there
are a number of different ways in which the younger
children could be making their mistakes.   They might
not understand what they are being asked to do;   or
they might not take in the information on which they
have to use their logic;   or they might not remember
it;   or they might understand, and take in and
remember everything perfectly, but be unable to perform the necessary logical manoeuvre.
  In many ways, the first three alternatives are
rather trivial (which is why this first sense of
logical development is so unimportant).   Children
do understand and take in and remember some things,
and any problem at all can be rephrased in such a way
that the child will know what he has to do and will
handle the information that comes to him effectively.
It is the fourth alternative which is crucial,
because if the child cannot make the necessary logical
move, if he simply lacks the logical ability or the
internal logical mechanisms, then no amount of re-
phrasing the problem will make the slightest difference.
53

This brings me to the second and much stronger sense of the term logical development. It is that young children initially lack and only rather gradually acquire the logical mechanisms which are needed to solve even the simplest logical problems. This in fact is the sense which has been adopted in all the theories of logical development of which I know.

The distinction between the two possible senses is that any one talking about development in the strong sense must be able to demonstrate that his experiments are not treating it in the weak sense. In other words, he must show that his unsurprising discovery that young children make mistakes is not simply a matter of some failure to take in or remember information. He must demonstrate that these really are logical errors.

One of the most striking things about most approaches to the question of logical abilities in young children is that this sort of precaution is often not taken and indeed that the need for it is frequently ignored.

A very striking example has always been our ideas about children's ability to make deductive inferences. The question here is a simple one. Can young children combine two separate items of information in order to come up with a solution which is, to them at least, a completely new one? This question demands a test in which the child is given two or more items, and is asked to combine them inferentially, and tests such as. these have an important place in the history of the experimental study of conceptual development.

One historical reason for paying attention to them is that it was this sort of test which apparently first attracted Piaget to child psychology. While spending some time at Simon's laboratory in Paris he was given some tests, devised by Burt, which involved syllogisms – John is bigger than Mary: Bob is smaller than Mary. Who is bigger, John or Bob? Piaget was deeply impressed by young children's failures on these apparently simple problems, and the experience seems to have set him off on the long and complex path which led to his insistent pronouncement that young children are basically illogical. Naturally his theory, among many other things, demands that children cannot link relational judgments in an inference until they reach the age of roughly seven or eight years.

Many others agreed with him, and this general consensus leads us to the second historical reason for

looking at inferences in children.   One could not
find two more disparate approaches to children, two
more divergent traditions, than Piaget's and the S-R
behaviourist tradition.   They disagree on practically
every point.   They are interested in entirely different
kinds of problems.   Their notions not only of what
children understand, but also of what causes their
understanding to improve are in total opposition.
And yet when it comes to deductive inferences they
speak with one voice.   From both sides we have the
clear statement that young children lack the internal
logical mechanisms to make whatever inference is in
question and do not acquire them before, at the
earliest, the age of seven or eight years.

     We can start with the behaviourist tradition, where
the most significant work has been done by Kendler and
Kendler (1967).   These are experimenters whose main
intent has been to uncover 'the biological continuum'
which they claim must exist between rat and (human)
college student.   Among other tasks they took the
question of inferences as something which might show
differences somewhere along this alleged continuum.

     Their starting point was the work of Maier (1936)
who in the late 1930s had given both rats and young
children spatial problems which could only be solved
by combining separate items of information.   For
instance, the children were first shown round a maze
which was actually in the shape of a swastika (experimenters must have been less sensitive to political
innuendoes in those days) and were then taken to a
particular part of it and required to find the most
direct way to another part.   They had to combine
their knowledge of the maze with their understanding
of where they were at that particular moment.   Children below the age of six failed this task quite consistently, though older than this they were more
successful.

     The experiment is not in itself at all convincing.
We can note, for example, that there was no check
that the young children who failed could remember the
information which they had to put together.   Therefore their failure might have had nothing to do with
a difficulty in co-ordinating separate items of information.   Instead they may simply have forgotten what
they had to combine.

     The Kendlers took care of this point at least in
some of their experiments, which led them in the end
to even more pessimistic conclusions than those of
Maier.   They took the precaution of making sure that

the children were thoroughly familiar with the items
they later had to combine.   Their basic experimental
situation involves a box with three panels.   The two
side panels have some sort of a handle and working
this handle produces an object which drops into a
tray set in its own panel.   In one panel this object
is a glass marble, in the other a steel marble.   So
much for the side panels.

The central panel is different.   Instead of a
handle it has a hole, and the child must learn that
dropping the steel marble, but not the glass marble
(or vice versa), has the effect of a small toy dropping
into the tray in that panel.   These then are the two
items of information, that one side panel produces a
steel marble, the other a glass one, and that placing
the steel marble in the central hole leads to a
reward.   Once both are learned thoroughly the child
is given the inferential problem, which involves
getting the reward from scratch.   He has to press
the handle which produces the steel marble and then
insert it in the hole.   He has to combine the two
segments.

The Kendlers' results on this sort of task were very
poor.   Five- and six-year-old children show no sign
of an inference, only a glimmer can be found in eight-
year-olds, and the only consistent success that could
be discovered was among a group of college students,
the peak of the continuum to which the Kendlers have
devoted their research.

At first sight this seems rather convincing evidence that young children cannot make inferences.
Certainly by making the children learn the separate
segments the Kendlers probably made sure that they
could remember the information which they were being
asked to put together.   However, some second thoughts
about the nature of the problem are surely justified.
It is all very arbitrary.   Pulling a handle produces
a steel marble for no visible reason.   Putting a
steel marble in a hole produces a toy, again for no
visible reason.   If there is no obvious logic to
these artificial associations (handle-steel marble,
steel marble-toy) why should the child be logical about
combining them?

There is now considerable support for this anxiety.
Cole, Gay, Glick and Sharp (1971), with some ingenuity,
set up a replica of the Kendlers' apparatus in the
middle of the Liberian bush and tested non-literate
Liberians, who did very badly indeed.   But the experimenters noticed that many of these people were overcome

with fear: the strange apparatus seemed too much for
them.   When they were given another task which had
exactly the same structure, but which involved familiar
and presumably more reassuring material (black and red
keys, boxes with corks) they managed to make the
inference perfectly well.

It turns out to be the same with children.   Simon
Hewson (unpublished material) has given children of
four years and upwards a series of tasks which involved familiar and understandable material, but which
were otherwise the direct analogy of the Kendlers'
problem.   For example, instead of having handles
which unaccountably produced marbles, he put things in
and out of drawers so that the child simply had to
learn which drawer to pull out in order to get a
particular marble.   These new tasks produced quite
different results.   Even four-year-old children
managed to make the inferential jump, though they
failed as soon as the Kendlers' more singular apparatus
was introduced.

We can conclude that in the Kendlers' experiment the
young children simply decided not to bother about
logic in a situation which to them seemed not to be
logical in any way.   We can also conclude that by
four they do have the ability to put together at
least some kinds of information inferentially.

Though the Kendlers' experiments were meant to be
a development of Maier's work with the swastika maze,
they involved a fundamentally different kind of
inference.   Maier's study was concerned purely with
space.   To solve it the child had to co-ordinate two
items of information which concerned only his position
and the position of things around him.   The Kendlers'
task, on the other hand, was concerned partly with
space but partly also with objects (the steel marble
leads to a toy).   This means that although we now
know that young children can solve the latter problem
we cannot be sure that they can make an inference
about space.

Yet the question is important, for we can only
perceive a limited amount of our spatial environment
at any one time.   Inevitably a great deal of our
behaviour must involve combining information about
different parts of the space around us which can never
be perceived at the same time.   It seems to be the
same with children.   A child will set off up the
stairs to fetch a toy from a particular room even
though the toy and the room are quite invisible when
he starts his journey.   Apparently, he is combining

two separate things (toy in room, stairs lead to room),
and this might very well be regarded as an inference.

There is however another way of looking at behaviour
like this.   It could simply be a chain of associations
(setting off in a particular direction and doing
various other things leads to the toy) rather than a
genuine inference (because the toy is in the room and
because the stairs lead to the room I must go up those
stairs).   So common observation cannot tell us whether
children link information about space inferentially.
We need an experiment.

Susan Somerville (unpublished material) gave some
five-year-olds a problem which could be solved by combining two items about space.   The task involved a
toy dog, cat, girl, boy, garden and house, and the
children were told where the boy and girl were (boy in
house, girl in garden) and whom each animal was with
(cat with boy, dog with girl).   From this information
alone they had to work out the position of each
animal.   To make sure that they were using spatial
relations alone to make the inference she threw in
some non-spatial items (e.g. girl drew a picture of
the cat) as well.

She found that the children could make the inference
perfectly well provided that they could remember the
items which they had to combine.   There seems to be
no doubt that by the time they go to school children
can make a spatial inference.   How soon in life this
ability appears is something which has yet to be discovered.

In fact Piaget (1954) has actually suggested that
even babies can make deductive inferences about space
by the end of their first year of life.   His evidence
which is based on observations about babies' reactions
to hidden objects is indirect, but the very fact that
he argued for the presence of an inferential ability
so early in life may surprise some who are more
familiar with his much more pessimistic statements
about other types of inferences.   But Piaget's main
concern in this area has been with transitive
inferences.

I know that when A > B and B > C, A must be greater
than C whatever the quantity involved.   To reach the
inferential conclusion about A and C, I must be able
to combine the two relations, AB and BC, and I must
also know that the continuum involved represents an
ordered series.

Piaget's (1970) argument is that the child of seven
years or so and younger simply cannot make a transitive

inference.   He is unable to realise that B can be simultaneously smaller than A and larger than C, and thus he cannot grasp the essential nature of an ordered continuum.   As a result he has to treat the two judgments (AB and BC) as entirely separate.

This basic inability, as Piaget is keen to point out, should have many serious consequences.   For one thing the child should not be able to measure or to understand why people do use measures, if he cannot grasp the fact that A and C could be connected through the common measure B.   Another consequence which Piaget suggests is that the child will not even understand many constant spatial relationships.   For example, the child will not understand that the water level in a tilted glass will always be horizontal, because he cannot take advantage of the perception that it is always parallel to horizontal features of the spatial framework like the top of a table.   He cannot work out that the level must be constant if, whatever the tilt, the level always parallels an unchanging feature.

No one could dispute Piaget's case for the importance of transitive inferences.   We are left with the question whether it is really true that children younger than seven or eight years really cannot manage to make them.

In fact all Piaget's evidence on this point turns out to be rather flimsy.   Broadly speaking he has pioneered two kinds of test, one which could be said to be basically passive, the other active.   In the passive tests the child is simply given all the essential information (A > B, B > C, or A = B, B = C) and is then asked the inferential question (A?C). All that he has to do is to make the inference.   Here is an example given by Piaget: 'We present two sticks to a child, stick A being smaller than stick B.   Then we hide stick A and show him stick B together with a larger stick C.   Then we ask him how stick A and C compare.   Pre-operational children will say that they do not know because they have not seen them together - they have not been able to compare them.'

It is easy to see from this example that the children are given all the necessary information and simply have to combine it.   It is also true to say that when children of five, six and even seven years are given the problem in this form, they often fail it.   As a result, it comes as no surprise that they tend to fail Piaget's more active test.

In the best known of his experiments on active

inferences Piaget (1953) wanted to find out whether
young children would spontaneously use measure to compare two lengths.   He built a tower of bricks on a
table, left a stick around which was the same length
as this tower from top to bottom, and then asked the
child to build another tower on the floor the same
height from top to bottom as the one on the table.
It was difficult to make a direct comparison of the
two towers accurately because they started from
different levels, and so the solution was to put the
stick against the existing tower, to find that tower
and stick were the same height and then to use the
stick as a standard for the height of the new tower.
Note that this solution involves an inference and also
two other things as well.   The child must recognise
that any direct comparison of the two towers will be
fallible, and he must find and use the measure.

In fact Piaget demonstrated that children below
seven years or so tended not to produce this solution.
They did not measure, and usually their two towers
were different heights.   He concludes from this, as
from the passive inference experiments, that these
children simply do not understand how to link two
relational judgments in one transitive inference.

This is the substance of Piaget's case which, it
is easy to see, is a fairly weak one.   Both sets of
experiments have serious weaknesses.   Two things at
least are wrong with the traditional experiment on
passive inferences.   The first concerns the children
who fail.   Piaget claims that they cannot make
inferences, but there is another possibility.   They
may not remember the information which they have to
put together.   There is no particular reason why
they should bother to do so.   So it is quite likely
that when children are asked the AC question they may
have forgotten what they were told about AB or BC
and that, if only they remembered, they could make
the inference.

It is very easy to control for this simply by
checking whether the child does remember AB and BC at
the time that he is asked the AC question.   Only if
he remembers that A > B and that B > C and still does
not reach the conclusion that A > C is it possible
to conclude that he cannot make an inference.   And
yet, despite the enormous interest in the problem of
inferences in children, despite the vast number of
experiments carried out on this problem since the
1920s, not one study managed to include this essential
control until 1970.

But this is not the only difficulty.   Three quantities (A, B and C) turn out not to be enough.   Five
are needed in order to ensure that children who produce the correct answer are not simply parroting
verbal labels remembered from the initial direct comparisons.   Suppose that there are five quantities,
initially presented in four direct comparisons (A > B,
B > C, C > D, D > E).   Note that three quantities
(B, C and D) are sometimes the larger, sometimes the
smaller, in these comparisons.   The inference that
can be made from these is that B > D, and since both
B and D, and C the quantity through which they can be
compared, are all equally often larger and smaller in
the initial comparisons the correct answer cannot be
produced by parroting.   Answering the BD question
correctly must therefore be an inference.

Some time ago Tom Trabasso and I (Bryant and
Trabasso, 1971) carried out two experiments, in which
we set out to meet both these requirements.   The
experiment involved two stages.   In the first the
children learned over many trials that A > B, B > C,
C > D, D > E.   A B C D and E were represented by
coloured sticks, and in one experiment the children
were given glimpses of their absolute lengths while
in the other they were not.   In the second stage of
each experiment the children were tested for their
recall of the original comparisons (AB, BC, CD, DE)
and were asked six new questions (AC, AE, BD, BE, CE);
of these the most important, as I have shown, was the
BD question.

We found that even four-year-old children could
answer this crucial question well above chance level
in both experiments.   It seems that by ensuring that
they remembered the necessary information well (as
indeed the memory tests established they did), we made
it possible for them to make a genuine transitive inference.   These children, we concluded, do possess
the logical mechanisms needed to make an inference.

These results have recently been confirmed (de
Boysson-Bardies and O'Regan, 1973), but these same
authors have disputed our conclusion.   They argue
that the children might have succeeded without actually
making a logical inference.   Their argument is a
complex one, but basically centres on the importance
of the end points of our series, A and E.   These
authors argue (i) that the children may recognise
that A being always large is the large endpoint or
that E being always small is the small endpoint or
both;   (ii) that they may notice also that in the

initial comparisons the endpoint B is always associated
with the large one A, and by association make B also
'large', and similarly make D 'small' when they notice
that the endpoint it is associated with, E, is the
small one; (iii) that when comparing B with D they
may decide that B is the larger because it is large
while D is small.

Actually this is such a complex train of thought
that it is difficult to believe that any child who can
manage it cannot also manage an inference. However,
it does seem that this is an alternative which was not
ruled out in our experiments. But a more recent
experiment by Susan Martin and myself makes it unlikely
that the endpoints have such effects.

Our experiments involved four quantities presented
in the following manner A > B, and Y > Z. (Again the
quantities were represented by coloured sticks whose
complete lengths the children never saw.) Notice
that this is not a series since B and Y are never compared. Some of the children, all of whom were four
years, were given just this information. The rest
were, in addition, taught that A was the longer and Z
the shorter of all four sticks; they were given endpoint training. Thus B has been associated with the
large endpoint and Y with the small endpoint for the
second but not for the first group.

Consider now what should happen when these children
are asked later how B and Y compare. If the endpoint
hypothesis is right the second group should, because
of the endpoint associations, answer that B > Y more
often than the first group who do not have these
associations. This did not happen. There was no
difference between the two groups' replies to the BY
question, and no sign at all that the second group
thought that B was larger than Y.

It seems then that the balance of the evidence
supports our contention that quite young children do
make transitive inferences. Certainly there is not
one convincing piece of evidence against this contention. Since we pointed out in 1971 that it was
essential to check for memory in these experiments,
no one has been able to produce one single instance
of a child who can remember the information essential
for an inference, but cannot combine it inferentially.

This leaves us with active inferences which test
whether the child can measure. There can be no
doubt that the child might have been confused about
what he had to do. After all he was asked to make
one tower as tall as the other, and it might not have

been clear to him that this meant the height from top
to bottom of each tower.   Certainly Piaget reports
that many simply lined up the summits of the two
towers, which suggests that they were thinking in
terms of absolute height rather than the length from
top to bottom.

However my co-workers and I have made many attempts
to make this and other measuring situations perfectly
comprehensible to even quite young children, and yet
we always come up with the same result, which is
again that young children do not use the intervening
measure.   Our conclusion is that although young children can make transitive inferences they do not
always put this ability to full effect.   Why not?

One possibility which we have yet to test is that
the children fail because they do not realise that an
inference is required.   A and C are present, but
present in such a way that a direct comparison between
them is likely to be wrong.   But if the child does
not recognise the fallibility of this sort of direct
comparison, he will not see the need to make an inference.   Why bother with the whole cumbersome process when a direct comparison apparently will do?

This could easily be tested in experiments in which
it is made abundantly clear to the child that a direct
comparison will not work.   But these are experiments
that are still to be done.   In the meantime I conclude that young children, even before they go to
school, can (i) make a deductive inference; (ii) make
a spatial inference; (iii) make a transitive inference.   How they put these inferences into effect in
real life remains as an important and educationally
relevant question.

REFERENCES

BRYANT, P.E. and TRABASSO, T.R. (1971), Transitive
Inferences and Memory in Young Children, 'Nature',
vol. 232, 456-8.
COLE, M., GAY, J., GLICK, J.A. and SHARP, D.W. (1971),
'The Cultural Context of Learning and Thinking',
London: Methuen.
DE BOYSSON-BARDIES, B. and O'REGAN, K. (1973) 'Nature',
vol. 246, 531-4.
KENDLER, T.S. and KENDLER, H.H. (1967), Inferential
Behaviour in Young Children, in Lipsitt, L.P. and
Spiker, C.C. (eds), 'Advances in Child Development and
Behaviour', vol. 3, Academic Press.

MAIER, N.R.F. (1936), 'J. Exp. Psychol.' (title not available).

PIAGET, J. (1953), How Children Form Mathematical Concepts, 'Scientific American' (November).

PIAGET, J. (1954), 'The Child's Construction of Reality', London: Routledge & Kegan Paul.

PIAGET, J. (1970), 'Genetic Epistemology', New York: Columbia University Press.

Chapter 3

THE OPERATIVE AND FIGURATIVE ASPECTS OF KNOWLEDGE IN PIAGET'S THEORY

Hans G. Furth

1   THEORETICAL PERSPECTIVE

Piaget is primarily interested in the nature of knowledge, and for him knowledge is concerned either with
states or with transformations of states.   In the
language of logic one could say that knowledge either
describes a thing or that it operates on a thing.   A
glass, for instance, can be observed as a state, something which has a certain shape; or it can be looked
upon as something that can be operated on, either
externally or internally, something that one knows
how to use, construct or repair.   All knowledge,
according to Piaget, implies not merely a reading of
but also a transformation of reality.   Consequently
static aspects of knowledge can be distinguished from
dynamic transformations.
    In logical terms there is a distinction between
descriptors (propositions or expressions that describe a certain state) and operators or combiners
(propositions that explain how to get from one state
to another).   This double aspect of knowledge is
vital in Piaget's theory.   One could say that the
whole of Piaget's theory is based on the assumption
that we know something if, and only if, we know how
to construct or transform it.   Piaget did not invent
this perspective, but he consistently built on it.
Consider that a person who knows how to construct a
chair certainly must know what a chair is; if one
knows how to set up a postal system one knows what a
postal system is.   If, however, a little child simply
observes a postman delivering letters but never tries
to understand how those letters reach their destination
or what the postman has to do with them, one could say
that his figurative knowledge of the postman may be

excellent, but his operative knowledge is quite
inadequate.

Piaget became a child psychologist in order to find
out how knowledge is constructed; for this purpose
he set out to observe children and to examine the
origins of adult knowledge. Piaget assumes that if
he knows how knowledge is constructed, then he should
know something about what knowledge is, because the
construction of knowledge reflects the *nature* of
knowledge, just as the construction of a chair reflects what a chair is, or the construction of a
glass, a glass. The word 'construction' obviously
relates to the operative aspect of knowledge.

To some extent Piaget has neglected the figurative
aspect of knowledge. In studying general structures
of actions and operations he has deliberately not
focused on the specific content of the operations.
So he discusses classification, or relation, or inference, and these rules of operations are general,
not limited to particular contents. However, by
stressing the operative-figurative distinction Piaget
points to the importance of content and individual
differences. Knowledge is not just rules of construction; knowledge implies the construction of
something specific, or the construction with something in particular. If one constructs with one
medium, the use of another medium *can* make a difference even though logically there is no change of
rules. Similarly, when dealing with operators or
combiners, it makes no difference whether one writes
A + B or B + A. But for a child it may make a lot
of difference. For instance, a transitivity problem
is presented in the form: A is bigger than B and B
is bigger than C. Many children will succeed in
knowing that A is bigger than C. However if the
problem is expressed in the form: B is bigger than C
and A is bigger than B, children who may succeed
with the first sequence could well be confused.
Logically, the operation is exactly the same, but
psychologically there may well be a difference.

There may also be individual differences. Piaget
records wide age ranges in the logical performance
of children. On certain tasks there are some five-
year-old children who seem to be at the stage of
formal thinking, and some twelve-year-old children
who have not even reached pre-operatory thinking.
Piaget, however, abstracted from these individual
differences, since his concern was to look for stable
structures that occur sequentially in time. These

structures are by definition operative structures,
which deal with general rules of organising, con-
structing and transforming, regardless of content.

The distinction between operative and figurative
aspects of knowledge stresses the fact that knowledge
is never in a vacuum.   It is not an idle activity
turned in on itself; knowledge always finally deals
with particular states.   It depends on our own perspective and interest whether we focus on the object
of knowledge as a *static* thing or whether we focus on
it as an *operative* rule.

If we focus on the figurative aspect of an object,
for instance a glass, attention would be directed to
its particular configuration: the accent is on the
particular, the special, the contingent.   The fact
that there may be a chip, some dust or some printing
on the glass becomes important.   The operative
aspect, on the other hand, would be primarily concerned with knowledge of what the object is and what
its function is.   It may be a special glass with a
particular use or material; it may be resistant to
breakage or have some other peculiar characteristics
relative to its use and handling.   This identification and interpretation of an object has to do with
the operative aspect, while the figurative aspect
deals with the static configuration, the descriptive
and observable.

It is, however, very important to understand that
these are not two different types of knowledge.   We
are dealing with two different *aspects* of the *same*
knowledge.   All figurative knowledge has some
operative components, because by definition knowledge requires some constructive contribution from
the knower, that is, from the person who knows something.   In the same way there can never be an
operative knowing that is not focused on some particular object, even if the object happens to be a
symbol.   Thus these aspects of knowledge are
different perspectives of the same whole.   One could
say that the figurative aspect deals with what is
usually called the 'observable', whereas the operative
aspect is that aspect of knowledge which has to be
inferred.   The difficulty is that one cannot define
a priori what is observable and what is inferrable
in the external world.

There are plenty of studies that show that what is
observable as a so-called fact is partly a function
of what the observer knows about the event in general.
What is observable to one person may not be observable

to another person.   For example, to us it is observable that certain lines on a window frame are parallel or vertical, but to a little child these 'facts' are by no means observable or comprehensible.   What is observable is always in part a function of the structures that the observer has developed.   Therefore one cannot divide the external world into things that are figurative and things that are operative.   Depending on the structures that the observer brings to the external world, one can identify the same stimulus as belonging to the operative or to the figurative aspects of knowing in practically any object.   These aspects change and what is the operative aspect to a young child may later become a figurative aspect for an older child.

Figurative aspects of knowledge by definition are present in any perception.   Perception means being in knowledgeable contact with some object that is present to the senses, and this demands that the knower pays some attention to the figurative components of the object.   Perception is therefore one instrument of figurative knowledge.

A second instrument of figurative knowledge, according to Piaget, is imitation.   Imitation has a rather important role to play in Piaget's system. In order to understand its function fully, we need to discuss Piaget's theory of schemes.

By definition all schemes are operative, and an operative scheme can be found at any cognitive-developmental stage, whether sensori-motor or operatory (operations).   The distinction operative-figurative is on an entirely different level from the distinction operatory versus sensori-motor.   Sensori-motor refers to a specific developmental stage, as does operatory with its three substages of pre-operatory, concrete operations and formal operations. Operative and figurative, however, refer to different aspects of the object of knowledge, regardless of stage.

Schemes are instruments of assimilation.   There may be all kinds of physical stimuli in the world, but if we do not have instruments for being in touch with these stimuli then, psychologically speaking, they do not exist.   If we do not have a scheme of a square, for instance, then we cannot perceive a square;   it is simply not there as far as we are concerned.   So the most essential aspects of knowledge are operative schemes that allow impinging stimuli to be psychologically assimilated.   This explains the importance of

these terms 'assimilation' and 'schemes' in Piaget's
theory.

The other important concept is accommodation.
Accommodation means the application of schemes to a
particular event or a particular object.   At the
outset we must understand that assimilation, schemes
and accommodation are three aspects of the same thing.
There is not one behaviour called 'assimilation' and
another behaviour called 'accommodation', and the
scheme does not really differ from assimilation.   A
scheme is an instrument of assimilation: a scheme
in so far as it assimilates is called assimilation;
the scheme in so far as it accommodates is called
accommodation.

Accommodation means the application of a general
scheme (and every scheme is general) to a unique
event (and every event is unique), and each event
changes in every second.   So there is always an
aspect of newness and an aspect of paying attention
to the particular.   And as attention is paid to the
particular, one can say that accommodation always
involves an aspect of imitation.   Visually, one's
eyes scan and thereby imitate the outline of the
object.   There is also imitation when an object is
handled.   The same scheme assimilates the single
object, but is applied differently: there are
different accommodations in the act of handling and
in the act of visually perceiving a given object.

Imitation can take place when the object or event
is not present.   When a child has gone beyond the
sensori-motor period and has reached the beginnings
of the operatory period, the child becomes capable
of symbol formation.   Symbol formation means imitation in the absence of a model.   If a child imitates
a glass that is not present, then he symbolises the
glass, and for that he makes use of imitation.   The
material that the child uses in the symbolisation
comes from figurative aspects of the things that he
dealt with.   So a child who has experienced a glass
of a particular size would imitate that particular
aspect.   In other words, in imitation, a child imitates a figurative aspect of an object.   Quite
generally, in every symbol formation, in every external or internal symbol, there is the figurative
aspect that provides the medium of the symbol.
Imitation is, in Piaget's terminology, the second
instrument of figurative knowledge.   And if this
imitation becomes internalised, then we have the
third instrument of figurative knowing, and that is

the mental image.   So there are three processes
involved in figurative knowledge: firstly, perception, and within perception there is accommodation
to a figurative component which is where figurative
knowledge comes from.   Secondly, in the absence of
the model there is external imitation in the form of
symbol formation, which takes its matter or medium
from the figurative component.   Thirdly, if the
symbol becomes internalised, we have what we experience as a mental image which could be a visual, kinaesthetic or sound image.   These are the three
sources, or instruments of figurative knowledge.
      The operative aspect, on the other hand, does not
come from an imitation of external objects and this
is a major difference between figurative and operative knowing.   The source of the *figurative* aspect
of knowledge is in the external world which is full
of configurations that we can imitate.   But the
understanding of the thing, the *operative* aspect,
does not come from imitating something that is outside.   Understanding is never observed in the outside
world, it is always an operative feedback from the
person's own activity.   So the source of figurative
knowing is the outside world, whereas the source of
operative knowing is the child's own activity on the
outside world.
      If a child understands the principle of commuta-
tivity, that A + B equals B + A, this, according to
Piaget, is operative understanding which cannot be
observed in the external world.   Obviously, a child
can observe that he has two apples here and three
apples there and that together they make five apples,
and that if he has three apples here and two apples
there he can again count five apples.   But there is
a difference between observing something as an empirical result, and understanding something as a logical
necessity.   When shown five elements in a certain
configuration with subsequent displacement so that
the initial state is transformed into another, many
children will say that the sum is still the same.
This is because they can count.   Children who have
to count to justify that the sum is still the same,
base their knowledge on a comparison of particular
states, whereas children who understand that numbers
do not change if the clustering of the configuration
of the elements is changed, do not have to count or
look at the empirical results; this knowledge of
conservation of number is at a different level than
the previous knowledge by counting.   Piaget refers

to stage-specific characteristics: a child who has
reached the operatory stage of numbers has a different
way of knowing numbers than a pre-operatory child, and
the most important characteristic of this knowledge is
that it is not based on the figurative knowing of
observable results.   The criterion of operatory
knowing derives, according to Piaget, from feedback
from the child's own activities, such as the activity of
ordering and displacing things and abstracting from it
the regulatory principle of commutativity.

The figurative and operative aspects of knowledge
are inseparable, as are the subject and the object.
The subject is the person who knows, and the object is
the thing that is known by the subject;   one cannot
have one without the other.   There is no object unless
there is also a subject to know it.   The operative
scheme and the known event are two different aspects
of the same thing.   Yet operative knowledge is
deductive, or at least it tends towards pure deduc-
tion;   it is not based on empirical results.   If, as
Piaget claims, the operative schemes do not derive
from the physical world, but derive from the activity
of the subject, the question can be asked: how is it
that these operative schemes have such an obvious fit
to the physical world?   How is it that mathematical
knowledge does not derive from the physical world?
This is an old philosophical question.

Piaget's answer to this is that the activity of the
organism is itself part of the physical world.   People
(subjects) are objects in the physical world and psychological activities share both physical and biological characteristics.   In this respect, one can
again see that the subjective and objective aspects
are not two entirely separate things.   The reason
why operative knowledge is not simply very important
for figurative knowledge, but is indeed absolutely
essential, is that one cannot know a state without
any kind of subjective operative contribution in the
first place.   Moreover, the greater our operative
knowing, the greater the transformation of reality
states.   But at the same time the better also our
figurative knowing.

2   THREE STUDIES

The difference between figurative and operative
aspects of knowledge can be particularly well illustrated in studies of memory, such as the studies devised

by Piaget and Inhelder, and extended in our own work.
As has been stressed in the theoretical discussion,
both operative and figurative elements are involved
in perception and image, but it is possible to distinguish them by positing that operative knowing is a
function of the child's stage of development and is
the code through which he transforms a situation into
something he understands.   The figurative component,
being concerned with the static here and now details
of an event, is linked to the perception and representation of a particular content, whether in image
or in recall.

Piaget showed children pictures of a tilted glass
on a table, half-filled with bright red liquid.
Children had no difficulty in recognising the picture
as a tilted glass half-filled with wine.   When the
children were asked to copy the picture, very few
five- or six-year-olds copied it accurately.   However, there may be a few children who accommodate to
the picture very well, pay attention to every detail
and copy it more or less accurately.   But when asked
two hours later to recall what they have drawn or
seen before, they do not reproduce an accurate like-
ness.   They draw what they know and understand;
they remember that they have seen a drawing of a
tilted glass, half-filled with wine.   In many cases,
this means drawing the level of the water parallel
to the base of the glass, not to that of the table,
or drawing a glass brim full, like an enclosed rectangle.   Piaget reports that certain children produced a deficient memory drawing after half an hour,
and six months later he went back to the children
and asked them to recall it again.   This they did,
and now they made a drawing that was better than the
first.   In other words, strictly speaking, as far
as their memory performance is concerned, the memory
improved between first and second trials.   This
finding is in some ways paradoxical because if memory
performance does anything it gets worse, not better.

In our experiments (Furth, Ross and Youniss, 1974)
we varied the conditions used by Piaget and Inhelder.
Children were presented with four stimulus pictures,
but for purposes of this discussion it is sufficient
to examine the results of the responses to one
picture - like Piaget's, that of a glass tilted from
the horizontal at an angle of 45°.   The area representing the liquid was entirely blacked in, with the
top edge clearly visible and paralleling the base line
of the picture, not of the glass (see Figure 1).

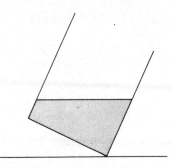

Figure 3.1

The sample consisted of 116 children aged five + to nine +.   The children were tested in their classroom, and were shown the picture.   Half the children were asked to copy the picture; half were asked to draw it after looking at it for fifteen seconds.   The results, showing the percentage of correctly drawn pictures (that is, partly-filled with the water level horizontal) can be seen in Table 3.1.

TABLE 3.1

Age	Copy (%)	Non-copy (%)
5	8	6
6	29	25
7	37	44
9	60	77

Notice the copy condition; it is rather revealing. The children saw the picture and were asked to copy it, but only 8 per cent of the five-year-olds and less than 30 per cent of the six-year-olds copied the horizontal water level as depicted.   Even by the age of nine many were unable to reproduce an exact copy. Indeed at all ages the performance in the copy condition was no better than in the short-term memory condition.   That is, many children did not reproduce the horizontal water level.

The children were retested after six months and again after twelve months.   The experimenter reminded them that they had seen some pictures and they were asked to recall and draw them.   Their drawings were coded into three categories: the first category

represents drawings correctly reproducing the important
characteristics of the original stimulus picture including the horizontal water level. The second, relevant modification, indicates that the child remembered
something important about the original stimulus
drawing.   There were three main types of relevant
modifications: the liquid parallel to the base of the
glass; the base of the glass adhering to the table,
but the sides tilted to form a parallelogram and
finally the liquid level tilted to be more vertical
than horizontal. · This last modification was more
frequent in the higher grades.   The third category is
called non-relevant modification.   In this case the
child would simply draw a glass and forget the tilt or
the half-full condition.   This category implies
absence of a specific memory for the original event.

TABLE 3.2   Results by age

Age	Reproduction	Trial 1 (%)	Trial 2 (after 6 mths) (%)	Trial 3 (after 12 mths) (%)
5 years	Horizontal	7	3	3
	Relevant modification	70	24	10
	Non-relevant modification	24	72	86
6 years	Horizontal	27	13	17
	Relevant modification	74	40	43
	Non-relevant modification	-	47	40
9 years	Horizontal	64	28	32
	Relevant modification	36	60	64
	Non-relevant modification	-	12	4

These results show a clear deterioration in memory
performance, particularly for the five-year-old children.   Even though the youngest children could take
notice of important aspects of the stimulus in the
immediate situation (only 7 per cent in the horizontal
category, but 70 per cent producing a relevant modification), after six months they produced fewer accurate

drawings but, most importantly, there was a dramatic
decrease in drawings that indicate specific memory
of the original and a corresponding increase in non-
relevant modifications. This trend was continued
in the drawings after one year. For the six-year-
old children there is also evidence of a regression:
the percentage of accurate drawings diminished, and
the responses were split almost evenly between relevant and non-relevant modifications after both six
and twelve months. However, the results for the
oldest group were different. Here the main change
was from horizontal to relevant modification, but
even so the majority six months or a year after the
first drawing seemed to deteriorate. They remembered
the half-filled glass, they remembered the tilt, but
they made errors on horizontality.

It is clear from these results that in most children the memory performance, over both six and twelve
months, indicates an apparent regression as far as
operative schemes are concerned. There were, however, 20 out of 160 children who showed an improvement
in their production, children who at first produced a
relevantly modified drawing, and after six months or
a year made a correct horizontal drawing. In general,
the results showed 17 per cent improvement and 66 per
cent deterioration in performance.

I will discuss these results in terms of the two
aspects of knowledge, operative and figurative, starting with those children who showed an improvement.
It is possible for an eight-year-old child to produce
at first a relevant drawing, without the horizontal
liquid level, and six months later a horizontal drawing. His operative knowledge may have developed
further so that now he has a better understanding of
what the drawing means. If one memorizes something,
one brings to bear one's understanding on the situation. If one's understanding is better, then one's
memory is also likely to be better. So what has
improved in this experiment is not the child's memory,
but his operative understanding.

The greater problem is really that of deterioration.
How is it possible that a child in January can make a
horizontal drawing and six months later in June when,
if anything, he should be more intelligent, he
deteriorates?

He remembered what to draw, but apparently he had
not fully understood the perception and the drawing
in the first place. In the first drawing, he imita-
ted the figurative component of the original and he

remembered the horizontal line as a figurative component.   The drawing was quite conspicuous - there was
a lively colour contrast, the line was big and he could
look at it and make a copy of it.   It is possible
that at this point the child really did not have the
scheme fully developed.   He had just enough of the
scheme to enable him to copy the drawing, together
with a figurative support, but after six months the
figurative support was no longer available.   So the
child produced a drawing that was more true to his
level of operative understanding the second time than
the first time.

What this suggests is that in a memory performance,
particularly this type of memory performance which is
strongly influenced by components of understanding, it
is possible for a child to copy something parrot-
fashion without understanding it, and then six months
later to forget it.   In the same way, if you ask a
child how much is nine and three, and he says that he
has forgotten, you know the child has not got the
operation of numbers.   Numerical operations are not
commonly memorized as a figurative knowing;   these
things are generally understood as an operative knowing even though, once they become routine, they may
appear to be handled as figurative knowing.   While
one can never be sure in a particular case whether a
child's performance reflects his figurative or operative knowing, globally the results of this experiment
are fairly clear.   If children make a better drawing
on the first than on the second trial, it is because
the figurative component helped them to make a drawing.   The drawing seems to indicate a higher operative level than is shown in memory performance six
months later when they no longer have this figurative
model to lean on.

These results illustrate what are figurative and
operative components in memory performance and it
seems that one can explain changes in memory performance very well as a function of the different contributions of figurative and operative components of
knowledge.   Naturally the figurative component is
stronger after one minute than after six months.
The figurative component is the essential memory
component - a recall of a particular figurative situation - whereas, in Piaget's terminology, operative
components are not things that one memorizes, rather
they are cognitive structures that one has.

Another example of the usefulness of separating the
figurative and operative component in memory is taken

from a study of the effect of labelling on recall.
The task (Furth and Milgram, 1973) was to recall the
names of a number of pictures which were presented
to children, aged four to twelve.   The pictures were
shown in different spatial and temporal conditions
which among other things affected ease of discovery
of categories.   For example, there were four pictures
of animals, fruit, tools and vehicles to be remembered.
We were interested to see how verbalization, that is,
labelling of the pictures during the original exposure,
would affect memory.

We discovered that the labelling condition had two
distinct effects on memory performance: one which we
called a direct primary effect, the other an indirect
organising effect.   To take the second effect first,
we observed that, particularly for the older children,
labelling facilitated discovery of the categories and
thereby indirectly improved recall in those conditions
where category recognition facilitated recall, or, on
the contrary, depressed memory performance where the
order of the pictures was not in line with the categories.   This then was an effect that is akin to
operative knowing and the effect differed as a function of the operative structures in the child (as
related to age) and of the categories in the original
picture array.   In contrast, the primary effect was
undifferentiated and was noticeable across the board
regardless of age or picture condition.   This direct
effect was slight compared to the selective powerful
influence of the other indirect effect.   It can be
related to the figurative aspect, in that labelling
apparently enhanced focusing on the perceptually given
features of the memory situation and thereby improved
memory performance.   In short, labelling during
presentation of the pictures to be recalled has two
distinct effects of which one is directly related to
memory and to figurative knowing whereas the other is
only indirectly related to memory, but directly to
organising activities and to operative knowing.

As a last example of using the figurative-operative
distinction I would like to consider a study undertaken
in our research centre at Catholic University in Washington, DC concerning transitivity thinking in young
children.   Bryant and Trabasso (1971) had claimed
that transitivity thinking (given A > B and B > C, it
follows that A > C) can be observed in children as
young as four years old.   The reason for young children's failure is not, as Piaget would assert, their
lack of reversible operations, but their limits in

memory capacity.   Consequently the authors trained
their children on the original pairs AB, BC, CD, DE,
after which the children spontaneously made rather
successful comparisons with the critical pair BD they
had not encountered before.   The conclusion: contrary to Piaget's theory these young children make a
correct logical inference of transitivity.

Here I would like to report a modified repetition
of the Bryant procedure to demonstrate that the performance of their subjects was not related to operative
knowing of the rule of transitivity but to a cumulative combining of figurative memory.   We argued that
children who understand (operative) transitivity
would differentiate between situations where transitivity reasoning is appropriate and those where it is
not, whereas children who build on (figurative)
memory would fail to distinguish the two situations.
Just as the infant who says 'mommy' to every female
adult is not credited with knowing what mother means,
we should not claim a logical operation in a subject
who does not know when and when not to apply it.   Two
tasks were used.   Task 1, which allowed operative
transitivity, was modelled after the Bryant and
Trabasso study.   In contrast, Task 2 did not allow
operative transitivity but it had a superficial,
figurative similarity to Task 1.

For Task 1 five pictures (A-E) were prepared, each
picture showing a stick figure of a sitting person of
apparently similar height with one distinguishing
characteristic from which the figure derived its
name.   During a first phase the children were trained
to make the following associations: when presented
with the pair AB they were to say that 'Mr Nose is
bigger than Mr Tie';   and presented with the pair BC
they were to say that 'Mr Tie is bigger than Mr Ear';
and then they were shown pairs CD and DE with similar
instructions.   Subsequently they were shown these
four pairs in random order and asked which of the
persons is bigger.   Both a verbal reply and pointing
were encouraged and errors were corrected.   After a
series of at least eight correct responses the test
phase started when no more corrections were given and
the children were presented in random order with all
possible pairs, both the ones they had seen before
and those not seen before.   In this case 24 of the
30 children (80 per cent) said on the critical comparison that B is bigger than D.   This is therefore
substantially a similar result to the one reported by
Bryant and Trabasso.

In Task 2 the experimenter referred, not to the relative size of the two persons, but to the colour of the button which they should get.   Specifically, we gave the children a red and a blue button and trained them that in the presentation of the pair AB 'the red button goes to Mr Nose and the blue to Mr Tie' (the child performed these instructions), in the presentation of the pair BC 'the red button goes to Mr Tie, the blue to Mr Ear', and similarly for the pairs CD and DE.   After they passed the criterion of eight errorless responses, they were requested during the test phase to make all possible comparisons, as on Task 1.   In this case 23 of the 30 children (77 per cent) put the red button with B, the blue with D.   In other words, these five-year-old children made a pre-dominantly transitive inference just as they had done on Task 1, but this time such an inference is logi-cally nonsensical.   I should add that for ten children the task order was 1-2, for 10 others it was 2-1, and an additional 10 children (who were only given one task) were then added for both Task 1 and Task 2. Inspection of results revealed no order effects.

We then gave both tasks to eleven-year-old children, 27 children for Task 1, 30 different children for Task 2.   The performance on Task 1 was quite similar to the results with the five-year-old group: on the critical BD comparison 81 per cent gave a 'transitive' response.   However, on Task 2 the two age groups differed on the critical response: only two (7 per cent) gave an illogical 'transitive' reply of red, three (10 per cent) gave an equally illogical 'intran-sitive' reply of blue, while twenty-five (83 per cent) gave the sensible reply 'I don't know.   This does not make sense.'   Table 3.3 contrasts the replies of the five- and the eleven-year-old children on all post-training comparisons.   The first four comparisons were trained; on the next five comparisons the interpretation of the reply is ambiguous because during training A was more frequently associated with red than with blue and E more with blue than with red. BD alone is the critical 'transitive' comparison.

TABLE 3.3   Percentage of replies to pairs of pictures on Task 2 in children (N = 30) aged five and eleven years

| Age | Reply | Training | | | | | | | | Critical |
		AB	BC	CD	DE	AC	AD	AE	BE	BD
5	Red	100	83	73	93	93	93	97	87	77
	Blue	-	17	27	7	7	7	3	13	23
11	Red	100	77	67	100	80	80	73	80	7
	Blue	-	10	7	-	7	7	7	7	10
	Non-sense	-	13	26	-	13	13	20	13	83

These different results on the critical trial BD demonstrate convincingly that different psychological processes were at the base of the performances of the older and the younger children.   The older children did not attempt to apply transitivity reasoning in Task 2; in contrast, the younger children showed an illogical transitivity, that is, they did not have transitivity at all.   Their apparent success on Task 1, just as their performance on Task 2, is easily explainable in the following terms.   When the children have to relate the pictures B and D which previously they had not seen together, they rely on the one figurative component which B and D have in common, namely C.   In the language of association theory, the combined presence of B and D evokes C and the respective response to B and D is then given on the basis of C: for Task 1, B is bigger than C and C is bigger than D, hence - omitting C - B is bigger than D; for Task 2, B gets red, C gets blue and C gets red and D gets blue, hence B gets red and D gets blue.

In conclusion, both eleven-year-old and five-year-old children performed alike on Task 1.   But Task 2 demonstrated that logical understanding of transitivity was present in the older but absent in the younger group.   In line with the figurative-operative distinction we can say that the figurative knowledge was similar in both age groups - and I pointed out how figurative associations can lead to what looks like a transitive performance - but they differed in operative knowledge, that is, the understanding of logical inference.

REFERENCES

BRYANT, P.E. and TRABASSO, T. (1971), Transitive Inferences and Memory in Young Children, 'Nature', vol.
232, 456-8.
FURTH, H.G. and MILGRAM, N.A. (1973), Labeling and
Grouping Effects in the Recall of Pictures by Children, 'Child Development', vol. 44, 511-18.
FURTH, H.G., ROSS, B.M. and YOUNISS, J. (1974), Operative Understanding in Reproductions of Drawings,
'Child Development', vol. 45, 63-70.

Chapter 4

OPERATIVITY, LANGUAGE AND MEMORY IN YOUNG CHILDREN

Eric A. Lunzer (1)

1 INTRODUCTION

Both the name of Jean Piaget and some of the main
features of his work are now so widely known that he
has become something of a legend in his own lifetime.
The sheer volume of his own writings is prodigious
(365 titles are listed in a Festchrift which appeared
in 1966 and the list is still growing). These have
engendered an even more voluminous body of writings
by critics and followers more or less concerned with
Piaget's ideas (cf. Modgil, 1974), and this leaves
out of account more incidental references. Yet it
remains the case that Piaget is too often a cult
figure, one who attracts either devoted admirers or
determined critics, but whose work is treated as
something apart from the main body of theory and
research. This is particularly apparent in the
recent edition of 'Carmichael's Manual of Child Psychology' (Mussen, 1970), where Piaget's theory is
given a chapter of its own, distinct from those on
learning, concept development, reasoning and language.
  If the findings on child development that derive
from Piaget have any scientific validity then this
divorce is to be deplored. In the course of a
research project entitled 'The systematisation of
thinking' we have been particularly concerned with two
aspects of the problem. In the first place, an
effort was made to establish more clearly the relation
between behaviour that might properly be regarded as
instancing operativity in Piaget's sense on the one
hand, and linguistic competence and memory on the
other. Operativity was defined as 'the degree to
which the subject can impose a coherent logical structure on input'. While the majority of the measures

under this heading mirrored the procedures originally
used by the Geneva school, the battery also included
a number of measures designed to estimate responsiveness to demonstration and guidance.   The remaining
procedures included measures of STM (short-term
memory) and LTM (long-term memory), the former, in
particular, being regarded as the major determinant
of operational level by McLaughlin, 1963 and Halford,
1968,   together with five tests of language acquisition.   The principal techniques used were correlation
and factor analysis.   The results of this part of
the study indicate that testing procedures derived
from the Piagetian concept of operativity are at
least as reliable as more conventional procedures.
Despite the relatively high correlations among the
relevant measures, the factorial analysis proved
successful in separating the operative aspect from the
symbolic (language).   Contrary to expectation, it was
found that nearly all measures of memory showed higher
correlations with the tests of language than they did
with tests of operativity.

The second major aim was to establish the relevance
of the Piagetian emphasis to the educational process.
To this end comparisons were made between the power
of the operativity measures on the one hand and the
language measures on the other in predicting achievement in the beginning stages of reading and mathematics.   It was found that operativity was more
effective as a predictor of reading and of mathematics.

The present paper is a brief account of the study
as a whole, and comprises the following sections.
Section 1 consists of a brief methodological description.   Fuller details will be found elsewhere. (2)
Section 2 is a summary and discussion of the results
of the first enquiry;   Section 3 is a first attempt
to describe operativity in terms of the structure of
psychological processes, using a flow-diagram to
sharpen the analysis, and Section 4 gives the findings
of the second enquiry.   Finally, Section 5 contains
a short discussion of some rather interesting results
obtained in the course of an ancillary study on
memory.

2 PROCEDURE

Subjects

The sample was taken from twenty-one schools in the
Nottingham region.   These schools were chosen after
consultation with the local inspectorate in such a
way as to provide an equal representation from three
socio-economic (SE) catchment areas, i.e. favoured
(mainly owner-occupiers, with a strong professional
element), average (skilled working class) and depressed
(central urban or the equivalent).   Seven schools
were chosen in each of these groupings and from each
of these five boys and five girls were selected,
yielding a total sample of 210.   All of the children
were aged between 5:6 and 6:0 at the time of first
testing, and all were native born.   Within these constraints, selection was made from the register, using
a table of random numbers.

Method

The enquiry was carried out in two phases.   The first
phase involved the administration of individual
measures of cognitive performance, and was carried
out in late 1971 and early 1972.   The second phase
was a shorter series of follow-up tests given about a
year later (early 1973).   These consisted predominantly of attainment tests, although they also
included replication of some of the procedures used
earlier, albeit on a limited sample.

Initial testing procedures

All of the tests given in the first phase were admin-
istered on an individual basis by members of the
research team, each of whom had developed a considerable expertise in his own area.   So far as possible
the order of tests was the same for the whole sample.
To avoid undue fatigue, each session was limited to
20-30 minutes, which meant that each child was seen
on 25-30 occasions.   The follow-up procedure was
similar, except that the testing was carried out by
diploma or higher degree students in the School of
Education, all of whom were experienced teachers.
   A full description of the procedures is given elsewhere (see note 2) and the following account is
necessarily brief.

Operativity

A total of nine tests were derived more or less
directly from the studies of Piaget and his associates.
Details of administration of these tests having been
given in a preliminary form in an earlier study
(Lunzer, 1970).   The tests used were: conservation
of number (1-1 correspondence), conservation of
length, seriation of rods, multiple seriation, classification (correct use of 'all' and 'some'), class-
inclusion, intersection (child is required to place
coloured shapes in the appropriate sector formed by
two or three overlapping hoops each of which should
define a given colour, shape or thickness), linear
and circular order (copying or reversing arrangements
of beads on a string) and haptic perception.   This
last test involved a considerable modification of
procedure as compared with that used by Piaget and
Inhelder (1956) so as to allow a more objective
scoring, taking into account the separate confusions
which a child can make or avoid, i.e. rectilinear
versus curvilinear, number of edges, proportion of
figure, size of angles, etc. (see Dolan, 1974 for a
more detailed discussion).

Learning

Four of the tests used in this part of the battery were
essentially measures of operativity, using a more
structured procedure with deliberate cueing in the
form of demonstration and correction.   These were
included with the idea of differentiating between the
ability to impose a spontaneous ordering on the
material provided and the ability to accept, to
replicate, and to transfer a systematic categorisation
when this is deliberately demonstrated or taught.
These measures were: (i) cross classification -
material to be classified first in one dimension
(e.g. colour), and immediately following this by
another (e.g. shape);   two posting boxes were used to
prevent a fourfold, two-dimensional classification
which is relatively easy and misses the essential
point, which is to ignore irrelevant criteria; (ii)
transformation - again the material consisted of
coloured shapes, and the child was shown by means of
examples how to 'transform' colour while retaining
shape and size, or to transform both shape and size
while retaining colour, etc.;   (iii) learning moves

and equivalences in a six group - the group chosen
was isomorphic with the rotations and reflections of
a triangle, although the material was specially
developed to be attractive and comprehensible to
young children (a rotating platform with three animals
occupying three 'stations'); (iv) learning a two-
group - here trial and error is used to acquire a
simple rule for choosing one of two objects to partner
a third, namely red light = 'match', green light =
'alternate'.

A fifth test was more nearly a measure of rote
learning using paired associates: linking geometrical
shapes with drawings of familiar objects (child learns
to guess the shape of the slot concealed by each of
three drawings and selects the shape he will put in
before exposing the slot). The sixth and final
measure of learning was originally included as a
test of LTM: the child is given ten repetitions of
a list of ten unrelated words and is scored for
accuracy in the last two presentations.

Language

The first two measures are well-known standard tests,
namely the English Picture Vocabulary Test (Brimer
and Dunn, 1962) and the Crichton Vocabulary Scale.
It will be recalled that the first of these involves
verbal production and recall (defining the meanings
of words) while the second involves recognition
(selection of a picture from an array). The third
test again involves production, being derived from
the Watts Language Scale (1944), and requires description of a picture. The remaining two tests were
of grammar. One was an adaptation of the comprehension section in the scale used by Fraser, Bellugi
and Brown (1963), and is a measure of the child's
ability to identify the grammatical cues signalling
passive voice, plural number, etc. To allow a
greater accuracy of scoring, the procedure was altered
by providing three multiple choice pictures rather
than just two. The final measure focused on a single
aspect of transformational grammar, namely the ability
to work through to an understanding of the deep structure of sentences having the form 'eager to bite' or
'easy to bite' and was based on the work of Cromer
(1970).

Memory

In addition to the list-learning referred to earlier,
the battery included four tests of STM and four of
LTM.   The former were: digit span and memory span
for unrelated words, reproducing a sequence of
animal pictures and reproducing a sequence of diagrams.   The presentation of sequence was audial for
the first two tests and visual for the second.
Since memory for visual presentation is known to be
facilitated by labelling (Flavell et al., 1966) it
should be noted that labelling was easier for the
animal pictures than for the shapes.   The interval
between presentation and recall was one day for all
LTM measures.   Two of these were stories read to the
child, who was subsequently asked (a) to repeat the
story and (b) to listen to a repetition and supply
details in gaps.   Each pair of scores was combined
to yield a single score for free recall and another
for cued recall.   Two of the tests were designed to
discriminate between memory for content and memory
for structure (cf. Piaget and Inhelder, 1973).   The
first consisted of a cross-classification in a matrix
arrangement (animals, vehicles, furniture, with two
or four supports).   The second was again a matrix
presentation, but this time ordered in two senses
(pictures of trees, seriated by colour and density of
foliage).   In this test the child was also asked to
observe and reproduce a sequence of transpositions
executed by the tester in such a way as to preserve
the ordering.   The scores for these two tests were
not combined in the analysis of data.   The last
memory test was again a test of visual recall, the
child being asked to name as many as he could of
twelve familiar objects following a sixty-second
visual presentation.

Standard tests of intelligence

In addition to the Crichton Vocabulary Scale, the
battery included two additional tests: Raven's Progressive Matrices (coloured version, 1961) and Ilg
and Ames's test of figure copying (1964).

Scoring

Standard procedures were developed for administering all of the above tests, including detailed instructions for scoring.   In general, each test yielded a single score.   For the most part there was a satisfactory distribution of scores, with discrimination right across the ability range.   The one notable exception was the third test of learning, structure of a six group, which proved too difficult for most of the children.

Follow-up

The principal procedures used in the follow-up were Schonnell's test of word recognition, the Neale Analysis of Reading Ability (1966) and a short test of mathematical reasoning which was specially constructed so as to test mathematical understanding as well as numerical competence.   These tests were given one year after the original enquiry to all of the children in the sample who were still available (N = 180 for mathematics and 183 for reading).   In addition, the memory and language tests were repeated with children in six schools, i.e. two from each of three SE groups. In this case the numbers actually followed up were reduced to 58.

3   LANGUAGE, OPERATIVITY AND INTELLIGENCE: RESULTS OF THE MAIN ENQUIRY

This discussion will centre on the following questions: (i) do the tests of operativity as defined have reliabilities that are comparable with more generally accepted measures such as the tests of language or Raven's matrices?   (ii) what are the general levels of correlation between tests?   (iii) what indications are there of a multi-factorial structure of ability at this age and in particular, how far is it possible to discriminate between language competence and operativity?   (iv) does the study provide some support for a close association between operativity and memory? and (v) do either the Piagetian measures or the specifically constructed learning tests provide a measure which is less sensitive to differences between higher and lower SE groups than standard tests of language and intelligence?

Reliability

Although this enquiry was not designed as a study of
the reliability of Piagetian tests, the select results
shown in Table 4.1 may be taken as a firm indication
that these procedures can be made as reliable as more
conventional forms of mental testing.

TABLE 4.1 Reliability of procedures used in the
main enquiry

	Test	Highest Corre-lation	with	Additional index and method
1	Cons. length	59	2	
2	Cons. number	59	1	
3	Seriation	61	4	
4	Mil. seriation	61	3	
5	All and some	49	4	
6	Class inc.	42	7	
7	Intersection	60	3	
8	Lin. and circ.	56	4	
9	Haptic rec.	54	4	0.86 TR (N=20)
10	Cross classif.	45	4	0.46 TR (N=18)
11	Transformation	53	4	0.77 SH (N=21)
12	2-group lng.	49	14	
13	Grammar	49	17	
14	Deep structure	55	17	
15	Watts	56	16	
16	EPVT	70	17	
17	Crichton	70	16	
18	STM digits	65	19	0.80 TR (N=20)
19	STM words	65	18	
20	STM shapes	46	21	0.70 TR (N=20)
21	STM animals	46	20	0.48 TR (N=20)
22	List learning	48	24	
23	Story recall	46	17	0.80 SH (N=200)
24	Story cued recall	51	17	
25	Kim's game	27	24	
26	LTM ser'n content	40	12	
27	LTM ser'n structure	41	29	
28	LTM matrix content	33	26	
29	LTM matrix structure	41	27	
30	Raven's matrices	45	7	0.58 TR (N=129)
31	Ilg and Ames	58	4	

TR = test retest
SH = split-half

The test retest figure is available only in the case of haptic recognition.   For the rest one may infer a comparable reliability from the high levels of correlation with similar tests.   It is true that the two standardised tests of language have a correlation of 0.70 and this is greater than the intercorrelation of any two Piagetian tests.   On the other hand, these tests have a larger number of items.   It is clear from the data given in   Section 4 that similar reliability and validity may be obtained by combining a number of Piagetian tests, as has been done in the present study.

Level of correlation between tests

Table 4.2 gives a convenient summary of the level of correlations found between the several scores yielded by the battery.   It will be seen that these are moderate rather than high, the majority being in the ranges 0.30-0.39 and 0.40-0.49.   Correlations within groups of related tests are somewhat higher than correlations between tests in different groups, but this is by no means invariable.   Despite the high reliability of many of the measures of memory, they rarely yield correlations of the same magnitude as operativity and language tests.   Correlations between operativity and learning tend to be somewhat higher than those between learning and language, as is to be expected from the design of several of these measures. The reverse is the case for the tests of memory.

Factor Analysis

The principal data from the various factor analytic procedures used are shown in Tables 4.3 and 4.4. Table 4.3 is based on oblique solution of the matrix, using Kaiser's 'Second Generation Little Jiffy' (1970). A preliminary principal components analysis yielded seven factors having eigenvalues greater than 1.   The seven columns of figures show the test loadings on rotated factors for the correlation matrix based on the whole sample.   Asterisks are 'salients' for interpretation.   Against each of these columns the table shows all the salients yielded by similar analysis applied to correlation matrices based on the two sexes taken separately.   To avoid cluttering the table, only salients are shown for these analyses, and

TABLE 4.2   Levels of correlation between cognitive measures

	Operativity	Language	Learning	Memory
Operativity	17,28,39,17	36,39,25,0	51,20,27,2	86,14,0,0
Language		0,50,16,34	45,45,10,0	76,20,4,0
Learning			50,40,10,0	78,22,0,0
Memory				67,19,9,4

Rows and columns correspond to groups of scores derived from Piaget tests (9), Language (5), Learning (5) and Memory (13).
The four figures in each cell represent the percentage of Z values in the range 0–0.29, 0.30–0.39, 0.40–0.49, and 0.50 and over.

TABLE 4.3 Factor analysis

Factor	I Full	B	G	II Full	B	G	III Full	B	G	IV Full	B	G	V Full	B	G	VI Full	B	G	VII Full	B	G
1 Cons. length	00			01			-09			-02			64*	+	+	01			-08		
2 Cons. number	-02			06			02			-06			71*	+	+	-05			05		
3 Seriation	75*	+	+	-12			-15			02			14			-02			10	+	
4 Mul. seriat'n	85*	+	+	-04			03			-05			-03			-01			-03		
5 All and some	52*	+		16			03			05			-15			02			-05		
6 Class inc.	06			-05			10			26	+	+	21			13	+		-21*	-	-
7 Intersection	46*	+	+	10			02			-04			24*	+	+	04			01		
8 Lin. & circ.	60*	+	+	-18			05			10			11	+		09			-09		
9 Haptic rec.	46	+	+	11			04			21		+	-11			04			-10		
10 Cross classif.	33	+	+	10			17			02			-09			11			-11		
11 Transformat'n	82*	+	+	-01			-04			-08			-14			-08	-	-	06		
12 2-Group lng.	45*	+		23			12		+	-03			-17			-09	-	-	21*	+	
13 Grammar	-14			53*	+	+	09			11			05			08			-18*	-	
14 Deep structure	15			58*	+	+	01			-20			-01			-02			19*	+	
15 Watts	22		+	56*	+	+	-07			03			-16		+	04			-08		
16 EPVT	-05			84*	+	+	00			-09			03		+	01			02		
17 Crichton	-06			73*	+	+	-08			15	+		06		+	-01			-01		
18 STM digits	00			-04			02			-07			-03			73*	+	+	03		
19 STM words	-02			06			-04			-04			-02			68*	+	+	03		
20 STM shapes	-09			-18			03			33*			12			15			28*	+	+
21 STM animals	-05			07			15			14		+	07			10			35*	+	+
22 List learning	00			-05			-01			46*	+	+	00			27*		+	00		
23 Story recall	02			-08			-10			72*	+	+	01			-11			13*		
24 " cued recall	-04			09			-02			74*	+	+	-11			-08			-04		
25 Kim's game	-15			08			17			31*	+		15			-02			-03		
26 LTM ser'n content	09			-08			78*	+	+	00			-08			-03			00		
27 " structure	-11			02			70*	+	+	-06			07			02			03	-	-

Factor	I			II			III			IV			V			VI			VII		
	Full	B	G	Full	B	G	Full	B	G	Full	B	G	Full	B	G	Full	B	G	Full	B	G
28 LTM matrix content	-14			18			40*	+	+	15	+		00			-07			-15		+
29 " structure	-03			09			41*	+	+	05			02			-01			04		
30 Raven's matrices	19			10			00			07			24*			-05			-01		+
31 Ilg and Ames	38*		+	-06			-08			10			21			04			-05		-
% contribution																					
Full	29.15			21.05			15.39			12.30			10.10			8.96			3.04		
Boys	30.9			25.5			13.4			8.7			13.6			11.7			6.7		
Girls	17.6			19.8			16.9			14.2			8.8			6.9			5.3		

they are indicated only by direction (+ or -).   It will
be seen that all seven factors are clearly interpretable
and that they are reproduced with only minor variations
when the sexes are taken separately.   Factor I is an
operativity factor, II is language, III is either
memory for logical arrangement or visual LTM (the tests
concerned do not allow a decision), IV is verbal
memory, V is conservation, VI is STM for audial presentation and VII has its highest loadings from the STM
visual tests.

One may conclude that the differentiation of ability
even at the age of five-six, is sufficient to allow one
to trace several distinct modes of variation in cognitive function.   The operative aspect is distinct from
the verbal aspect, and each of them manifests itself
in several quite different tests.   The learning
measures do not yield a distinct factor, which is con-
sonant with the view that conceptual learning depends
above all on the existing level of conceptual functioning (Inhelder, Sinclair and Bovet, 1974).   On the
other hand, conservation tests do not factor with the
remaining tests of operativity (cf. Tuddenham, 1970).
Somewhat less expected is the failure of the   class-
inclusion tests to load on Factor I.   Its artificiality
is recognised by Kohnstamm (1967) and others.   The
present data lead one to be a little sceptical about
the importance attached to the test both by Piaget
himself (Inhelder and Piaget, 1964) and by Kofsky (1966).

It should be pointed out that the factor structure
is not the result of chance, since it reappears for
each of the sexes.   Nor is it due only to the particular mode of rotation.   The same seven factors
appeared with almost equal clarity in the varimax
solution.   The oblique solution has the advantage
that it is sharper (there being more high loadings and
also more near-zero loadings on each factor), and that
it is probably more faithful to the psychological
reality (one would expect the several aspects of cognitive ability to be correlated).   It has the further
advantage that the relations of the matrix can be
further explored by examining the correlations between
factors, as has been done in Table 4.4.   Despite the
very high correlation between Factors I and II, they
give two distinct higher-order factors, again corresponding to the verbal/symbolic aspect and the operative
aspect of cognitive functioning.   One notes that the
principal contributions to the latter are Factor I and
Factor V (conservation).   No less noteworthy, however,
is the fact that all of the memory factors have sub-

TABLE 4.4   First order factor correlations and loadings on second order factors

	II	III	IV	V	VI	VII	I´	II´
I Operativity	0.778	0.620	0.605	0.745	0.424	0.261	0.12	0.77*
II Language		0.486	0.829	0.620	0.590	0.455	0.59*	0.31
III LTM visual			0.519	0.315	0.638	0.336	0.40	0.22*
IV LTM verbal				0.454	0.648	0.492	0.85*	-0.01
V Conservation					0.283	0.157	-0.25	0.95*
VI STM verbal						0.489	0.85*	-0.20
VII STM visual							0.88*	-0.43

TABLE 4.5 Standard scores and F ratios for upper and lower socio-economic groups

	Upper SEG		Lower SEG		F-ratios	
	Boys	Girls	Boys	Girls	SES	Sex
1 Cons. length	114	106	94	92	4.6*	1.3
2 Cons. number	109	104	99	99	6.2**	0.4
3 Seriation	108	112	96	94	19.9***	0.4
4 Mil. seriation	108	108	96	94	14.4***	0.4
5 All and some	104	107	90	91	23.3***	0.0
6 Class inc.	98	103	94	99	2.1	6.8*
7 Intersection	106	101	91	94	10.3*	0.3
8 Lin. and circ.	102	106	93	97	6.5***	5.8*
9 Haptic rec.	106	106	95	93	9.9***	0.4
10 Cross classif.	100	102	93	100	1.6	3.2
11 Transformation	103	109	90	98	10.3**	6.3*
12 Two-group lng.	107	102	91	96	8.9*	0.3
13 Grammar	96	99	91	92	6.2**	1.8
14 Deep structure	106	101	96	97	3.8*	0.0
15 Watts	106	106	91	94	14.2**	0.5
16 EPVT	109	103	94	89	17.5***	7.1**
17 Crichton	107	101	91	87	17.5**	2.3

	Upper SEG		Lower SEG		F-ratios	
	Boys	Girls	Boys	Girls	SES	Sex
18 STM digits	99	102	95	98	1.3	6.2*
19 STM words	99	101	93	95	2.5	3.0
20 STM shapes	96	101	99	96	0.4	0.8
21 STM animals	101	100	93	96	3.8*	0.4
22 List learning	99	101	96	96	3.5*	0.5
23 Story recall	99	103	96	94	3.6*	1.3
24 Story cued recall	98	101	95	94	4.4*	0.1
25 Kim's game	97	93	95	90	4.0*	0.1
26 LTM ser'n content	100	101	93	96	3.4*	1.5
27 LTM ser'n structure	99	100	96	98	1.3	0.3
28 LTM matrix content	97	99	95	94	2.6	1.1
29 LTM matrix structure	98	100	89	93	6.7**	1.8
30 Raven's matrices	106	101	96	99	3.1*	2.3
31 Ilg and Ames	108	108	97	97	11.0**	2.1

stantial contributions to the first higher-order factor,
and these are invariably greater than their loadings on
II (the operative aspect).   In one sense this is not
surprising inasmuch as storage and retrieval must of
necessity rely on symbolic coding (Merriot, 1974).
The present finding can also be taken as contra-
indicating the speculations of McLaughlin (1963) who
sought to explain the development of operativity by
reference to increase in STM.   Nevertheless one should
stress that it is not argued that operativity is independent of STM anymore than it is independent of
language, only that it is a distinctive aspect which is
sui generis (see next section).

Language, operativity and social class

A two-way analysis of variance was carried out on the
scores obtained from each of the measures to test the
effect of social class and sex.   The two sets of F
ratios for main effects are shown in the last two
columns of Table 4.5.   It will be seen that while sex
differences were generally negligible (girls were
superior in tests 6, 8, 11 and 18, and boys, surprisingly, in 16, EPVT), there are marked social class
differences for nearly all measures of operativity as
well as for language.   The relative magnitude of
these differences is brought out in the first four
columns of the table in which the means for the
favoured groups (high SE) and disadvantaged groups
(low SE) are expressed as deviations from a standard
score of 100 with s.d. of 15 derived from the intermediate group.   The smallest differences occur in the
memory tests - when both lower and upper SEG scores
are marginally lower than those of the intermediate
group.

    These results clearly indicate that tests derived
from Piagetian principles do not tap a dimension of
ability which is independent of the effects of social
class.   Clearly they do not enable one to decide to
what degree the underlying differences are innate and
due to heredity and assortative mating, and to what
degree they are acquired and due to learnt modes of
handling experience.   The parallel results for
language are entirely expected.

4   OPERATIVITY AND STRUCTURE

We conclude from the foregoing section that Piaget's
distinction between the symbolic and the operative
aspects of cognition is supported by the psychometric
evidence.   But the word 'aspect' is itself too meta-
phorical a term to explain the nature of the distinction.   In Section 1 operativity was defined as the
ability to impose a logical structure on input.   But
'ability' is itself a psychometric term rather than a
description of a process.   It is therefore of some
interest to consider the place of operativity in a
genuinely psychological description of cognition, i.e.
a description of the process itself as opposed to a
statement about variation of output measures - which
is all that factor analysis can yield.

   To this end, it was decided to attempt a theoretical
representation of the process involved in the solution
of one of the tests used in the enquiry: intersection
of classes.   The result is presented diagrammatically
in Figure 4.1.   Suppose a child has been shown two
overlapping hoops, with the instruction that he must
put 'all the yellow shapes' in one, and 'all the square
shapes' in the other.   He has also been alerted to
the intersection, with the explanation that any piece
put there will be in both hoops at once.   The pieces
in front of him include yellow, squares, yellow squares
and others.

   The conventions adopted for this diagram are arbitrary but quite simple.   The use of boxes for
'operations' (not in Piaget's sense) and diamonds for
'tests' is standard.   To these have been added closed
circles to represent nodes.   The nodes are points at
which different paths are taken at differing levels
of maturity or proficiency.   The small closed diamonds
also represent choice-points, but the outcome of these
is a function of level of satiation and not of competence.   Successive letters in the alphabet represent
successive levels, lower case letters being used when
the process indicated may be superseded at some later
level.

   The diagram differs from the usual flow-chart chiefly
in that it shows the successive levels of behaviour
within a single representation.   The assumption is
that more primitive levels of behaviour continue to be
within the competence of the more mature subject, and
indeed that given unfavourable conditions he is liable
to regress.   Thus, in one sense, the figure may be
thought of as a representation of the programming as

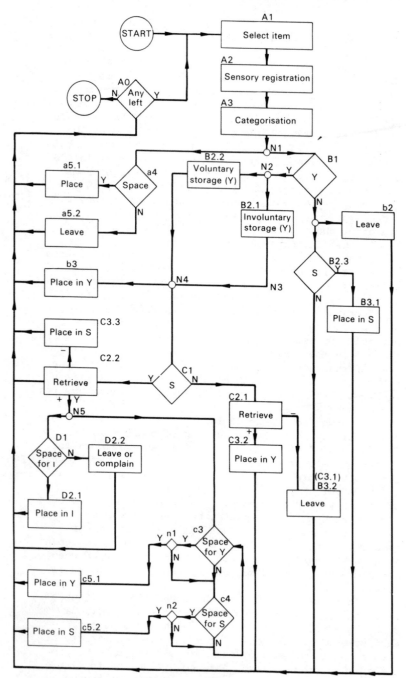

FIGURE 4.1   Flow-diagram for solution of intersection task

it actually exists in the child of seven and over.
Only a part of the diagram would be necessary to describe the behaviour of younger children.   On the
other hand, interest will centre chiefly on the
choice-points between alternative lines of behaviour,
and it is reasonable to assume that the effect of
these will be especially evident during periods of
transition, when the child sometimes succeeds but is
quite liable to regress.

Item selection (A1), sensory registration (A2) and
some initial categorisation (A3) are taken to be
common to all levels under consideration.   At the
node N1, older children (above the age of three to
four on average) will test whether or not the piece
is yellow.   But very young children will fail to go
on to make this test because they cannot integrate a
goal and a sub-goal within a single plan (cf. Miller,
Galanter and Pribram, 1960; Woodward, 1972).   The
overall plan is to put pieces in hoops and this yields
the sequence (a4, a5.1) or (a4, a5.2).

At the five-year level, nearly all children will
proceed from N1 to B1, testing for yellowness.   If
the piece is not yellow, a few children will fail to
test whether it is square, even though they might have
placed it in the proper circle had the test been
positive.   This contingency is represented in the
diagram by the right-hand fork at N3.   The majority
of children who pass at N1 to level B will go on to
B2.3, testing for squareness.   (It makes no difference
in what order tests Y and S are taken.   When S is
tested before Y, all Ys should be read as Ss and vice
versa.)   This will be followed by B3.1 or B3.2,
depending on the outcome of the test.

If the piece is yellow, that outcome may be
deliberately stored (verbal coding?) or it may be
stored only incidentally.   Since this is a function
of competence, the choice is represented by a node, N2.
The next node is more critical.   At N4, some children
(a majority at age five) will simply accept the fact
of yellowness and put the piece in the yellow hoop.
Others (the majority at age seven) will go on to test
for squareness.   Since this represents a higher level
of competence it has been indexed as C1.   A negative
outcome to this test is less interesting.   The child
who successfully retrieves the information that the
piece is yellow places it in the yellow hoop (C3.2).
If he fails, he leaves it (C3.1).

When the outcome of C1 is positive, failure in retrieval that the piece is also yellow (C2.2) produces

the uncomplicated output of placement in the square
hoop (C3.3).   When the retrieval is successful, the
behaviour enters the critical node for solution of the
intersection problem, N5.   A successful outcome
entails looking actively for an appropriate space to
represent the fact that the piece is both yellow and
square.   In other words, the child looks for the
intersection of the two hoops.   This yields the
sequence (D1, D2.1) - or (D1, D2.2 if the hoops do not
overlap and are immobile).   Failure to reach this
level may lead to oscillation between the yellow hoop
(c3) and the square hoop (c4).   This follows from the
assumption that the child is not immediately satisfied
with either squareness or yellowness, having progressed
beyond the node N4 and having retrieved all the relevant information at C2.2.   This represents exactly the
state of affairs hypothesised by Piaget in his discussion of successive stages in equilibration (1957).
However, since the child is under pressure to respond,
it is supposed that after a very few such oscillations,
that pressure will overcome his hesitancy.   It is
this contingency that is represented in the diagram
by the two possible outcomes c5.1 and c5.2.   The
'switches' at n1 and n2 have quite different determinants from the nodes N1-N5.   Their 'setting' will be
a function of the motivational state of the subject
and not his cognitive competence.

   Although the flow-diagram is a representation of
events which are in general unobservable, it is not
arbitrary.   Thus each of the key nodes has been included at a precise point in the chart on the basis of
observed divergences in the behaviour of real subjects
performing the task.   In particular, an earlier
version of the chart featured only one path from C2.2
to D1, omitting the vital node at N5.   In other
words, it was assumed that a subject who was aware
both of 'yellow' and of 'square' would automatically
choose the intersection placement.   The inclusion of
the new node and of the loop route, c3, (n1), c4, (n2),
c3..., was dictated by the observation that many children betrayed their indecision by the hesitancy of
their behaviour.

   In point of fact, this particular section of the
figure is the only one which brings out what it is
that drives the child towards a more satisfying, but
more demanding, solution, this being the D route in
the present case.   However, it is not difficult to
imagine that the child who at N4 continues on the B
route and places the piece in the yellow sector (b3)

is liable to notice that it is also square if, for
instance, identical pieces end up in different sectors
as they are liable to do when following the B strategy.
This might lead him to reflect on the alternatives at
N4, and thereby launch him on the higher level C.
Thus the present account and the accompanying diagram
are chiefly limited by the fact that only one section
of the behaviour is shown, with all its variants.
It seems probable that, in general, progress from a
lower level to a higher is achieved by integrating
two lines of behaviour within a single path, where
previously the two paths existed only as alternates,
so that on any given occasion only one of the two was
functional.   If this is so, then the recall of previous behaviours and their outcome is crucial to the
development of operativity.

It is hoped that further exploration of process
analysis will eventually reach a point when it becomes
possible to construct a programme to simulate their
development on a computer.   For the present, it is
instructive to note that it is impossible to find
appropriate labels for those aspects of the diagram
which correspond to the operative aspect.   There is
not the same difficulty in the case of language.
Although the intersection task is non-verbal, language
is implicit in voluntary storage (cf. Section 5).
Nor would it be difficult in the description of any
task to insert an 'operation' (rectangle) to denote
verbalisation or rehearsal.   The difficulty which
attaches to the labelling of operativity otherwise
than by the nodes, is that operativity does not correspond to any part of the process, but rather to its
structure.   The level of operativity consists simply
in the complexity of the behavioural line which is
governed by the selection of one path or another, at
successive nodes.

Again, it is not argued that the selection of a
higher level of operativity is not influenced by
language.   For instance, voluntary storage (labelling)
at B2.2 as opposed to involuntary storage at B2.1 will
facilitate both the selection of route C and the retrieval of information at C2.2.   (Similarly, level
of operativity plays an important part in the acquisition of language.)   However, despite the interdepen-
dence of the two aspects and their mutual facilitation,
they are theoretically distinct as well as factorially
distinguishable.

5   PREDICTION OF ATTAINMENT

The present section deals with the predictive power
of the tests used in 1972 when tested against the
measures of reading and mathematical understanding
which were taken in 1973, when the children concerned
were one year older.

All of the multiple regression calculations to be
reported were devised from the programme REGRAN given
by Veldman (1967).   The programme is admirably suited
to the task of evaluating the relative contributions
of a number of predictors by comparing alternative
'models'.   The basic technique consists of first
selecting a small number of good predictors which
will act as a reference model.   It is then possible
to remove one or more predictors from the basic
model, and test the significance of such reduction by
analysing its effect on the squared multiple correlation and computing an F-ratio.

Ten predictors were included in the original set.
With one exception, (Crichton Vocabulary), each of
these predictors is the unweighted average of standardised scores on several related tests.

The ten predictors were:

1	Conservation	- average of tests	1 and 2	
2	Operativity	- "	3-9	
3	Conceptual learning	- "	10-12 and six-group*	
4	Simple learning	- "	22 and posting*	
5	Language	- "	13-16	
6	Crichton	- "		
7	Audial STM	- "	18 and 19	
8	Visual STM	- "	20 and 21	
9	LTM	- "	23-26 and 28	
10	LTM structure	- "	27 and 29	

* See Section 2.   These tests were not included in
  the factor analysis data because of relatively poor
  discrimination.

TABLE 4.6 Prediction of attainment based on cognitive measures taken in Year 1

Standard predictor set	Word recogni- tion	Neale compre- hension	Mathematical understanding
R^2	0.4312	0.2901	0.4934
R	0.6566	0.5386	0.7025
1 Conservation (Beta et)	0.0200	-0.0167	0.2063
2 Operativity	0.2258	0.1669	0.2492
3 Complex learning	0.2069	0.0716	0.1099
4 Simple learning	0.0308	-0.0041	0.1152
5 Language	0.0595	0.0596	0.1335
6 Crichton Vocab.	0.0770	-0.0182	0.0333
7 STM auditory	0.0312	0.0910	0.0440
8 STM visual	0.2583	0.2584	0.1156
9 LTM content	-0.1115	0.2102	-0.0689
10 LTM structure	0.1069	0.1069	0.0233
Reduced predictor sets (omitted items)			
1 and 2 Piaget measures	0.6415	0.5303	0.6500
F ratio	2.979*	1.073	11.842**
3 and 4 learning measures R	0.6420	0.5365	0.6918
F ratio	2.878	0.274	2.480
5 and 6 language measures R	0.6510	0.5372	0.6942
F ratio	1.108	0.181	1.916
7-10 memory measures R	0.6136	0.4387	0.6925
F ratio	4.129**	5.911**	1.164
N	183	183	180

The principal results of the analysis are given in Table 4.6. The β-weights show that operativity and conceptual learning scores contribute more powerfully to the prediction of attainment in reading and mathematics than do the measures of language, a result which is borne out by the F-tests for reduced models. The second outstanding feature is the high independent contribution of the two measures of STM (visual) for reading.   In the case of the Neale test of comprehen-

sion, it is the measures of memory for stories which
make the principal contribution to prediction, while
in the test of mathematics understanding, conservation
contributes more than seriation and the remaining
operativity measures.

In view of the common factorial structure of operativity and conceptual learning, it was of some interest
to study the effect of deleting both sets of measures
as compared with the deletion of language predictors.
The result of the operation (Table 4.7) confirms the
overriding significance of the operative aspect for
word-reading and mathematics.

Table 4.8 shows that these relationships hold good
for SEG groups 1 and 3, taken separately, as well as
for the total sample.   The slightly anomalous result
of SEG group 2 may be due to sampling error.

That differences in operativity affect the learning
of reading while differences in language skills have
no independent effect, may seem paradoxical.   After
all, reading is a linguistic skill.   Nevertheless the
present result should have been predictable.   While
it is true that language is essential to the learning
of reading, it does not follow that differences in
language skills at age six play any significant part
in determining differences in learning to read.
Because the language used in texts is simple, differences in linguistic ability do not greatly affect the
child's ability to profit from instruction.   By and
large, all but the poorest speakers are familiar with
the words and the structures met with in initial
readers.   On the other hand, the processes that
figure in tests of operativity: classification,
seriation, reflexion, analysis, are very much those
that are required in learning to read, e.g.

(i)   that there is a one-one correspondence between
the temporal sequence of words as spoken and the
left to right spatial sequence of words as printed -
with spaces between words corresponding to (possible)
minimal pauses in speech,

(ii)   that there is an approximate one-one correspondence between the left to right spatial sequence
of letters and the temporal sequence of phonemes,

(iii)   the strategy of forming a temporal synthesis
of meaningless vocal syllables obtained by following
a left to right sequence to form a meaningful word
(Roberts and Lunzer, 1968).

A second point that emerges from the data in Table
4.7 is the fact that the tests of visual STM make a
highly significant and independent contribution to the

TABLE 4.7 Comparative effects of operativity and language in predicting attainment (β weights)

	Schonell word recognition		Neale comprehension		Mathematical understanding	
	Language	Operativity	Language	Operativity	Language	Operativity
1 Conservation	deleted	0.0350	deleted	-0.0111	deleted	0.2202
2 Operativity	deleted	0.2626	deleted	0.1800	deleted	0.3013
3 Complex learning	deleted	0.2245	deleted	0.0788	deleted	0.1341
4 Simple learning	0.0871	0.0375	0.0231	0.0000	0.1575	0.1240
5 Language	0.1873	deleted	0.1342	deleted	0.2928	deleted
6 Crichton Vocab.	0.1453	deleted	0.0085	deleted	0.1328	deleted
7 STM auditory	0.0463	0.0477	0.1075	0.0951	0.0502	0.0568
8 STM visual	0.2672	0.2681	0.2577	0.2623	0.1195	0.1333
9 LTM content	-0.0774	-0.0748	0.2315	0.2135	-0.0544	-0.0366
10 LTM structure	0.1659	0.0466	0.1327	0.1879	0.1270	0.0177
R	0.5991	0.6510	0.5201	0.5372	0.6151	0.6942
R^2	0.3589	0.4238	0.2705	0.2886	0.3784	0.4820

TABLE 4.8 Comparison of the effectiveness of language and operativity in the prediction of attainment in the three socio-economic groups: values of R based on two predictor models

criterion	SEG 1	SEG 2	SEG 3	model
Schonell word recognition	0.559	0.702	0.670	language
	0.640	0.689	0.710	operativity
Neale comprehension	0.585	0.547	0.712	language
	0.687	0.552	0.676	operativity
Mathematical understanding	0.423	0.670	0.724	language
	0.547	0.758	0.803	operativity

prediction of reading.   On the face of it, this could
be explained by the importance of letter sequence in
reading, paralleling the sequence of symbols in the
Animals and Shapes Tests.   But it should be noted that
the reading situation differs from the test situation
in that the reader is not required to memorise the
visual sequence since the text remains in front of him.
Conversely, the reader does have to retain audial
elements (e.g. the first syllable of a two-syllable word
or the earlier words in a long sentence), to make sense
of what he reads.   Yet the contribution of audial STM
is negligible.   One might speculate that if nearly
all children possess a minimal level of competence in
this area, then differences between them might be of
less importance.   A similar explanation was given for
the relative lack of influence of language as an independent predictor.   Nevertheless the lack of influence
of STM (audial), despite its high reliability, runs
counter to much recent theorising, and certainly merits
further enquiry.

6   A COMPARISON OF CONCURRENT AND FORWARD PREDICTION

As noted in the Introduction, a number of the tests
given in 1972 were replicated in 1973 with samples of
50-60 children.   The data from this ancillary study
are summarised in Table 4.9.   They are confined to
the measures of language and memory.   The long-term
reliabilities of the tests vary considerably, and the
figures for STM digits, EPVT and Crichton are
strikingly high.   Memory for classification and
seriation (LTM, content and structure) produces much
lower reliabilities, as might be expected from the
brevity of the test, taken in conjunction with the
complexity of the situation.   However, the most
remarkable feature of Table 4.9 is the fact that forward prediction is superior to concurrent prediction
for nearly all measures of memory, at least in the
prediction of reading.   Similar findings for the
tests of grammar and deep structure are doubtless due
to the fact that these instruments tend to 'ceiling
off' by the time the subjects are nearing seven years
of age.   But this line of explanation cannot be used
for any of the tests of STM.
     If the present data are supported in replicatory
studies, it seems to follow that the tests of memory
do not measure the same abilities at different ages.
This could be due to one of two reasons.   It could be

TABLE 4.9   Long-term reliability and correlations with attainment for memory and language, concurrent and predictive

		1973 Replication	Reading 1973	Comprehension 1973	Mathematics 1973
STM digits	1972	0.74	0.31	0.37	0.41
	1973		0.28	0.44	0.40
STM words	1972	0.50	0.36	0.47	0.50
	1973		0.00	0.19	0.19
STM shapes	1972	0.31	0.45	0.39	0.43
	1973		0.14	0.26	0.35
STM animals	1972	0.54	0.60	0.65	0.47
	1973		0.51	0.62	0.56
List learning	1972	0.35	0.26	0.43	0.25
	1973		0.27	0.36	0.35
Story recall	1972	0.24	0.39	0.62	0.51
	1973		0.23	0.34	0.27
Cued recall	1972	0.67	0.54	0.71	0.63
	1973		0.50	0.61	0.53
LTM content	1972	0.32	0.40	0.53	0.40
	1973		0.29	0.42	0.45
LTM structure	1972	0.16	0.26	0.43	0.27
	1973		0.21	0.34	0.41

	Year				
Watts	1972	0.51	0.16	0.15	0.29
	1973		0.42	0.27	0.64
EPVT	1972	0.79	0.23	0.32	0.36
	1973		0.22	0.31	0.36
Crichton	1972	0.70	0.41	0.20	0.37
	1973		0.41	0.37	0.45
Grammar	1972	0.46	0.27	0.15	0.55
	1973		0.12	0.13	0.22
Deep structure	1972	0.22	0.48	0.35	0.35
	1973		0.00	0.22	0.20

that the process that leads to performance is not the
same for these children when they are a year older as
that which was invoked when they were first tested.
Alternatively, it could be that while the process is
the same, the contribution of the several components
of that process differ in the sense that individual
differences are irrelevant beyond a critical point.
For instance, in the case of very young children,
memory for visual sequence would be determined in part
by their ability to discriminate between the forms
they are given.   But while such discrimination continues to be part of the process of memorisation and
reproduction, one might surmise that the capacity for
making such discriminations ceases to be an important
factor once a sufficient level of competence has been
reached.

Perhaps the most likely interpretation is that
between five and six many children do not engage in
spontaneous verbal rehearsal when asked to memorise
(cf. Flavell et al., 1966), whereas a year later this
tendency is more nearly universal.   Differences in the
performance of memory tasks at the earlier age would
then reflect that tendency while one year later it
would no longer have the same importance.   If it is
further assumed that the beginnings of reading, and to
a lesser extent of arithmetic, require a verbal media-
tion which is spontaneous, it would follow that children who acquired that tendency sooner would be more
successful in their initial approach to scholastic
tasks.   Thus, although by the time this second set of
measures was taken, nearly all of the sample had made
the necessary adjustment, those who had made it
earlier would have had a longer opportunity to progress.

In view of the relatively small numbers and the
absence of experimental controls, this interpretation
must for the present be tentative.   Much less tentative is the conclusion that operativity is distinct
from language, and that tests derived from Piaget can
be made sufficiently reliable and robust to be of
considerable value in the assessment of initial individual differences in cognition.

NOTES

1   The writer wishes to acknowledge the support of the
    SSRC and the collaboration of T. Dolan, J.E.
    Wilkinson and D. Bond.
2   'The development of systematic thinking' by E.A.

Lunzer.   Report to the Social Sciences Research
Council.

REFERENCES

BRIMER, M.A. and DUNN, L.M. (1962), 'English Picture
Vocabulary Tests', Educational Evaluation Enterprises.
CROMER, R.F. (1970), Children Are Nice to Understand:
surface structure clues for the recovery of a deep
structure, 'Brit. J. Psychol.', vol. 61, 397-408.
DOLAN, T. (1974), The Haptic Recognition of Geometric
Shape, M. Phil. Thesis, Nottingham University.
FLAVELL, J.H., BEACH, D.R., and CHINSKY, J.M. (1966),
Spontaneous Verbal Rehearsal in a Memory Task as a
Function of Age, 'Child Development', vol. 37, 283-99.
FRASER, C., BELUGI, R. and BROWN, R. (1963), Control
of Grammar in Imitation, Comprehension and Production,
'J. Verb. Lng. Verb. Beh.', vol. 2, 121-35.
HALFORD, G.S. (1968), An Experimental Test of Piaget's
Notion Concerning Conservation of Quantity in Children,
'J. exp. Child. Psychol.', vol. 6, 33-43.
ILG, F.L. and AMES, L.B. (1964), 'School Readiness',
New York: Harper & Row.
INHELDER, B. and PIAGET, J. (1964), 'The Early Growth
of Logic in the Child', London: Routledge & Kegan
Paul.
INHELDER, B., SINCLAIR, H. and BOVET, M. (1974),
'Learning and the Development of Cognition', London:
Routledge & Kegan Paul.
KAISER, H.F. (1970), A Second-generation Little Jiffy,
'Psychometrika', vol. 35, 401-15.
KOFSKY, E. (1966), A Scalogram Study of Classificatory
Development, 'Child Development', vol. 37, 191-204.
KOHNSTAMM, G.A. (1967), 'Piaget's Analysis of Class-
Inclusion: Right or Wrong?', The Hague: Mouton.
LUNZER, E.A. (1970), Construction of a Standardised
Battery of Piagetian Tests to Assess the Development
of Effective Intelligence, 'Research in Educ.', vol. 3,
53-72.
McLAUGHLIN, G.H. (1963), Psycho-Logic: a possible
alternative to Piaget's formulation, 'Brit. J. Educ.
Psychol.', vol. 33, 61-7.
MERRIOT, P. (1974), 'Attributes of Memory', London:
Methuen.
MILLER, G.A., GALANTER, E. and PRIBRAM, K.H. (1960),
'Plans and the Structure of Behaviour', New York:
Henry Holt.
MODGIL, S. (1974), 'Piagetian Research, A Handbook of

Recent Studies', London: National Foundation for
Educational Research.
MUSSEN, P.H. (ed.) (1970), 'Carmichael's Manual of
Child Psychology', New York: Wiley.
NEALE, M.D. (1966), 'Neale Analysis of Reading
Ability: Manual of Directions and Norms', London:
Macmillan.
PIAGET, J. (1957), Logique et équilibre dans les
comportemonts du sujet. In Logique et équilibre,
'Etudes d'Epistémologie Génétique', vol. 2 by L.
Apostel, B. Mandelbrot and Jean Piaget, Paris: Presses
Universitaires de France, 27-117.
Hommage à Jean Piaget (PIAGET) (1966), 'Psychologie et
Epistémologie Génétiques: Thèmes Piagétiens', Paris:
Dunod.
PIAGET, J. and INHELDER, B. (1956), 'The Child's Con-
ception of Space', London: Routledge & Kegan Paul.
PIAGET, J. and INHELDER, B. (1973), 'Memory and Intel-
ligence', London: Routledge & Kegan Paul.
RAVEN, J.C. (1961), 'Guide to the Crichton Vocabulary
Scale with Progressive Matrices Sets A, Ab, B', London:
H.K. Lewis.
ROBERTS, R.G. and LUNZER, E.A. (1968), Reading and
Learning to Read, in E.A. Lunzer and J.F. Morris (eds),
'Development in Human Learning', London: Staples
Press and New York: American Elsevier.
SCHONELL, F.J. (1942), 'Backwardness in the Basic
Subjects', London: Oliver & Boyd.
TUDDENHAM, R.D. (1970), A 'Piagetian' Test of Cognitive
Development, in W.B. Dockrell (ed.), 'On Intelligence:
the Toronto Symposium on Intelligence', 1969, London:
Methuen.
VELDMAN, D.J. (1967), 'Fortran Programming for the
Behavioural Sciences', Holt, Rinehart & Winston.
WATTS, A.F. (1944), 'The Language and Mental Develop-
ment of Children', London: Harrap.
WOODWARD, M. (1972), Problem-solving Strategies of
Young Children, 'J. Child Psychol. & Psychiatr.',
vol. 13, 11-24.

Part three

EXAMINATIONS OF PIAGET'S THEORIES

Not all Piaget's theories have been uncritically accepted. Particularly his theory of formal operations, the description of reasoning in terms of propositional calculus, has been subjected to stringent examination by psychologists and also by logicians and epistemologists. Peter Wason presents some of the objections raised to the theory of formal reasoning, and examines the theory in terms of his own independent studies of reasoning. Piaget has stressed in his analyses the structures of intellect, the formal qualities rather than the content: Wason shows this to be an erroneous emphasis, demonstrating the importance of content or meaning in formal reasoning.

Professor Hotopf's criticism of Piaget's theory of perception is of considerable importance. Piaget has constantly contrasted perception and intelligence, insisting that the operativity and reversibility that characterise the latter are not part of the former. He has studied various visual illusions and has provided an explanatory model of perception based on these which he then extends to the more complex types of perception which characterise our adjustment to the world. Professor Hotopf critically examines the theory and the experiments both in terms of their internal consistency and in the light of experimental evidence from his own research and that of others working in the field of visual illusions. Piaget's view of perception is certainly different from that of many other psychologists. Whereas he argues for the distinction of perception from other cognitive processes, insisting that perception is directed by intelligence and is to be distinguished also from mental imagery, for many cognitive psychologists perception is an integral part of the individual's

cognitive congress with the world.   It is this
difference in how perception is understood that is
clarified and illuminated in the second paper of
this section.

Chapter 5

THE THEORY OF FORMAL OPERATIONS – A critique

Peter C. Wason

It would be presumptuous for me to try to expound all
the features of the most mature stage of human intelligence which Piaget calls *formal operations*.   Instead
I shall be mainly concerned with my own research and
that of my associates although I should stress at the
start that its implications are co-incidental;   my own
experiments were not designed to investigate Piaget's
theories.

Furth, in his illuminating book, 'Piaget and Knowledge' (1969), reminds us of the scope of the theory:
'Although the formal operational stage is considered
a final one in terms of structural changes, it is conceived as a dynamic equilibrium that is wide open to
limitless elaborations and particular applications.'

It could be claimed, however, that scope is not a
virtue in a theory.   Popper would argue, just as he
did about psychoanalysis, that the strength of a
theory lies in the extent to which it forbids the
occurrence of certain events.   Indeed, there is a
semblance between Freud and Piaget.   To quote Furth
again: 'What dreams were to Freud, the psychoanalyst,
developmental observations are to Piaget, the epistemologist.'   Wittgenstein pointed out the charm which
psychoanalysis has for many, and the same could be
said for genetic epistemology.   One aspect of its
charm resides in the aesthetic appeal implicit in the
idea that content gradually becomes subordinated to
form with the growth of knowledge.   However, Anne
Clarke (personal communication) has pointed out that
the appeal of the theory to educationists resides more
in its idea that the child learns 'naturally' through
exploration.   To resist the seduction of charm we
have to be especially critical, always remembering
that criticism is generally a mark of respect and I hope
that in this case it will ultimately prove constructive.

119

It is necessary for my thesis to say something
about the salient features of the concrete operational
stage which is assumed to precede formal operational
thought.   Its substage of preoperational thought is
characterised essentially by irreversibility;   it
lacks a structure which makes possible the inter-
iorised action associated with intelligence.   This is
best illustrated by selecting just one feature in the
child's thought which is drastically (and surprisingly)
different from the adult's;   the familiar lack of
conservation of physical properties could have been
cited, but I prefer the less well-known studies of
class inclusion.   Consider this protocol (Inhelder
and Piaget, 1964, p. 61) of a child of five who has
been shown a row of seven blue circles, five blue
squares and two red squares.

> What did we have? - *Blue circles and red and blue*
> *squares* (right) - Are all the circles blue? - *No*
> (wrong) *because there are [blue] squares and*
> *circles.* - Are all the red ones square? - *Yes,*
> *because there were only the squares.* - Are all the
> circles blue? - *No* (wrong), *there were circles and*
> *squares [blue].*

It is as if the class of circles and the class of
blue things are assumed to have the same extension:
the child fails to appreciate that all the circles are
blue because some blue shapes are not circles.   The
transition from preoperational thought to concrete
operations proper, characterised by the acquisition
of reversibility, is best illustrated in relation to
seriation:

> Many years ago, Piaget and Szeminska studied the
> development of seriation using 10 small rods rang-
> ing from 9 - 16.2 cms together with a set of rods
> of intermediate length for subsequent insertion
> in the completed series.   We found three distinct
> stages.   In the first, the child cannot arrange
> the ten initial elements in order.   He arranges
> them in sub-series of 2, 3 or 4 elements, which he
> cannot then put together.   At the second stage,
> he manages the initial seriation empirically by a
> process of trial-and-error.   He can only insert
> the additional elements by further trial-and-error,
> and he usually has to start again from the begin-
> ning.   At the third stage, which starts at 7-8
> years, the child proceeds systematically by looking
> for the smallest (or largest) element first, then
> for the smallest among those remaining, etc.   This
> procedure, and this alone, may be regarded as

properly operational, because it implies an awareness
that any given element is both larger than the preceding and smaller than those that succeed it (e.g.
E > D,C etc. and E < F,G etc.).   This operational
reversibility is accompanied by the ability to
insert the new elements correctly, without trial-
and-error (Inhelder and Piaget, 1964, p. 250).
In his later writings Piaget (1972, p. 35) has summarised the transition succinctly: 'Thus, the innova-
tion introduced at this stage consists in using the
relations > and < not by excluding one from the other
or by non-systematic trial-and-error, but simultaneously'.

In the mature stages of concrete operational thought
Piaget assumes an isomorphic relation between logical
'groupings' and the structure assumed to underlie the
child's overt responses, a view which is quite alien
to Anglo-Saxon psychology and epistemology.   It is
not, of course, assumed that the child is following a
rudimentary calculus.   In fact, the operations are
called concrete because they are not yet independent
of content; they are restricted to the manipulation
of things.

Formal operational thought implies that operations
can be performed on operations.   Mathematical groups
(such as the Klein group) are assumed to be elaborated
through 'reflection' on concrete operations, and these
allow the real to be seen as just one among many possibilities.   Inhelder and Piaget (1958) assert that the
adolescent can abstract the variables in a complex
causal problem, and subject them to a combinatorial
analysis which nicely exhausts the possibilities.
Piaget admits that this process is not always conscious, but the important point is that performance
is assumed to entail a cognitive structure which is
fully describable in terms of the logic of the propositional calculus.   For example, one typical task
is to deduce the necessary and sufficient condition
for producing a yellow colour from four flasks of
colourless liquids.   It is argued that the adolescent
will systematically test each of the sixteen combinations of the four flasks.   More important, it is
claimed that he *knows* that this is the way he must
proceed; he has advanced beyond the stage of trial-
and-error.

Such an interpretation has not gone unchallenged.
During 1969 the late Cyril Burt corresponded with me,
and expressed his general scepticism about Piaget's
conclusions.   One letter in particular is of some
historical interest:

Towards the close of the First World War, when I was
a lecturer at John's, I was fortunate enough to have
Russell next door at Trinity. He was then revising
his 'Principia' for a fresh edition; and, when I
asked whether he thought his theories and notation
could be usefully applied in my studies of reasoning (instead of the Keynes-Joseph 'Logic' on which
I had been brought up at Oxford), he replied:
'Used as a method of analysis it would be both
appropriate and illuminating but used as a standard
for critical evaluation it would be not only inappropriate but highly misleading.' Piaget seems
to me to have fallen into the trap thus indicated.
After a series of ingenious experiments and valuable
psychological observations, he suddenly assumes the
Cambridge logician's academic gown, and judges the
children's performances in terms of the continental
version of the Russell-Whitehead symbolism. I am
thinking of his ideal adolescent who is supposed to
perform a combinatorial analysis yielding 16 alternatives and to test them systematically. He forgets that the Russell-Whitehead-Carnap logic is
modelled on the mathematician's ideal: it is not
the logic of everyday life....

I think Russell's point was that the propositional
calculus, which he had done so much to formalise,
would be misused if it were taken to reflect any so-
called 'laws of thought'.

Bruner (1959) in his well-known review of Inhelder
and Piaget (1958) is less critical of the existence
of formal operations, but much more critical of the
supposed mechanism which causes the transition from
concrete to formal operations. For Piaget this
consists in the lack of stability of the rather vague
concept of a self-regulating 'equilibrium'. But for
Bruner social and cultural factors provide the
motivating force:

the adolescent differs from the child not simply in
that he uses a propositional calculus that deals
with possibilities rather than merely with actual-
ities, but rather that he is *forced* to deal with
possibility by the nature of the tasks that he
undertakes and by the nature of the unfolding and
development of his drives and the social connexions
required for filling them. It is not equilibrium
that keeps him back in the concrete operational
stage and not a new equilibrium that brings him
forward. It is the vicissitude of coping with
demands - internal and external.... Logical

structures develop to support the new forms of
commerce with the world.   It is just as plainly the
case that the pre-operational child, protected by
parents, need not manipulate the world of objects
unassisted until the pressure for independence is
placed upon him, at which time concrete operations
emerge.   So the concretely operational child need
not manipulate the world of potentiality (save on
the fantasy level) until pressure is put upon him,
at which point propositionalism begins to mark his
thinking.   And indeed, it is the case that such
propositional thinking *never* emerges in any full-
scale sense.   It is no surprise then, that children of intellectually under-privileged families
or of manual workers tend to be less challenged in
terms of a sense of possibilities and do not
develop what we commonly speak of as an abstract
gift.

In contrast, Lunzer (1973) has disputed the existence of a stage of formal operational thought because
in practice its unique defining characteristics are so
difficult to identify.   In a series of meticulous
studies he, and his associates, have offered simpler
interpretations of adolescent reasoning.   Indeed, he
now repudiates his earlier views (Lunzer, 1965) and
argues that there are no advances in thinking from
childhood to adolescence which 'are sufficiently
homogenous and distinctive to warrant the use of the
general term *formal reasoning* in opposition to the
term *concrete reasoning*'.

In 1966 I published a problem which consisted of
four cards and a sentence (Wasonl 1966).   At that
time it seemed little more than a puzzling curiosity.
Nevertheless I carried out an experiment on it
(Wason, 1968) because if one discovers something
which clever people can't do it seems worth while
trying to find out why they can't do it.   It became
known as the 'selection task' although recently Lunzer
has given it the more appropriate name: 'the four-
card problem'.   It is only fair to say that some of
my respected colleagues considered it ridiculous
(especially after failing to understand it) because
it was so unlike anything which anyone had seen before,
either inside or outside the laboratory.   Far from
seeming a limitation, this struck me as a peculiar
virtue because it provided a potential instrument to
probe inferential powers unaffected by past experience.   It stood in stark contrast to the ingenious
realistic causal tasks devised by Inhelder and Piaget.

In its original form the cards showed the following
four symbols: A, D, 4, 7, respectively. The subjects
knew that each card had a letter on one side and a
number on the other side. Their task was to name
those cards (and only those cards) which would need
to be turned over in order to determine the truth
value of the following sentence: 'If there is a vowel
on one side of a card then there is an even number on
the other side.' The solution is 'the A and the 7',
but the vast majority of highly intelligent subjects
say 'the A and the 4', or 'only the A'. The problem
is certainly difficult. Two professors of logic
have, after considerable thought, come to grief on it.
So did a leading mathematical psychologist whose sole
comment was not illuminating: 'a computer could
easily be programmed to solve that.' Some people
take a long time to see the solution, and a few even
dispute its validity. And yet, contrary to the
belief of some experts the problem is formally fairly
simple. In our opinion it is the effort to try to
solve such an unusual problem which has allowed clever
people to read undreamt of difficulties into its
structure: the difficulties exist only in their
brains. (I stress this because I have been told
that a group in Germany is working on its philosophical implications.)

After an extensive series of experiments (Wason
and Johnson-Laird, 1972) we have postulated that complete insight into the problem coincides with the
attempt to try to falsify rather than verify the
test sentence (Johnson-Laird and Wason, 1970). More
recently, Jonathan Evans (1972, 1973) has argued that
unenlightened solutions are not so much governed by
verification per se, but by an even more primitive
tendency to 'match' the sentence with the cards.
He has shown that given a sentence in the form, 'if p
then not q', the subjects correctly select the named
valued p and q. My immediate response to his
studies was one of scepticism. It seemed to me
likely that his subjects were ignoring the negative
because of its notorious difficulties. Hence I suggested that we collaborate in an experiment in which
the subjects write down their reasons for selecting
(and not selecting) each card (Wason and Evans, 1974).
The results showed that my supposition had been wrong.
The subjects tended to give logically impeccable
reasons for selecting the negated consequent term.
This suggested that they had gained insight into the
structure of the problem, but we argued that no such

insight had been gained.   Rather it seemed to us that
the reasons were rationalisations of an intuitive response in terms of the negative context of the task.
Current research on such 'dual processing' may enable
us to understand it better.

This preliminary account of the problem should
persuade you that it is not its difficulty which is
at all interesting.   Rather its interest lies in the
fact that in the 'normal task' (with an unnegated
test sentence and abstract material) the errors are
consistent and that subjects do not respond in accordance with their own interpretation of the test
sentence, i.e. they acknowledge that 'p and not q'
falsifies the sentence, but still fail to select not
q as potentially relevant.   They are deceived by
superficial simplicity.

Looking at the responses alone, as our American
friends are inclined to do, we might fairly claim that
our results are inconsistent with formal operations.
Our subjects conspicuously fail to 'isolate the
variables and subject them to a combinatorial
analysis'.   But it is the qualitative features of
performance which are more illuminating because they
are reminiscent of concrete operations.   Again and
again, the subjects seem tied to perceptual data:
'The cards not mentioned in the sentence have nothing
to do with it';   'Presumably only those which I can
see are correct.'   The next experiment (Wason, 1969)
revealed a more subtle resemblance.

I had developed a technique for probing the errors
by asking the subjects about the consequences of the
two alternatives on the other side of the two correct
cards.   This involved them in contradictions or conceptual inconsistencies.   In the experiment they
knew that every card had a triangle on one side and
a circle on the other side, but they knew only that
the colour of the shape on the other side was *either*
red *or* blue.   The cards consisted (face upwards) of
a red triangle, a blue circle, a red circle, and a
blue triangle respectively.   The test sentence was:
'Every card which has a red triangle on one side has
a blue circle on its other side.'   Hence the solution is, 'the red triangle and the red circle'.   The
following is a dialogue with one articulate and con-
fident subject who never gained any insight at all.
He had originally selected the red triangle and the
blue circle, the two symbols named in the test
sentence.
E: 'Your task is to tell me which of the cards you

need to turn over in order to find out whether the
sentence is true or false.'

S: 'A red triangle on one side ... although there
were some in which both sides were red ... I don't
know how many of them.   At present we have two
cards which could satisfy those conditions ... so
you only have two cards to choose from: the red
triangle and the blue circle.'

E: 'What could be on the other side of the red
triangle?'

S: 'A red circle or a blue circle.'

E: 'If there were a red circle on the other side,
could you say anything about the truth or falsity
of the sentence?'

S: 'It would be untrue.'

E: 'And if there were a blue circle, could you say
anything about the truth or falsity of the
sentence?'

S: 'It would be true.'

E: 'By the way, what was your choice of cards to turn
over in order to find out whether the sentence in
front of you is true or false?'

S: 'The red triangle and the blue circle.'

E: 'Are you quite happy about this choice?'

S: 'Quite happy, as the other two do not agree with
the statement made.'   [Only the mentioned cards
count.   The subject has just failed a *weak hypothetical contradiction test*: he agrees that a
red circle on the other side would falsify, but
fails to see the relevance of the red circle card.]

E: 'What could be on the other side of the red
circle?'

S: 'A red triangle or a blue triangle.'

E: 'If there were a red triangle on the other side of
the red circle, could you say anything about the
truth or falsity of the sentence?'   [This is a
strong hypothetical contradiction test because it
refers to an unselected but relevant card.]

S: 'The statement would be meaningless because it
doesn't apply.'   [This sometimes happened in the
previous experiment; the subject refuses to
sanction the validity of the inference.]

E: 'In fact it would be false.'

S: 'It could be, but you are not doing it that way
round.   The statement would be untrue in any case,
no matter what is on the other side.' (sic).
[Irreversibility?]

E: 'If there were a blue triangle on the other side,
could you say anything about the truth or falsity
of the sentence?'

S: 'No.'
E: 'Are you quite happy about needing to turn over just
     the red triangle and the blue circle in order to
     find out whether the sentence is true or false?'
S: 'Yes.'
E: 'Please turn over the red triangle and the blue
     circle and tell me whether the sentence is true or
     false.'
S: 'The sentence is true.'   [There is a blue circle
     on the other side of the red triangle and a red
     triangle on the other side of the blue circle.]
E: 'I am now going to turn over the red circle, and
     I want you to tell me whether you still think the
     sentence is true.'   [This is a *concrete contra-
     diction test*: there is a red triangle on the
     other side.]
S: 'Wait a minute.   When it's put like that the sen-
     tence is not true.   Either the sentence is true,
     or it is not true.   You have just proved one thing
     and then you have proved the other.   You've proved
     a theorem and then its corollary, so you don't know
     where you are.   Don't ask me about the blue tri-
     angle because that would be meaningless.'
E: 'Are you quite happy about needing to turn over
     just the red triangle and the blue circle in order
     to find out whether the sentence is true or false?'
S: 'There is only one card which needs to be turned
     over to prove the statement exactly: the red tri-
     angle.   Strictly speaking, you don't need the
     blue circle.   You must find every card with a
     red triangle on it and turn it over, but there is
     only one.'
E: 'But you just said when the red circle was turned
     over the sentence was false.'
S: 'That is doing it the other way round.'
E: 'The problem is very difficult.   Very few people
     get it right.   What we are interested in is why
     they don't get it right.'
S: 'I am a member of Mensa.   I wasn't going to tell
     you that until afterwards.'
     This is another dialogue with a five-year-old boy.
'Do you have a brother?', 'Yes', 'What's his name?',
'Jim', 'Does Jim have a brother?', 'No'.   It demonstrates the irreversibility characteristic of pre-
operational thought, but is it any more irreversible
than admitting that a red circle on the other side of
a red triangle would falsify, and then denying that a
red triangle on the other side of a red circle would
do so?

In a recent experiment, carried out in collaboration
with Evelyn Golding, irreversibility of this kind
became the most characteristic feature of the protocols.   The subjects had to determine the truth value
of one or other of the following two synonymous sentences: 'Above each number (N+) is a letter (L+)', or
'A letter (L+) is above each number (N+).'   (We presented the paper without using logical notation,
partly because psychologists seemed to dislike p's and
q's, but mainly because the notation of the propositional calculus seemed inappropriate.)   The test
sentences have the surface structure of a declarative;
they are assertions.   And yet their deep structure is
that of the following conditional: 'if there is a
number below, then there is a letter above.'   The
fact that they were no easier to process suggests that
the phenomena in question are not a function of a conditional surface structure.

An attempt was first made to program the subjects
with the conditional truth function by presenting
four fully revealed cards, and asking them to pick
out the *one* which falsified the sentence, i.e. no
letter (L-) above a number (N+).   The subsequent task
material consisted of four partially masked cards (see
Figure 5.1).   After the subjects had made their choice
of cards (usually one number and one letter), the two
correct ones were simultaneously unmasked and shown
to be identical: no letter (L-) above a number (N+)
(see Figure 5.1).   Since the subjects had nearly
always selected one of these cards i.e. (N+) but not
the other, i.e. (L-), they were confronted with an
inconsistency and asked to account for it.   Similarly,
if the subjects had correctly selected no letter (L-),
but incorrectly selected the letter (L+), the other
two cards were unmasked and shown to be identical.
However, we shall not be concerned with the attempt to
correct this minor error.   The protocols, of which
the following are representative, speak for themselves.   (The convention is adopted that the first
symbol refers to that part of the card originally
visible, and the second to that part originally
masked.)

(i) N+L-: 'I saw there was a number at the bottom
and therefore the sentence could be true or false.'
    L-N+: 'I saw there was a blank at the top which
meant there was no letter so the sentence had to be
untrue.

(ii) N+L-: 'There was a number showing - the other
space was covered up and it was possible it could have
been a letter.

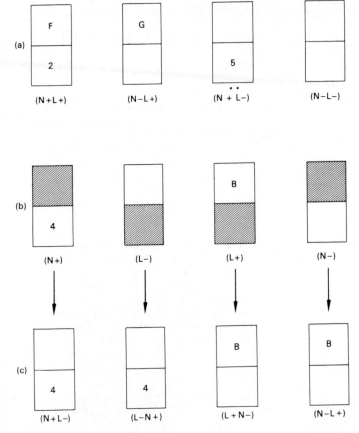

FIGURE 5.1 The material used by Wason and Golding (1974)
(a) the inspection cards;   (b) the masked task cards;
(c) the unmasked task cards.   For (a) the falsifying
card is indicated by asterisks.   The test sentence is
either, *Above each number is a letter,* or *A letter is
above each number.*

      L-N+: 'There was a blank and it was preventing
the sentence from being true.   I knew it already.'
(iii) N+L-: 'The sentence could have been untrue if
this space had been a blank and not a letter.'
      L-N+: 'Was untrue anyway because there was not
a letter, so it was definitely untrue.'
 (iv) N+L-: 'Because it was a number and it stood a
chance of being wrong.'
      L-N+: 'Could have been two blanks.'
  (v) N+L-: 'I knew there was a number and if there
was a letter above it it would prove it.'
      L-N+: 'I did not think there was a number and

it might have been two blanks which would not prove anything.'

(vi) N+L-: 'That was the only one which could definitely prove it untrue.'

L-N+: 'If it had been a blank which it could have been you did not know that it was not anyway.'

Are these remarks rationalisations of error, or do they reflect the initial interpretation of the stimulus material? Either way it appears that an inference is sanctioned in one direction only, i.e. when it starts with a visible symbol; a blank confers no such warrant. And even when the cards had been revealed as identical, the thought processes tended not to reverse. Less than a third of the subjects were correct when the task was performed again, and even less when new lexical material was substituted. (One curious comment arose in discussing this experiment. A colleague, who knew the previous experiments, and was conversant with symbolic logic, asked to be given the solution because the knowledge that not q implies not p was obviously useless as an algorithm for grasping a conditional sentence expressed as an assertion.) Very recently we have acquired some evidence that the inconsistent utterances, elicited by confronting the subjects with contradictions, have their origin in differences between the functioning of the left and right hemispheres of the brain. When critical information is fed directly to the left (verbal) hemisphere, by tactile stimulation of the right hand, performance is substantially improved (Golding, Reich and Wason, 1974).

Some earlier studies, however, did bridge the gap between my problem and those of Inhelder and Piaget. My first hunch was to present the problem in a realistic guise. The beneficial effects of so doing were demonstrated by Diana Shapiro (Wason and Shapiro, 1971) and (independently) by Lunzer, Harrison and Davey (1972). Shapiro used a story about four journeys in which destinations and modes of transport were named on the cards. Lunzer et al. used graphic material. But the most brilliant experiment was conducted by Johnson-Laird, Legrenzi and Sonino Legrenzi (1972). In the experimental ('thematic') condition the subjects had to imagine they were postal workers whose task was to determine whether the following rule had been violated: 'If an envelope is sealed, then it has a 5d. stamp on it.' The task material consisted of four envelopes showing respectively the back sealed, the back unsealed, a 5d. stamp

on the front, a 4*d*. stamp on the front.   The solution
is to select the back sealed and the 4*d*. stamp on the
front.   In the control ('symbolic') condition the rule
referred to arbitrary symbols on the front and back of
the envelopes.   There were twenty-four subjects who
each received two versions of the thematic problem and
two versions of the symbolic problem in different
orders.   The results are shown in Table 5.1

TABLE 5.1   Frequency of solving both problems, one
problem and neither problem (N = 24) (after Johnson-
Laird, Legrenzi and Sonino Legrenzi, 1972)

	Thematic	Symbolic
Both problems correct	17	0
One problem correct	5	7
Neither problem correct	2	17

There were obviously no transfer effects whatsoever
between the two kinds of problem; in fact, only two
subjects acknowledged any logical relation between
them.   Lunzer et al. (1972) had obtained a similar
result, and it led him to reject a 'strong' form of
the theory of formal reasoning:

> If it is true that, once he is alerted to the
> logical structure of the problem ... a subject
> will reason in accordance with it, the same subject
> should not immediately revert to an intuitive
> pattern of thinking when an analogous, but slightly
> more difficult problem is posed.

Recent research (Gilhooly and Falconer, 1974;
Bracewell and Hidi, 1974; Van Duyne, 1974) has attempted to isolate the variables which contribute to the
beneficial effects of realistic guise - with slightly
differing results.   In my research unit Petrus van
Duyne has succeeded in manipulating the arbitrariness
of the test sentence in a remarkable experiment which
involved a serial task consisting of sixty-four
trials (sixteen blocks each consisting of four
stimuli).   There were four independent groups:
(a) ABSTRACT e.g. 'If a vowel is on one side of an
    envelope, then there is an even number on the other
    side.'   Complete insight responses = 19.3 per cent.
(b) ARBITRARY e.g. 'If L.B. MILL is on one side of the
    envelope, then there is PRINTED MATTER REDUCED RATE
    on the other side.'   Complete insight responses =
    49.0 per cent.

(c) SIMULATION e.g. 'If there is PRINTED MATTER REDUCED
RATE on one side of the envelope, then it must be
left open.'   Cards with words on them were substituted for real envelopes.   Complete insight
responses = 87.0 per cent.

(d) REALISTIC e.g. 'If an envelope is marked PRINTED
MATTER REDUCED RATE, then it must be left open.'
With real envelopes as stimuli.   Complete insight
responses = 98.0 per cent.

The trend across these four conditions was highly
significant, but when it was broken down the difference
was most pronounced between the Arbitrary and Realistic
conditions.   Van Duyne (personal communication) has
plotted these results, combined with previous ones, to
illustrate how different components which go to make
up 'realistic guise' affect the subject's grasp of
the problem (see Figure 5.2).   The curve illustrates
rather nicely the importance of semantics in problem
solving.   But it is a little depressing too because
it suggests that the critical appreciation of falsification is aroused, not by invoking a calculus, but by
assimilation to more mundane experience.   And when
this experience is subsequently stripped away, what
looked like the understanding of abstract structure
has also been shown to vanish.   Experience is not
just necessary to induce understanding; it is evi-
dently necessary in order to maintain it.   It is
somewhat ironical that, after so much research, this
conclusion which implies a severe limitation on reasoning powers, might well seem highly plausible to the
layman.

In summary: our results suggest that reasoning is
radically affected by content in a systematic way,
and this is incompatible with the Piagetian view that
in formal operational thought the content of a problem
has at last been subordinated to the form of relations
in it.   It is all the more incompatible when it is
remembered that nearly all our subjects were not just
intelligent adolescents, but highly selected university
students.   Burt (personal communication) said that my
early results 'furnish one of the most conclusive
proofs that the theory of formal operations requires
modification.'   However, I would settle for the more
modest conclusion of Halford (1972) that they show
that: 'If adults have what Piaget calls formal operations, then Piaget has done very little to specify
the conditions under which they will be observed.'

Looked at in another way, the results are a testimony
to Piaget's insight into the concepts of irreversibility

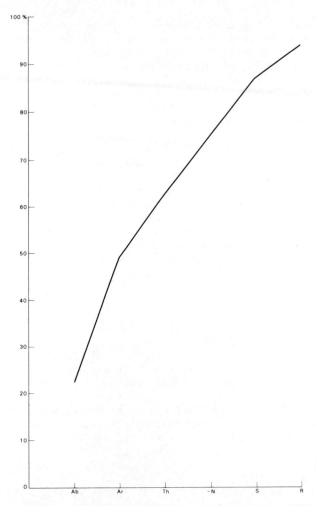

FIGURE 5.2 Mean percentage of complete insight responses
as a function of task material (N = 184) (after Van
Duyne)
Ab = Abstract condition computed from Wason and Shapiro
     (1971), Johson-Laird et al. (1972), Van Duyne
     (1974), Van Duyne (in preparation) N = 72
Ar = Arbitrary condition computed from Van Duyne (in
     preparation) N = 24
Th = Thematic condition computed from Wason and Shapiro
     (1971) N = 16
-N = Realistic condition but less natural realism com-
     puted from Van Duyne (1974) N = 24
 S = Simulation condition computed from Van Duyne (in
     preparation) N = 12

and concrete operations in thinking.   These are the
most distinctive features of our research.   But they
appear at what would seem to be the wrong stage as a
function of the *novelty* of the problem.   It is this
novelty which makes adults reason like children.
     The criticism can be deflected if the theory is
construed as one of competence rather than performance,
as has been pointed out to me by Apostel and by
Jonckheere (personal communications).   For in that
case the stages mark an upper bound which individuals
can be expected to attain only under ideal conditions.
But this raises difficulties in devising critical
tests of the theory because contrary evidence can
always be evaded by invoking the concept of *horizontal
décalage* - the fact that tasks differ in the extent
to which they resist and inhibit the application of
cognitive structures.   All that we have done is to
show that even mature intelligence is much more affected by content or meaning than the theory of formal
operations seems to allow.

REFERENCES

BRACEWELL, R.J. and HIDI, S.E. (1974), The Solution of
an Inferential Problem as a Function of Stimulus
Materials, 'Quarterly Journal of Experimental Psycho-
logy', vol. 26, 480-8.
BRUNER, J.S. (1959), Inhelder and Piaget's 'The Growth
of Logical Thinking': I A psychologist's viewpoint,
'British Journal of Psychology', vol. 50, 363-70.
EVANS, J.St.B.T. (1972), On the Problem of Interpreting
Reasoning Data: logical and psychological approaches,
'Cognition', vol. 1, 373-84.
EVANS, J.St.B.T. and LYNCH, J.S. (1973), Matching Bias
in the Selection Task, 'British Journal of Psychology',
vol. 64, 391-7.
FURTH, H.G. (1969), 'Piaget and Knowledge', London:
Prentice-Hall.
GILHOOLY, K.J. and FALCONER, W.A. (1974), Concrete
and Abstract Terms and Relations in Testing a Rule,
'Quarterly Journal of Experimental Psychology', vol.
26, 355-9.
GOLDING, E., REICH, S.S. and WASON, P.C. (1974), Inter-
hemispheric Differences in Problem Solving, 'Perception',
vol. 3, 231-5.
HALFORD, G.S. (1972), The Impact of Piaget on Psychology in the Seventies, in 'New Horizons in Psychology',
vol. 2, ed. P.C. Dodwell, Harmondsworth: Penguin Books.

INHELDER, B. and PIAGET, J. (1958), 'The Growth of
Logical Thinking from Childhood to Adolescence', London:
Routledge & Kegan Paul.
INHELDER, B. and PIAGET, J. (1964), 'The Early Growth
of Logic in the Child: classification and seriation',
London: Routledge & Kegan Paul.
JOHNSON-LAIRD, P.N. and WASON, P.C. (1970), A Theoret-
ical analysis of Insight into a Reasoning Task,
'Cognitive Psychology', vol. 1, 134-48.
JOHNSON-LAIRD, P.N., LEGRENZI, P. and SONINO LEGRENZI, M.
(1972), Reasoning and a Sense of Reality, 'British
Journal of Psychology', vol. 63, 395-400.
LUNZER, E.A. (1965), Problems of Formal Reasoning in
Test Situations, in 'European Research in Cognitive
Development', ed. P.H. Mussen, 'Monogr. Soc. Res. Child
Development', vol. 30, 19-46.
LUNZER, E.A. (1972), The Development of Formal Reason-
ing, in 'Cognitive Processes and Science Instruction',
ed. K. Frey and M. Lang, Burn-Stuttgart, Vienna: Huber
and Baltimore.
LUNZER, E.A. (1973), Formal Reasoning: a reappraisal,
paper presented to the second annual conference of the
Jean Piaget Society, Philadelphia.
LUNZER, E.A., HARRISON, C. and DAVEY, M. (1972), The
Four-card Problem and the Development of Formal Reason-
ing, 'Quarterly Journal of Experimental Psychology',
vol. 24, 326-39.
PIAGET, J. (1972), 'The Principles of Genetic Epistem-
ology', London: Routledge & Kegan Paul.
VAN DUYNE, P.C. (1974), Realism and Linguistic Com-
plexity, 'British Journal of Psychology', vol. 65, 59-67.
WASON, P.C. (1966), Reasoning, in 'New Horizons in Psy-
chology', vol. 1, ed. B.M. Foss, Harmondsworth:
Penguin Books.
WASON, P.C. (1968), Reasoning about a Rule, 'Quarterly
Journal of Experimental Psychology', vol. 20, 273-81.
WASON, P.C. (1969), Regression in Reasoning? 'British
Journal of Psychology', vol. 60, 471-80.
WASON, P.C. and SHAPIRO, D. (1971), Natural and Con-
trived Experience in a Reasoning Problem, 'Quarterly
Journal of Experimental Psychology', vol. 23, 63-71.
WASON, P.C. and JOHNSON-LAIRD, P.N. (1972), 'Psychology
of Reasoning: structure and content', London: Batsford.
WASON, P.C. and GOLDING, E. (1974), The Language of
Inconsistency, 'British Journal of Psychology', vol.
65, 537-46.
WASON, P.C. and EVANS, J.St.B.T. (1974), Dual Processes
in Reasoning?, 'Cognition', vol. 4 (in press).

Chapter 6

AN EXAMINATION OF PIAGET'S THEORY OF PERCEPTION

W.H.N. Hotopf

In 1942 there was published in the 'Archives de Psychologie' a research paper on the Delboeuf illusion by
Piaget and his colleagues Lambercier, Boesch and von
Albertini.   This was the first in a series of some
fifty articles in that journal published during a
period of over thirty years entitled 'Recherches sur
le Développement des Perceptions'.   The results of
these researches in so far as they contributed to a
detailed theory of perception in relation to Piaget's
theories concerning the development of knowledge and
intelligence were published in 1961 in a book called
'Les Mécanismes Perceptifs', first published in an
English translation in 1969 under the title, 'The
Mechanisms of Perception' (Piaget, 1969).   This book
included researches as yet unpublished in the 'Archives
de Psychologie', but since then there has been some
further work reported in that journal, as well as work
related to Piaget's theory published in other journals.
In this chapter however I shall confine myself to
Piaget's book, because it constitutes a detailed description of his theory, and his theory is what I am
interested in.

It is important when considering Piaget's theory to
bear in mind the date when the book was published.   A
lot of research in visual perception has been carried
out since 1961, and of course none of this is mentioned
in Piaget's book.   It is indeed doubtful whether it
would have received much attention from Piaget even had
he written the book later.   Very little mention is
made of other psychologists' pre-1961 experiments or
indeed of their theories, except briefly and perhaps
opportunistically to assimilate points they have made
to his own theory.   The major external influence upon
Piaget seems to have been Gestalt psychology and it is

with regard to this in the main that his book may be
regarded as taking up a position.

Given that this is the case, why, it may be asked,
should much time and space be devoted to a theory put
forward such a comparatively long time ago when so
much research has been carried out since.   Logically
speaking, unless one regards a theory as merely an
abstract description of experimental evidence, there
is no reason why subsequent work should be incompatible
with a theory developed earlier.   However one can also
say that Piaget's reputation and influence is such as
to make his theory still important for consideration.
Indeed in the field of visual illusions the theory is
frequently referred to and gives rise to experiments
though, it must be admitted, these relate only to a
very simplified form of the theory.   Though highly
critical of the theory, I believe that in its fully
developed form it is of some interest for its own
sake.   At all events I shall largely confine myself
to the theory rather than to its experimental evidence.
The theory fits the experiments loosely in the sense
that the evidence is often indirect and highly interpreted.

Piaget starts in his first chapter with a consideration of a set of illusions called 'primary illusions'.
He discusses or mentions about sixteen of these illusions including those such as the illusion of rectangles (where the longer side is overestimated in
relation to the shorter side), 'angle' illusions such
as the Zöllner and Poggendorff, the Müller-Lyer and
Delboeuf illusions and the illusion of filled space.
These illusions are identified by two characteristics.
Firstly, they decrease with age.   This does not mean
from birth but from the age of five, the earliest age
from which he could get experimental data.   Secondly,
they occur even when eye movements are precluded by
brief tachistoscopic presentation, something which
leads Piaget to say that they result from 'simple
field effects'.

Piaget holds that all these illusions can be
accounted for in terms of a general formula, called the
Law of Relative Centrations, which includes in its
terms certain dimensions of their display.   Most
important among these dimensions are two lines in the
horizontal and/or vertical orientations which differ
in length and hence give rise to a length contrast
effect, of which for Piaget the simplest illustration
was the illusion of rectangles.   That such a comparison is involved, often in the form of an implicit

rectangle, Piaget tries to show for every one of the
illusions mentioned.   I will describe this in more
detail later in order to give the reader a clearer
understanding.

Having arrived at his descriptive formula, Piaget
in his second chapter essays an explanatory model.
This model was suggested in particular by his discovery of the 'error of the standard' according to
which the standard increases in apparent size if, in
psychophysical studies, it is fixated separately in
every judgment made with regard to a different comparison object.   On the other hand, if it can be
seen simultaneously with a set of comparison objects,
so that it does not need to be so carefully fixated
each time a comparison is made, the opposite effect
will result.   From this and other evidence Piaget
inferred that fixation or relative foveality of vision
resulted in an increase in apparent size.   By the
same token what was more recently fixated or fixated
longer, for a certain limited range of times, would
also be increased in apparent size.   Greater attention
would have the same effect.   If we now grant that a
longer line presented near to a shorter one is more
attention-compelling, more likely to be fixated or to
attract the fixation point towards itself, then we
would account for the main factor in the explanation
of the primary illusions.   The explanatory, physiological model Piaget then develops out of these and
similar considerations, postulates that a line consists of a large number of minute parts, each one of
which has to be matched - 'encountered' to use his
technical term - by a different neural unit or 'ocular
micro-movement'.   These encounters are a function of
the number of 'centrations' (Piaget's word for acts
of fixation and attention) that the line receives.
The more it receives, and the rate of increase is
exponential, the more nearly the apparent size will
match the objective size.   The more frequently an
illusion is displayed the greater the likelihood that
the discrepancy in number of encounters and hence of
centrations between the long and short lines will
decrease.   Piaget describes this closer matching of
relative numbers of centrations as 'decentration'.
There is clearly an analogy here with the gradual
development away from egocentricism that characterises
his approach to the evolution of stages in intelligence.
Piaget emphasises the independence of his psychological finding, the Law of Relative Centrations, from
his physiological model.   Even if the latter were

wrong, this would not invalidate the relationship that
the formula expresses. He goes on however in the
third, fourth and fifth chapters of his book to rely
on his explanatory model to give credibility to his
treatment of secondary illusions.

Secondary illusions are ones which increase with
age (i.e. from five onwards) or increase with age up
to a certain point. They were the consequence of
perceptual activities involved in exploring the world
so as to be able to adapt to it better. Piaget
points to the evidence of grosser, less skilled eye
movements of young children which are not so finely
related to the details of a display. In so far as
eye movements became more finely graded and the
visual scene continuously explored, so there should
be a constant relative equalising of centrations which
should reduce primary illusions. However, eye movements are also structured by the structure existing in
objects. In so far as more information might be
present in the upper than in the lower part of a
display level with the eyes, (1) so new relative centrations would be learned leading to relative overestimation in size of objects in the upper part of the
field. For example, in comparing the lengths of two
vertical lines, one above the other, the upper would
be judged longer because more fixated, even though
they were both of the same size and therefore no
length *contrast* effect could be operating as with
the primary illusions. Then again the viewer would
learn to make use of more distant parts of the field
and employ them as a frame of reference in making
judgments of orientation instead of relying on 'egocentric assimilation' to his 'line of regard'. He
would however initially have difficulty in making
comparisons between such distant objects. Consequently when he was first developing the use of
frames of reference at the age of about ten years he
would do less well in making such judgments than both
younger and older subjects.

Piaget distinguishes a number of different kinds
of perceptual activity, which may or may not be defined,
such as exploration (eye movements along a line),
transports ('the activity by which the perception of
one element is carried over and applied to the second
element which is at a sufficient distance to require
a second centration'), transpositions (eye movements
involved in comparing one pair of elements with
another pair, which seems to imply two transports in
succession), referrals, regulation (including hyper-

regulation), composition, schematisation and so on.
He makes further distinctions within a particular type
of perceptual activity such as ones between directional and dimensional transports, spatial and temporal
transports, and distance transports (distinguished
from ones confined to the frontal parallel plane).

Generally speaking what these kinds of perceptual
activity do is· to relate centrations at greater dis-
tances in space and time. In so far as such relating
is done there is an evening out of centrations (in
other words, decentration) so that one element is not
exaggerated at the expense of another. As an illustration of this we can quote evidence he gives in
which two lines which are separated from one another
are compared in length. Whether they were correctly
judged or not he found depended upon whether the
transports (eye movements) from one line to the
other were 'reciprocal' or not. When they were not,
i.e. when the eyes moved from one to another but not
back again, then this former line, the one not re-
ceiving a return movement, was underestimated, because
it would have received fewer centrations.

Piaget's procedure is to give evidence for all
sorts of perceptual tasks involving such distortions
as errors of anticipation (effect of ascending and
descending series in psychophysical tasks); the
central tendency; size constancy, whether over- or
under- and its relation to judgments of distance;
relative frequency of different types of judgment in
Michotte-type causality judgments; effects in
studies of apparent movement and of time; and to
show how these vary with age. In accounting for
the relationship he uses evidence of eye movement
studies, experiments where no eye movements were
possible (short exposure tachistoscopic studies) or
fixation was controlled, where the separation between
standard and the comparison object was varied or the
time interval, and from all these he tries to work
out in a very interpretive fashion, with accumulations
of instances, the most close-fitting general account
in terms of his theory's predelictions. There are
two things in particular he is concerned to establish -
the dependence of perception on prior activity and,
related to this, the learned nature of perceptual
effects. I shall say something about each of these
and then conclude this section by considering the
relation between secondary illusions and Piaget's
explanatory model.

We have seen that secondary illusions are by defi-

nition consequent upon prior movement, but what about
primary illusions?   Piaget holds that it is not
possible to measure these before the age of five.
The possibility exists then that they are the consequence of perceptual activities which take place in
the first five years of life.   It will be remembered
that there were two criteria for primary illusions -
their decline with age and their being field effects,
by which he meant that eye movements were not necessary for their perception.   The first is obviously
not relevant in deciding this question, so for Piaget
it depends upon the second.   He decides in the
affirmative on the basis of an experiment which he
claimed showed that field effects could derive from
perceptual learning.   In this experiment when simple
figures like squares, circles and triangles have their
outlines merely suggested by corners, short arcs and
the like and are superimposed upon one another, then
five-year-olds had difficulty in picturing them but
seven-year-olds had greater success.   Piaget attributed this to the development of 'virtual' lines, a
concept which we will see he is particularly attached
to and which implies that the children learn to see
lines which are not there, thus yielding an immediate
'field' effect.   In Piaget's words during the second
stage of learning the subject

> imagines possible virtual lines but constructs
> them by successive approximations, thanks to
> explorations, transports, transpositions and above
> all to anticipations which allow him, bit by bit,
> to build up the best form.   Finally, in the
> third stage, the virtual line is perceived imme-
> diately and of necessity, even in the absence of
> any sensory support or indication that the virtual
> line is restricted to joining the segments actually
> given (p. 197) (2)

In their detailed report of the study however, Piaget
and von Albertini (1954) do not present evidence that
the children actually saw the 'virtual' lines in the
way such lines known as 'virtual contours' are seen
in certain well known demonstrations of 'good'
figures by Gestalt psychologists (cf. Kanizsa, 1974).
It appears to have been an inference from the older
children's success.   From this experiment, then,
Piaget infers that field effects *are* compatible with
an illusion being secondary and goes on then to argue
that primary illusions involving 'Euclidean' or, as
some call them, 'geometrical' figures, are, contrary
to the Gestalt view, likely to require some preliminary

learning such as the 'elementary activities of fixation ... of locating, of segregating, of noticing
differences in length between neighbouring elements,
or appreciating directions within the figure, etc.'
(p. 201). Piaget does indeed frequently refer to
perceptual processes becoming unconscious and auto-
matic, giving rise to 'field' effects, due as he once
put it to the operation of 'crystallisation, auto-
matisation or sedimentation (according to the preferred
figure of speech)' (p. 212), a characteristic dis-
closure incidentally of his looseness in use of
terminology, so confusing in one given to the invention of new terms of art.

The significance of his rejection of field effects
as a differentiating criterion however lies in his
involvement with the Gestalt approach and opposition
to its nativist bias. Not only does he take trouble
to explain the characteristics of good figures in
terms of their being less likely to bring about differential centrations because of the absence of
inequalities of dimensions and to give evidence of
their change with age which we have just described,
but also his approach to size constancy, perception
of cause and apparent movement is mainly motivated to
providing arguments against the nativist position of
the Gestalt psychologists and Michotte, as well as
experimental evidence for regarding these phenomena
as learned as a result of perceptual activities.
His argument is however very involved, the evidence
extremely detailed and rather indirect, so I will not
attempt to describe it here.

Our last question concerned the relation between
Piaget's explanatory physiological model and the
secondary illusions. What this, it will be remembered, involved was the relative exaggeration in
apparent size of material which was more centrally or
more frequently or more recently (within a time span
that has been left unspecified) fixated or more
closely attended to than that which it was compared
to. Instances of this were mentioned above when referring to the overestimation of objects higher in
the field of regard and when describing reciprocal
transports. It must be said however that with many
of the secondary effects it is difficult to see how
this explanation can apply. Perhaps purely temporal
transports which are successive comparisons made
without eye movements can be explained in terms of
differential attention, though Piaget nowhere invokes
this when using differences in temporal transports to

account for the stronger and more lasting effect in
adults as compared with children of the central tendency in judging the lengths of rods. It is very
difficult however to see the relationship between
Piaget's explanatory model and another effect of
temporal transports and transpositions, namely
schematisation, a concept already well known to those
familiar with Piaget's treatment of operations.
Since sensori-motor activities give rise under certain
circumstances to schematisations so too, Piaget
argues, should perceptual activities. He then
applies this to the explaining of perceptual categorisation in which he includes the 'good' figures
of Gestalt psychology. The activities give rise to
schemes and these then control later perceptual
activities controlling presumably the way a person
looks at an object. Feature analysis for Piaget
would then entail a succession of eye movements and
acts of attention leading to a cognitive decision or
categorisation, activities which would eventually
sediment into an apparently immediate impression
which would be a field effect. Piaget writes about
deforming schematisation but the only experimental
evidence he gives is of cases of good figure categori-
sations, and not of what he calls 'empirical perceptual schemes'. Some connection might be worked out
between an overestimation of size and the observed
distortion of a 'good' figure, but how could this
apply to his empirical schemes, seeing a hand with
parted fingers rather than a fan of lines to use an
example from an experiment by Brunswik that Piaget
himself quotes. This makes us more conscious of the
obvious, namely, that throughout Piaget has been
dealing with *size* effects. He has assimilated
various illusions such as the angle illusion to simple
overestimation of line length, but what about illusions of brightness and colour, or for that matter
brightness and colour constancy? Perhaps this is
the reason why his treatment of constancy which he
regards as learned - 'a perceptual scheme of conservation' (p. 233) as he calls it - is confined to size
constancy.
    It is true that he makes brief mention of the size-
weight illusion and refers to 'perceptual activities
(including decentring, relating, transporting, transforming, etc.)' (p. 189), connected with the perception
of sound and music. These may be activities but
what movements are they meant to be? Contractions of
the middle ear muscle, turning the head towards the

source of sound maybe, but to regard all the distortions
and illusions which sound perception is prolific in as
secondary to motor activity would appear a tall order
even for a theorist as resourceful and pertinacious as
Piaget.

It would seem that Piaget gradually forgets his
model as he develops his theme of developing perceptual activity in response to the structure of the
world.   There are one or two signs of early forget-
fulness as when he account, as we mentioned on p. 139
above, for the child's errors in judging the orientation of obliques in terms of his assimilation of
their direction to his line of regard.   How is this
source of error a relative centration?   Similarly, he
writes of how the development of perceptual co-ordinates from about seven to nine 'progressively hampers'
a child making comparisons of length between lines of
different orientation, but once 'this system has been
constructed' there is improvement.   And when he comes
to the perception of causality, movement and time, all
pretence to use his model has been dropped.   Instead
his constructs, transpositions, compositions, regular-
isations and so on are used as though they are themselves explanations.   One example of this apparent
circularity may be given from his treatment of anticipations.   He describes an experiment in which
adults show a quicker development of anticipation but
when later the anticipated events stop occurring, they
cease, in response to this, to anticipate much
earlier than children do.   'These findings', writes
Piaget, 'are very characteristic of an activity
having a double aspect of reinforcement with age and
of increasing regulation with age, in the sense of a
damping or a gradual extinction when the anticipation
is not confirmed' (p. 188).

The truth is that Piaget, with the ground he has
to cover, wishing to extend his treatment of perception
from visual illusions to more complex types of perception implicit in our successful adjustment to the
world, has not the time to work out relationships at
the microscopic level of his explanatory model, if
indeed, as may be thought, it were possible at all.
He has certain purposes.   These are to show perception
in accordance with his general theory as advancing
developmentally from the egocentric to the objective
as a result of activity but also to show that every
advance sows the seeds of decline.   There is for
Piaget always unreliability in perception.   And when
we come to the last part of his book, we see the
reason why.

In this last part Piaget raises the issue which we
may guess was his long-range purpose in writing his
book - what is the relation between perception and
intelligence?   He starts off by taking fourteen
points of difference between the two in a way that
seems to involve a lot of redundancy.   What he does
here is to compare what he calls 'primary perception'
with what we might call pure intelligence, i.e. that
achieved in its most highly developed level of formal
operations.   What 'primary perception' is is not
easily determined in view of Piaget's argument that
perception at the age of five was in fact secondary,
the product of earlier meaningful perceptual activities.
Perhaps we should take it as the sort of ideal type
that philosophers once operated with when they talked
about sense data.   Piaget's comparison of the two
sounds somewhat derogatory to perception.   The following extracts may illustrate this.

> perception is subordinated to an object of which it
> supplies a direct knowledge: ... by contrast, in-
> telligence can evoke the absent object by means of
> a symbolic process (p. 285).
> Perceptual field effects are not only subordinated
> to the presence of the object but also to limiting
> conditions of spatial and temporal proximity: ...
> but intelligence, which can relate any elements,
> whatever their spatio-temporal separation, can, in
> thought, equally well dissociate neighbouring
> objects and reason on them in isolation (ibid.).
> Perception is essentially egocentric from every
> point of view....   The essence of the operations
> of intelligence is, on the contrary, the achieve-
> ment of knowledge, which is independent of the
> ego, independent of a particular individual's
> point of view (pp. 285-6).
> Primary perception constitutes an indissociable
> totality which can be described as 'rigid' ...
> while an operational totality exhibits the primary
> and fundamental characteristic of being mobile in
> the sense that the subject himself can decompose
> and reconstitute it at will (p. 287).
> while perceptual compositions are both incomplete
> and poorly delimited, for want of abstraction,
> operational compositions are both well delimited
> and, in the present context, complete (p. 288).
> A last fundamental difference between perceptual
> and operational structures summarises, but is more
> general than the preceding ones; operations are
> reversible and perceptions are not (p. 292).

Having drawn these distinctions, Piaget then re-
considers them but this time instead of contrasting
perception and intelligence at their greatest
difference he takes into consideration their various
stages of development.   This is like lowering a
ladder from formal operations down to the mundane
level of sensori-motor activities whilst considering
perception in terms of what it actually is.   He is
recognising that there is no true primary perception
in the sense of pure phenomenalism.   Perception we
might say is riddled with inference and meaning.   We
have the constancies, the stability of the spatial
framework, all those features of perception that it
is the aim of theories of perception to explain.

What Piaget now notes is - given that intelligence
evolves according to his view of it from the earliest,
most primitive level of organisation, that of sensory
motor activity - might not this or perhaps pre-
operational representational intelligence itself in
their turn have evolved from perceptual structures?
Could conservation for example have developed from
constancy, deductive thinking from perceptual
inference?   Piaget considers each of the previously
established differences and contrasts perceptual with
operational structures.   It is however clear where
for Piaget the answer lies.   Operational structures
are primary.   Given that what we actually see is
determined by previous perceptual activities (the
case he advanced in the second part of the book),
'since perceptual activities themselves are only
varieties of sensory-motor activity, it is likely
that they too are subordinated from the beginning to
sensory-motor activities as a whole' (p. 296).   Or
again

> sensory-motor and representational forms of decen-
> tration could not derive in any simple way from
> those forms of decentration which are initiated
> by perceptual activities, because new connections
> are involved which concern action as a whole and
> not only perceptions corresponding to a single
> sensory modality (p. 299).

Reasoning according to Piaget depends upon abstractions,
but 'the dissociation of perceptual forms from their
content is very limited' (p. 305).   'Schematised and
generalised actions are constructions on the part of
the subject and not just abstractions from the properties of the object' (p. 303).   The difference is
summed up thus: 'the compositions of intelligence
can be complete because their delimitation is a matter

of choice, while the compositions of perception, in
which the freedom of choice does not exist, must be
probabilistic' (p. 304).

The fight Piaget puts up between intelligence and
perception is I feel a sham.   It is rather boring
to read not only because of the repetitive nature of
the statements but also because it is obvious how it
is all going to end.   Nevertheless the arguments from
which we have quoted which Piaget advances for holding
intelligence primary and that to which perception is
affiliated are not the end of the matter.   The arguments, says Piaget, are simply hypotheses and he then
has a chapter reporting a number of experiments which
for him confirm his hypotheses.   I will not however
report these since, as with all his work, this could
only be done at length owing to his very detailed
evidence-accumulating, in- and not at all de-deductive
way of thinking.   It is difficult to see how anybody
taking perception in the way Piaget does, could have
believed our conceptions could have derived from it
and one wonders why Piaget has given so much time to
this question.

In fact, as Piaget makes clear in his final chapter
and indeed indicated in the Introduction, he takes
himself to be combating both the approach of the
empiricists in epistemology and that of the Gestalt
psychologists.   The attack on empiricism reads oddly
since his own system of psychology is decidely empiricist in the sense in which this is normally understood, that our concepts and categories are learned
rather than innate.   But what he is clearly opposed
to are phenomenalist approaches that derive our
knowledge from association of ideas or of sensations
whether in the hands of philosophers like Locke or
Hume or introspectionist psychologists like Wundt.
As for the Gestalt psychologists, he attributes to
them the notion that more complex processes derive
from perception.

I turn now to detailed consideration of the most important aspects of Piaget's theory.   These are the
formulae he derives from his study of the primary
illusions, his explanatory physiological model and
his final conclusions concerning the relationship of
perception and intelligence.   The first and second
are important in the light of what Piaget wrote in his
introductory chapter concerning correct scientific
procedures in the use of a 'purely relational language'
(p. xxi) and in establishing, in contrast to the

Gestalt psychologists who were merely descriptive (3)
in their approach, an explanatory theory. They are
important too in that the relational statement, the
Law of Relative Centrations, was extremely ambitious
and made possible his explanatory physiological model,
which in accounting for the secondary illusions
claimed to be immensely powerful. As for the last
aspect of Piaget's theory, the relation between intelligence and perception, which I have just described,
his long involvement with epistemological issues is
well known and it is likely, as I have already suggested, that it was his interest in the part played in
knowledge by perception that initiated the long series
of perceptual studies published in the 'Archives de
Psychologie' which eventuated in the book under
consideration.

 The primary illusions, dealt with by Piaget, consist of the illusion of rectangles, the horizontal/
vertical illusion or T figure (where either the vertical or the horizontal divides the other line in two),
the 'angle' illusions (such as the Zöllner and
Poggendorff), Münsterberg's shifted chessboard pattern,
curvature-estimation illusions, illusions of parallelograms (including the Sander parallelogram) and of
trapezia, the Müller-Lyer and Delboeuf illusions and
illusions of divided lines and filled spaces. All
these illusions are derived basically from length
contrast between two lines which lie in the horizontal
or vertical orientation (4) and are either at right
angles to one another or at 180°, i.e. aligned with
one another. The length contrast is expressed in
terms of the relationship between the difference in
length between the two lines multiplied by the length
of the shorter line, as expressed by the formula

$$(L_1 - L_2)L_2,$$

where the first is the *length* of the longer, and the
second the length of the shorter line. (Piaget also
employs A and B as *names* of these lines.)   In accounting for the illusion Piaget makes use of three more
symbols to produce the full form of his Law of Relative Centration thus:

$$P = \frac{(L_1 - L_2)L_2}{S} \times \frac{nL}{L_{max}}$$

where P is the measured illusion, S is the surface, n

is the number of separate comparisons between the
longer and the shorter and L_{max} is the length of the
longest line in the illusion figure.   In the case of
rectangles S will be the area of the figure and L_{max}
will be the length of the longer side or of the diagonal, where that is considered;   in the case of
lines forming extensions of one another, L_{max} is the
total length of the two lines and S is the square of
L_{max}.   The apparent arbitrariness of this Piaget
promises to clear up in his explanatory model.   The
use of n is confined to those cases where one line is
divided into two by the other line (except in the
case of the T figure where Piaget oddly omits n from
the formula), as in the Delboeuf illusion which for
Piaget depended upon the contrast in length between
the diameter of the inner circle and the distance of
its circumference on either side from the circumference of the outer circle.   In such cases Piaget
held two 'separate comparisons' would be made.
Lastly, the term L in the equation Piaget defined as
'the given reference length', justifying its inclusion
on the grounds that for the equation to represent a
relation between lengths the same number of lengths
had to be present in the numerator as in the denomi-
nator.   Piaget does not state any rule for determining
which line length should be chosen in any particular
case nor can I, looking at the ways in which he
realises this equation for different illusions, find
out by induction which it is.
    This then is the 'mathematical expression of the
systematic deformations proper to perceptual structures' (p. 5), at least as far as the primary
illusions are concerned.   There are two other claims
he makes for it.   One, that all the illusions to
which it applies, the primary illusions, decrease in
size from the age of five on.   Two, that 'the distribution of errors has the same form at all ages at
which experimentation is possible' (p. xix);   i.e.
the same relationship holds between the terms of the
formula giving the size of the error, independently
of variation of size with time.   These are indeed,
as Piaget asserts, ambitious claims though some of
the thrill of the first one is reduced when we remember
that the distinction between primary and secondary
illusions was dropped later on in the book (see pp.
141 and 142 above), when Piaget hypothesised that all
illusions are in fact secondary, not only in time but,
as I earlier implied, in status as compared with
actions, i.e. the perceptual activities.

How well does Piaget's evidence measure up to his
claims?   I find this question impossible to answer
as a whole because, quite apart from the validity of
Piaget's data, the exposition, detailed and involved
as it is, is too obscure to follow.   I have already
referred to some lack of clarity in his definition of
his symbols; elsewhere in his book he often does not
define them at all, leaving the reader to work them out
by inductive procedures.   In his self-absorption
Piaget seems unaware of his reader trying to follow
him.   Again and again one needs but does not get
diagrams to clarify what is being measured in one or
another version of a particular illusion figure.   The
clarity one should expect with a mathematical approach
is sadly lacking.

But we can, I think, assess Piaget's approach by
considering certain aspects of it which will affect its
prima facie plausibility.   This can be shown by considering the way he derives from a rectangle type of
illusion the 'angle' illusions, which manifest a regression to right angles tendency, and the Müller-Lyer
illusion, all of which on the surface seem so very
different from the rectangle illusions.   In doing this
we will confine ourselves to the length contrast effect.

Piaget relates the regression to right angles effect
(tendency of acute angles to be over- and obtuse angles
underestimated) to the Müller-Lyer effect (the length
of the arms of acute angles are under- and those of
obtuse angles overestimated) and to the illusion of the
median (tendency within an isosceles triangle of the
line bisecting the bisector of the apex angle to appear
nearer to the apex if the apex is acute and further, if
obtuse, than it really is).   The central feature in his
explanation of all these illusions is his belief that
the orientation of obliques is perceived in terms of
their relation to the horizontal and vertical.   Figure

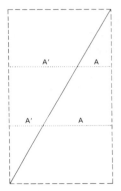

FIGURE 6.1

6.1 (taken from Figure 7 in Piaget's book) illustrates
an oblique which forms one arm of an acute angle which
has the form of an inverted V.

For Piaget each arm of the inverted V has an imaginary
reference rectangle in terms of which its orientation is
judged.   This is shown in the Figure by broken lines.
With regard to this rectangle, Piaget then postulates
virtual lines parallel with its side which cross the
oblique, two of which are shown also as dotted lines,
in Figure 6.1.   A length contrast effect is then set
up between the parts of each line that are on either
side of the oblique.   In Figure 6.1 the upper dotted
line will have A' exaggerated at the expense of A, and
the reverse will hold for the lower dotted line.
Since the longer part will appear still longer and the
shorter still shorter the effect is to increase the
slope of the oblique in the direction of 45°.   Of
course the opposite effect will result from the vertical virtual lines, but Piaget held that since there
were fewer of these the horizontals would win out.
The same thing is considered to happen with the other
oblique line, forming the other arm of the inverted V,
with the result that the apical angle as a whole will
be seen as nearer a right angle.

Piaget quoted as evidence for his theory experiments
in which rectangles with diagonals drawn in them showed
a reversal of the usual illusion of rectangles because,
instead of the inequality of the sides being exaggerated, they appeared more equal.   In other words, they
became more like squares with the implication that the
slope of the diagonals came nearer to 45°.

Piaget goes on to derive the illusion of the median
by means of the same reasoning but since the argument
is complicated I will leave it and pass on to the
Müller-Lyer illusion, or rather to the illusion of
the sides of trapezia from which Piaget derives the
Müller-Lyer.   It would take too long to give a full
account of his complex explanation.   I will say only
enough to give the key idea upon which his explanation
depends.   In the case of the trapezia the shorter
sides are over- and the longer sides are underestimated, so once again we have an apparent reversal of the
length contrast effect.   Piaget explains this
reversal by reference once again to an imaginary
rectangle shown by the broken lines that have been
added to the trapezium in Figure 6.2.   Again we have
'virtual' lines.   This time they are the difference
between the long and the short line in the trapezium
(A' in Figure 6.2).   Piaget argues that the virtual
lines are 'a genuine part of the figure ... because
the apprehension of obliques always involves reference

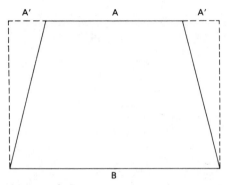

FIGURE 6.2

to verticals and horizontals' (p. 39).   A' is by
definition smaller than B and when it is also smaller
than the side of which it is a continuation (A in
Figure 6.2), then *both* A and B will be overestimated
in contrast with it.   It is not however clear why A
should be more overestimated than B though Piaget
suggests that since A' will by contrast be *under*-
estimated and since A' is the difference in length
between the two sides, then this diminution in the
difference between the two sides will favour the
shorter rather than the longer (i.e. A rather than B).
It is as though the virtual rectangle shown in Figure
6.2 can only be conceived as shrinking.
     But what happens when A' is longer than A?
Piaget describes the results of an experiment which
showed that the degree of relative overestimation of
A increased up to the point where A and A' were equal
and thereafter declined.   But one would expect *under*-
estimation when A' was greater than A and the greatest
amount of overestimation when A' was much smaller than
A, not when it was about equal.   The answer is that
when the other factors in the Law of Relative Centrations such as the surface, S (the height multiplied
by the width of the virtual rectangle into which the
trapezium fits), and the longest line in the figure,
L_{max} (i.e. B in Figure 6.2), are taken into account,
then the experimental findings are found to agree
with those predicted by the formula.
     Turning to the Müller-Lyer figures, Piaget points
out that these can be seen as parts of double trapezia
and quotes evidence to show that applying the same
formulae to them does equally well.   But however much
this may be so, it is obvious that we are very far
removed from any simple length contrast effect of the
kind that would be understood in the case of the

rectangles illusion.   In the case of an illusion like
the Zöllner, for example, we are to imagine rectangles
of which the transversals are the diagonals, and
within these rectangles we are further to imagine a
number of virtual lines, parallel with the sides of
the rectangle, and crossing the transversal, upon
which the contrast effects depend and adding up in
such a way that the sum determines the opposite of the
rectangle illusion and hence the illusion we observe
in the Zöllner figure.   Still more far-fetched seems
to me the notion of the Müller-Lyer figure being seen
as two trapezia and these two trapezia being seen as
rectangles.

    And yet Piaget is certainly thinking in terms of
centration, i.e. in terms of the way in which we are
likely to look at a figure.   When for example he
comes to deal with the Delboeuf illusion he has a
situation similar to that postulated in the case of
the trapezium illusion, namely, one which depends in
part upon a contrast between a line and two other
lines, albeit virtual ones, on either side of it, as
can be seen by comparing A with A' in Figure 6.2 with
these same lines in Figure 6.3.   Now when discussing

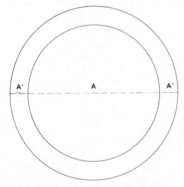

FIGURE 6.3

the trapezium illusion and in a way very characteristic of his mode of procedure throughout his book, that
is to say, in a discursive, pondering, tentative
manner, Piaget considers three relations between A, A'
and B, asking himself which one of these relations he
should choose for the $(L_1 - L_2)L_2$ part of his
formula.   He decides upon the relation $(B - 2A')2A'$
as 'the appropriate one'.   But when he comes to the
Delboeuf illusion he chooses instead $(A - A')A'$.   How
does he justify this choice?

The answer illustrates how very subjective his application of his formula is:

The explanation is simple: in the case of trapezia
... the value B corresponds to the longer base,
hence to a line *separately represented in the
drawing and quite distinct* from A (the shorter base).
In the present case, on the contrary, B is the
diameter of the larger circle which contains a
smaller circle: the relation which is *perceptually
obvious* is not that which unites B to its parts,
2A', but that which unites A to A' (p. 52, my
italics).

This shows the extent to which Piaget appears to be
making up the rules as he goes along, something which
adds to the difficulty in following him. Less un-
charitably expressed, one could describe it as
illustrative of the extent to which, deeply immersed
in his problem, he is feeling his way. Remarks
similar to that we quoted above appear elsewhere when
he is dealing with primary illusions though they are
more common in other parts of his book. Thus he
explains certain discrepancies from his own findings
of those of others in terms of their use 'of much
larger figures, where it is possible to evaluate A
independently of B ... and where the effect of verti-
cality has overwhelmed that of the semi-rectangle'
(p. 14) or again, 'it is as if the subject was
influenced by only one of the two semi-rectangles
instead of by the whole figure' (ibid.), and 'No
doubt the reason is that ... the circular form becomes
sufficiently noticeable and "pregnant" for the evaluation of F (the height of a chord) to be made as a
function of the vertical and horizontal diameters at
one and the same time' (p. 29). These are welcome
signs of Piaget's continuing sensitivity to subtle
influences but they ill accord with the hypothetico-
deductive mathematical stance he claims to be taking
up.

We might indeed rechristen Piaget's book 'The
Mathematico-Inductive Theory of Perceptual Deformation'
for inductive is what he obstinately remains. This
is evident in his statements on the form of the Law
of Centrations (5) - 'Experimentation has shown that
the main objective dimensions which determines the
subjective variations in illusions is not simply the
absolute difference [between the longer and shorter
line], but this difference multiplied by [the shorter]
and divided by a product which will be provisionally
labelled the surface of S' (p. 6), but also in his

recognition that some of the primary illusions he
deals with have secondary components (e.g. Munsterberg's shifted chessboard illusion, the Oppel-Kundt
illusion of divided spaces, the horizontal-vertical
illusion, illusions of parallelograms).   In other
words, in some forms there is an increase rather than
a decrease with age with arguments being devloped in
each case as to how the two influences might operate,
but with no clear statement as to how in the case of
any new illusion we should proceed in order to determine what part is primary and what secondary.

At the end of his chapter on the primary illusions
Piaget comments on the different constituent relations
entering into the different illusion figures.   We
have already shown how these differ as between the
trapezia and Müller-Lyer illusion on the one hand and
the Delboeuf on the other.   Piaget confesses that
'an impression may have been created of a sometimes
bewildering diversity of component relations', but
adds - 'a retrospective glance indicates that these
constitutive relations reduce to six varieties' (p.
67), which he then lists.   How very characteristic
that a chapter devoted to showing how the illusions
could be accounted for in terms of a single law should
end with a generalisation that is like a discovery,
one moreover that is in keeping with Piaget's basic
trade, fundamentally, as a taxonomist.

But in contrast to those Popperians who follow
their master in extending logical objections to induction to the belittling of the role of observation in
the framing of theories to the degree of calling the
latter 'guesses', it may be asked are not these
'inductive' procedures important, indeed necessary, in
formulating general laws?   The answer to my mind must
be yes.   But in formulating a mathematical theory
one must be able to show how it applies in a principled way and this is what Piaget does not do.   Also,
and we have so far refrained from making this criticism, if one is going to employ a mathematical theory
then one must also employ mathematical, that is to
say statistical, methods of assessing the data, which
Piaget nowhere does, so that one has to treat his
claims with regard to the success of his theory with
reservation.   Perhaps one should say that Piaget's
theory is still in the workshop, and his book like a
television documentary in the ciné-verité style shows
him surrounded by his assistants chipping away at it,
as experiment follows experiment and the theory is
tested from a hundred different angles, a small

adjustment made here, a changing of a part there - *if only* one could feel that there would come a moment when the theory would be wheeled out and the moment of truth faced.   Instead his style of procedure suggests that any such test would be putting the theory at the mercy of an insufficiently understood complex reality, one which in detail he continually studies, aware of the dangers of centration, striving by experimental and thinking activities everlastingly to approximate decentration, the perfect fit of reality to the mind's eye.

I have been discussing Piaget's Law of Relative Centrations and shown how it is less firm than its mathematical form and the kind of claim Piaget makes for it would lead one to expect.   But as I showed earlier Piaget gives it a physiological interpretation. (6)   Could this clear up the apparent arbitrariness of the formula?   In particular, can it explain his use of S and L_{max} which complicate the length contrast formula which in itself, given the relative stability of the phenomena to which it refers, is at least plausible?   Let us look more closely at Piaget's model.

He postulates that the more centrations a given line receives the more encounters there will be between the minute parts of which, he further postulates, the line is composed and neural units of some kind in the perceiver's brain.   The more there are of these the nearer the perceiver is to seeing the correct size of the line, something which Piaget describes as progressive overestimation of the line though it is really progressively less underestimation.   This assumed error in the perception of a line on its own he calls 'elementary error 1'.   Now when two lines are exposed close to one another the longer will attract more centrations, and therefore will be relatively less underestimated in length;   in other words, there will be length contrast.   This relative error he called 'elementary error 2'.   The more frequently the two lines are seen together the more centrations they are in the long run likely to receive and this results in less underestimation.   Now since many of the encounters on a given line that take place in time will be ones already made, the curve showing lessening underestimation will be a negatively accelerated one.   Consequently the difference between the two lines being compared will reduce with time - the length contrast effect will diminish.

But though this might serve to explain the decline

in time of the primary illusions it does not seem to
be what Piaget has in mind, for he introduces the
concept of 'couplings' between encounters.   He nowhere describes what sort of process coupling is but
the word itself suggests some kind of relationship
between encounters on the two lines.   He does however give a formal statement as follows:

> If encounters on L_1 in time t number αN, and βN
> on L_2 (when $L_1 = L_2$ or when a part of L_1 is of the
> same length as L_2), there will be said to be com-
> plete coupling between the encounters on L_1 and
> those on L_2 at a given moment, T, if $\Sigma\alpha N = \Sigma\beta N$, and
> incomplete coupling if $\Sigma\alpha N \gtrless \Sigma\beta N$ (p. 88).

The difficulties of interpreting this may serve as
an example of the powder Piaget puts in the reader's
eyes in his desire for mathematical precision.   The
symbols, αN and βN, were earlier defined by Piaget in
this way.   N is the number of 'encounterable ele-
ments' of which a line is said to be composed and αN
or βN stands for the number actually encountered
during time t. α and β obviously stand for fractions
but the use of the same symbol N for the number of
elements in both L_1 and L_2 would seem to suggest that
the number of elements in each line were the same.
Is this what is implied by the second clause in the
parenthesis above - 'or when a part of L_1 is of the
same length as L_2'?   Presumably $\Sigma\alpha N = \Sigma\beta N$ would then
mean that the sum of $\alpha N_1 + \alpha N_2 \ldots N_n$ would yield
exactly the same proportion of N in the case of that
part of L_1 (which, by the way, stands for the *length*
of a line, not for its name) that was the same as L_2
yielded by $\beta N_1 + \beta N_2 \ldots \beta N_n$.   This would be better
expressed as proportionate, in contrast to dispro-
portionate, coupling because *complete* coupling (when
$\Sigma\alpha N = \Sigma\beta N$) should entail that $\Sigma\alpha N$ and $\Sigma\beta N$ each
equalled N.

However, when Piaget later gives an illustration by
carrying out some calculations with arbitrary amounts,
his illustration suggests that by totally complete
coupling, he means that every element in one line
should be coupled with every element in the other
line.   This is indicated by his giving as the number
of couplings that are possible between two lines of
equal length the square of the total number of
encounters that can occur on each of them.   As for
the term S in the Law of Relative Centrations, this
represents 'the collection of possible couplings
compatible with the structural relations of the given
figure' (p. 106).   For example, when comparing the

length of two unequal parallel lines Piaget shows that it is the sum of four different sets of couplings, those (i) between the shorter line and an equivalent length of the longer one, (ii) between the shorter line and the rest of the longer line, (iii) between a 'virtual' line, extending the shorter to the same length as the longer, and the part of the longer that is of the same length and was coupled with the shorter in (i), and (iv) between the same 'virtual' line as in (iii) and the rest of the longer line.

As for L_{max} - but I think I have said enough to indicate the difficulties of interpreting Piaget and how unlikely his model is to succeed in its *explanatory* function.   Before leaving Piaget's model however there is one nagging difficulty about it, even when interpreted simply in terms of the relation between relative attention and apparent size, that should be mentioned.   Possibly an attempt to account for this difficulty was responsible for the obfuscation of the theory I have been describing.   The difficulty concerns the relation between temporary effects and permanent effects.   Both the error of the standard, as well as what Piaget says concerning 'illusions ... sometimes [being] completely eliminated under repeated presentation of the figures' (p. 95) in the course of one experiment (due to increase in the number of couplings), appear to be only temporary effects. Certainly, if they were permanent, errors of the standard should decline with age but Piaget nowhere indicates that this does happen except as an incidental result of different kinds of eye movements. Then again, unless the effects of decentration were considered to be extremely specific, it is scarcely credible that the matching of elements of figures with neural elements necessary for correct vision should take so long.   As we all know, the 'primary' illusions remain effective throughout our lifetime. But if the effects *are* considered to be specific to each illusion figure - and how different must one figure be from another for the effects not to transfer? - then the theory by being confined to these very specific effects must forfeit the ambitious claims Piaget makes for it.

So far I have used internal criteria in assessing Piaget's theory of primary illusions, concentrating on questions of internal consistency, bringing out the assumptions upon which it depends and so on.   I have not considered it in the light of contrary experimental evidence.   A great deal of work has been done on visual illusions since the publication of Piaget's book.   I will draw on this only to the extent of dealing very briefly with three points rather crucial to Piaget's theory and general approach.

First, there is the notion, fundamental to his extension of the length contrast effect to the 'angle' illusions, that obliques on their own tend to be seen nearer to the halfway position between the horizontal and the vertical (i.e. 45°).   Using alignment judgments to infer perceived orientation, experiments have shown that obliques tend either to be seen as more horizontal than they actually are, which is the so-called Zehender illusion (Wundt, 1886; Zehender, 1899; Obonai,1931; Goldstein and Weintraub, 1972; Day, 1973), or to be seen as nearer the horizontal or vertical according to which of these co-ordinates is in fact nearer to the oblique (Bouma and Andriessen, 1968).   Which of these two different effects occur seems to depend upon whether the variable which is to be aligned with the oblique is itself a line or only a dot (Curthoys, Wenderoth and Harris, 1975), but neither of them agrees with Piaget's theory and the second is its opposite.   A complication in using the alignment method is however spatial anisotrophy of the kind suggested by the horizontal/vertical illusion, which Day and Dickinson (1976) suggest could account for the Zehender illusion.

Second, there is the question of the amount of interpretation necessary to relate a theory to the experimental evidence advanced in its support. Piaget's evidence is often very indirect.   His evidence for saying that obliques tend to the halfway position, which was that the rectangle illusion is reversed when the rectangle has a diagonal drawn on it, is a good example of this.   Even cases where the evidence seems much more closely related are not necessarily reliable as Virsu and Weintraub (1971) showed when criticising Piaget and Vurpillot's study of overestimation of the curvature of small arcs (one of the primary illusions studied in Piaget's book) which was inferred from underestimation of the lengths of the chords of the arcs.   Virsu and Weintraub showed that two different instructions requiring the execution of exactly the same task yielded opposite results.   These instructions were, for one group of subjects, getting them to locate the centre of the circle of which the arc formed part and, for the other, getting them to find a point equidistant from the two ends and the middle of the arc.   The first group showed apparent over- , and the other, apparent under-estimation of the curve.   Virsu (1971) gives further evidence on the dangers of expecting visual illusions to obey the laws of logic.

Third, there is the question of the degree to which visual illusions can be regarded as simply structured.   Piaget does, it is true, from time to time suggest that illusions are more complex than his accounting for them, in so far as they are primary, by the Law of Relative Centrations would suggest. Concerning the parallelogram illusions, for example, he admits that they 'give rise to multiple systematic errors ... which are often very complex (and include some secondary effects)' and that he does not 'pretend to have exhausted [their] analysis ... in terms of the general law of primary illusions' (p. 30).   Never-theless there breathes a hope that ultimately they can be dealt with in terms of the primary/secondary dichotomy.   As work on visual illusions progresses, however, a strong case is emerging for moving away from particular illusions, used as jousting grounds for the unhorsing of rival theories, to recognising instead that a multiplicity of influences act on every illusion in varying degree.   We are accustomed to thinking of each illusion figure as showing a different effect such as length distortion (Müller-Lyer), orien-tation distortion (Zöllner) or alignment distortion (Poggendorff).   Each figure is however multiply dis-torted though drawn in such a way as to betray only one of these distortions.

We can see this multiplicity of factors even in such a simple illusion as the horizontal/vertical illusion.   If the figure is drawn with the vertical bisecting the horizontal, the length contrast effect mentioned earlier (Künnapas, 1955; Piaget and Morf, 1956(a)) is present; if drawn with the two lines separate and the vertical below the horizontal, we get what might be called the pure horizontal/vertical effect (Piaget and Morf, 1961); but if the vertical is drawn above the horizontal, a much stronger effect is obtained due to the tendency to overestimate elements placed higher in the field relative to those placed lower (Piaget and Morf, 1956(b); Piaget and Lambercier, 1956).   I have drawn here upon the work of Piaget himself, together with that of his associates; as we have seen, he regards the two latter effects as secondary illusions though his account of how they derive from perceptual activities is difficult to follow and unconvincing.

When we come to a more complex figure like the
Poggendorff illusion (Figure 6.4), upon which a good

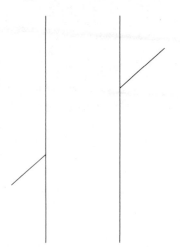

FIGURE 6.4

deal of research has been carried out in recent years,
the task of accounting for it in terms of a single
theory becomes all the harder.   Depending upon how
the Poggendorff figure is drawn and orientated, at
least seven factors can be regarded as affecting the
size of the illusion.   First of all, we get a small
effect even without the parallels in Figure 6.4.
This is known as the Zehender illusion.   As mentioned
above, Day and Dickinson consider this to be due to
the same factor as that responsible for the 'pure'
vertical/horizontal illusion.   If space is more
stretched in the vertical than the horizontal dimension, then the Zehender illusion would indeed follow. (7)
The Zehender illusion would not however be contributing
to the total Poggendorff illusion if the parallels were
horizontal instead of vertical, and Day and Dickinson
(1976) have shown this to be the case.   Second and
third are effects due to change in the apparent
orientation of the transversals.   The first of these
is the regression to right angles effect, which is
exemplified in the Zöllner illusion and the Wundt and
Hering figures.   If in Figure 6.4 the perceived
angles of the transversals each appear nearer a right
angle than they really are, then the illusion will
follow, i.e. the transversals will not appear aligned,
but the top right one will appear too high for the
bottom left one.   That this regression to right angles
does in fact take place has been shown by Hotopf and

Ollerearnshaw (1972(a) and (b); see also Hotopf and
Robertson (1975)). The second orientation effect
is the assimilation of oblique lines to the horizontal or vertical depending upon which co-ordinate is
nearer (Bouma and Andriessen, 1970; Weintraub and
Krantz, 1971; Hotopf, Ollerearnshaw and Brown, 1974).
As Bouma and Andriessen and also Curthoys, Wenderoth
and Harris (1975) have shown, this effect can be distinguished from the Zehender effect.   Figure 6.5
(a and b) shows a Poggendorff illusion with the trans-

a   b   FIGURE 6.5

versals nearly vertical, an effect which works in the
opposite direction from the Zehender illusion and cannot at such a large angle be attributed to the
regression to right angles effect.   In Figure 6.4
however the transversals are nearer the horizontal
than the vertical, consequently assimilation to the
horizontal would add to the illusion.   Had they been
at an angle less than 45° to the vertical then, as
Hotopf, Ollerearnshaw and Brown (1974) have shown,
the illusion would have decreased.
   Next we have the contribution of two kinds of
contrast effect.   The first of these is that shown
in the rectangle illusion.   This operates in the
following way.   The parallels in Figure 6.4 form a
rectangle.   Now if the width of this rectangle were
reduced by contrast with its height, the two parallels
would appear nearer than they really are.   This once
again should cause the transversals no longer to
appear aligned; the upper right one should appear
too high for the lower left one as indeed it does.
Tong and Weintraub (1974) and Day and Dickinson (1976)
have shown that the size of the illusion does vary
inversely with the apparent distance apart of the
parallels.   The other contrast effect works in the
opposite direction.   This is the divided line illusion

where a line in the context of a short line looks
longer than when it is seen in the context of a long
line, as Figure 6.6 shows.   Hotopf and Robertson (in

FIGURE 6.6

preparation)   have shown that when the Poggendorff
illusion is drawn as in Figure 6.5 then 6.5(b) yields
a bigger illusion than 6.5(a).   The apparent mis-
alignment in 6.5(b) is seen in the context of a much
shorter line than it is in 6.5(a).   In Figure 6.4
however, where the transversals are at a much smaller
angle than in Figure 6.5, the divided line illusion
should work to reduce the total illusion.   It is the
only one of our seven factors which operates against
the Poggendorff effect shown in Figure 6.4.

The sixth factor is the one upon which the Müller-
Lyer illusion depends, namely, the apparent shortening
of the arms of acute and lengthening of the arms of
obtuse angles.   In the case of the Poggendorff figure
(Figure 6.4) this would mean that the upper right and
lower left transversals will be displaced in upward
and downward directions respectively, which will again
produce the Poggendorff effect.   Attempts to demonstrate this by presenting one of the transversals in
an orientation at 90° to the other, as in Figure 6.7,

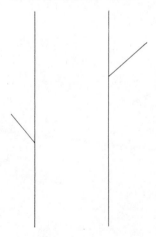

FIGURE 6.7

which should reduce the illusion because both will be
displaced in the same direction have however been

unsuccessful (Hotopf and Ollerearnshaw, 1972 (b); Day,
1974).   The reason for this seems to be a seventh
factor, which I will call the alignment displacement
effect.   An illusion involving alignment displacement
that has been known since the time of Wundt (1886) is
illustrated in Figure 6.8.   The single line does not

FIGURE 6.8

appear to be collinear with the lower of the two
parallel lines to the left of it but to be displaced
in the direction of the other parallel line.   The
same effect is shown in Figure 6.9, where the single
line seems to be displaced in the direction of the
perpendicular to the line with which it is objectively
collinear.   Experiments I have been carrying out
show these effects to be operating in addition to the
Zehender illusion.   In Figure 6.10 where the upper

FIGURE 6.9

and right-hand line is aligned with the lower tip of
the lower and left-hand line, it again appears displaced

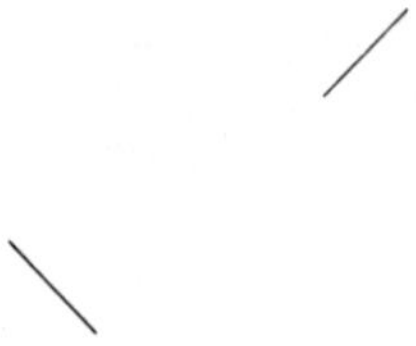

FIGURE 6.10

in the direction of the centre of the lower left-hand
line.   Now in the case of the Poggendorff figure
(Figure 6.4) each of the lines that has to be aligned
with the other has a second line, the vertical
parallel, extending both above and below its point of
intersection.   If however it is the part of the
second line that is nearer to them that exerts on
the transversals the displacement effect shown in
Figure 6.9, then there should be a double displacement effect in the direction of the Poggendorff
illusion.   Again, experiments that I have conducted
show that this is the case.   Figure 6.10 also shows
that there should be an additional displacement
effect in the opposite direction to that of the Müller-
Lyer illusion, which might account for the failure to
find a reduced illusion in Figure 6.7.   One other
effect that could be accounted for in terms of the
alignment displacement effect is the well-known and
anomalous finding that the Poggendorff illusion sometimes fails to occur when the parts of the parallels
that form obtuse angles with the transversals are
removed, as shown in Figure 6.11 (Brentano, 1894;
Green and Hoyle, 1964;   Restle, 1969;   Weintraub and
Krantz, 1971;   Krantz and Weintraub, 1973;   Day, 1973).
It is clear that in Figure 6.11 the alignment dis-

FIGURE 6.11

placement effect should now work in the opposite
direction from the normal Poggendorff effect.   That
we do not often get a negative illusion but only a
reduction or no illusion at all would be expected
owing to factors working in the opposite direction,
particularly the regression to right angles and the
Zehender and Müller-Lyer effects.

So much for our seven factors, six of which should
be contributing to the amount of illusion observed in

Figure 6.4.   Possibly still other factors enter in,
such as a horizontal/vertical contrast tendency
(Hotopf, Ollerearnshaw and Brown, 1974), optical blur
(Chiang, 1968; Glass, 1970) and even inappropriate
constancy scaling (Gillam, 1971).   Of course other
workers in this field might advance different lists
from the above and argue that some of my factors
could be accounted for in terms of others, but the
general argument that there are many illusion-pro-
ducing factors at work which one experiences as soon
as one starts measuring particular illusions and
systematically varying variables such as size and
orientation, is widely accepted (Robinson, 1972;
Weintraub and Krantz, 1971; Goldstein and Weintraub,
1972; Krantz and Weintraub, 1973; Tong and Weintraub, 1974; Weintraub and Tong, 1974; Day and
Dickinson, 1976).   Developmental studies of visual
illusions as well as ones using them in personality
testing and cross-cultural studies (e.g. Gough and
McGurk, 1967; Gough and Delcourt, 1969; Gough and
Olton, 1972), in so far as they are based upon single
rather than systematically varied sets of figures,
are obviously weakened by neglect of these considerations even if only because their reproducibility
depends upon the accident of similar dimensions,
orientations and angles being employed in subsequent
studies, an 'accident' which is indeed likely to
occur given the strongly conventional element in the
drawing of visual illusion figures.

   That there should be such a variety of factors
operating in the case of illusion figures should not
be surprising in view of the great complexity of the
visual system, a fact which we psychologists living
in a more macroscopic world are inclined to forget.
Theoretical prejudices rationalised as a 'law of
parsimony' bolster this attitude.   But only by
accepting these stubborn facts in some variety is
one likely to be forced to create a well-articulated
and powerful theory.   It is paradoxical that Piaget
by assimilating so much to his simple formula and
rather featureless explanatory model should be in
effect so much denying structure and articulation.
It might indeed be held that this is a pervasive
aspect of his theorising as we shall see as we turn
once again to the arguments at the end of his book on
the relation between perception and intelligence.

As we saw in the last part of Piaget's book, he held
that 'knowledge' and intelligence could not derive

from perception but rather that sensory-motor activities
in the first place preceded perception and that every
stage in advancing cognition further 'enriched' it so
that perception was both literally and figuratively very
much in the second place.   I did not however describe
his evidence for this for the reason that it did not
seem possible that anybody could hold the position that
Piaget was attacking.   So let us first consider his
claim that empiricist phenomenalist epistemological
theories on the one hand and the Gestalt psychologists
on the other had in fact done this.   Piaget nowhere
spells out, let alone considers in detail, what the
theorists he is opposing say.   There are a great
variety of phenomenalist theories but, although they
operate with the concept of sensation, they all make
use of memory and generally of imagery (8) too.   In
these are included kinaesthetic imagery, learned movements and compound ideas or sensations, i.e. ones not
restricted to a single modality.   This is of course
well known but surely makes possible a much more
plausible theory than the one Piaget imagines.
Similarly, the Gestalt psychologists did not present
a theory of the kind Piaget suggested.   What they did
was to identify the fields of forces operating in the
brain using the same terms as those used in accounting
for perceptual structures, e.g. continuity, contiguity,
closure, set and Prägnanz.   They attempted to demonstrate the operation of these concepts in memory and
action.   Changes of the kind that took place in
problem-solving, to which learning was assimilated,
were conceived as reorganisations under tensions
induced by new factors whose course could be described
once again in field terms.   The stress upon insights,
which were the phenomenal aspects of reorganisations
in brain fields, might be taken to imply the basic
role of perception in problem-solving but the
experiences involved in insights were conceptualisa-
tions and reconceptualisations of problems.   In so
far as these may be called 'perceptions' they are
perceptions in the *judgmental* sense of the word, as
for instance, when we might say of one of Köhler's
apes that he was able to *perceive* the branch of a tree
as a tool to pull in a banana from beyond the bars of
the cage.   However true to the phenomenological
approach one might be in reporting, or requiring to
be reported, such data, they are not the restricted
sense-perception data that Piaget alone considers.
Though one may not accept such magisterial constructions as Koffka's 'Gestalt Psychology' or for that

matter phenomenalist associationist accounts, pre-
ferring instead Piaget's stress on the effects of
attempts at adaptive activity and the formation of
primitive and gradually more elaborate schemes, the
case Piaget puts forward for perception is very much
of a straw man, a private notion perhaps of Piaget's
own.

But there is something more profound that is wrong
with the climax of Piaget's book.   One becomes aware
in reading it of a continuous denigration of perception as compared with intelligence.   It was to give
the reader some impression of this that I quoted from
his book on p. 145 above a number of extracts in
which he compared the two.   Piaget's attitude is
akin to that of mystically inclined philosophers such
as Plato with their low regard for images, for mere
appearances, which belie and betray in contrast with
Reason's clear illumination of the truth.   And this
of course is what Piaget's whole book is about.
Perception always means centration.   Decentrations
achieved through growing intelligence give rise to
new centrations.   Although we tend to objectivity
we never attain it.   All experiments on perception
yield error and variance.   The 'compensations' that
may be achieved as with size constancy and distance
are never perfect;   there is not complete invariance;
we do not, in other words, have reversibility.   This
only intelligence can achieve.

But why one may ask should perception be thus
singled out for derogatory treatment?   Why not
memory, learning, or indeed problem-solving?   Experimental psychology has certainly suggested the unreliability of the first of these.   We are after all
interested in faulty perception and in forgetting in
order to discover the factors determining them.
Hence we impose conditions of perception and memoris-
ing we would scarcely ever be satisfied with in our
normal adaptive functioning.   Studies of learning
and problem-solving tend on the other hand to be
achievement-oriented, though this does of course
depend upon the motive of the research.   Compare for
example Thorndike's, Köhler's and Ruger's investigations, into learning, insight and problem-solving.
In recent times the work of Wason and his colleagues
has admirably illustrated the inadequacies of our
performance of certain formal operations.   Even
highly intelligent people carrying out long sequences
of simple arithmetical calculations without the use of
machines produce a high proportion of errors. (9)

We might render the argument ad hominem and accuse
Piaget himself of errors of reasoning.   His theory
of perception is that perception could only be made
perfect if attention is evenly, or has come to be
evenly, distributed over the whole figure.   Under
those conditions of decentration, he argues, there
should no longer be illusion.   But this fails to
take into account the function of attention.   We are
unlikely to be able to get the information we need
unless we centre upon one part rather than another.
What after all is the point in no longer having
visual illusions?   Unless the illusions can be
shown to be seriously dysfunctional, it doesn't matter
if we have them.   Those who have worked on visual
illusions have not on the whole been interested in
the question of the practical harm they might do.
Clearly this would be related to the kind of perceptual task which the particular thing we were trying
to do depended on.   It is unlikely that at the level
of everyday activities as opposed, say, to flying
space craft, they would make much difference.   But
for the establishing of Piaget's case this is the
kind of study (i.e. establishing that they do make a
difference to our normal daily activity) that should
be carried out.
    The problem is however more complicated than this.
We have referred to the 'function' of attention and
we may be reminded thereby that one of the great
merits of Piaget's approach is that it is a function-
alistic one.   But what possible function can be seen
to exist in his explanatory physiological model.   It
is simply large and empty.   Truly functional physiological models are ones making use of concepts such
as lateral inhibition to sharpen the image and repress
interference, or filtering to reduce the amount of
information that has to be handled, and so on.   From
the operation of these processes it is believed
illusions must follow.   Good perception in one
situation may be shown to depend upon bad perception
in another.   Showing this is investigating its
causal mechanics.   This is what has to be taken into
account to get a true idea of decentration though it
may be doubted whether this is not too global a concept
to be of use for any but the most coarse analysis.
Piaget might perhaps be criticised for insufficiently
fine articulation of his concepts and for insensitivity
to their distinctive logical properties.   This might
be indicated by his treatment of perception as merely
an inferior kind of intelligence whereas of course

perception has quite different functions.   We would
never know that we were capable of reversible operations unless our perception, and for that matter our
memory, could be relied on.   Perhaps Piaget is
guilty of a logical confusion, as between process and,
to speak loosely, product.   We have both symbols and
formation - and transformation - rules for combining
them and relating their combinations.   We can see or
hear the symbols and we can operate the rules.

When dealing with perception Piaget seems to be
dealing with the *process* of seeing the symbols whilst
when dealing with intelligence he is dealing with the
rules themselves - not with the operating of them.
But why, one may ask, should Piaget concern himself
with the rules, with, say, the calculi of classes,
relations and propositions?   Are not these the pro-
vince of the logician and not of the psychologist?
The answer is that he takes elaborate human inven-
tions such as these as actually operating at his
stage of formal operations.   His arguments are not
however of the kind that Chomsky proposes with regard
to the syntax of ordinary language, because he considers these rules to have developed in each individual
as a result of that individual's continually developing
adaptive interrelation with the environment, though
one may speculate as to whether Piaget has not
borrowed, wrongly in my view, some plausibility from
Chomsky's rather different conception of a language
acquisition device.

This is not of course to deny that rules of *some*
kind may operate whose nature we may deduce from
studies of types of errors, latencies of responses,
etc.   But then rules are likely also to underlie
perception, including perception of symbols.   Indeed
it seems to me likely that rules operating in the
registering of signals, their codings, recodings and
multiple transformations will be found to constitute
an engineering achievement by Nature more impressive
by far than those last little bits that are likely
to happen in conscious reasoning.

NOTES

1 We might mention, though Piaget does not, the face
   on a body, the eyes in the face and the upper as
   opposed to the lower half in a line of print.
2 Page numbers which are given in brackets refer to
   the English edition of Piaget's book.   Where a

number of quotations are given in succession from
the same page, the page number is only given for
the last of these.

3 Piaget characterises them thus but of course they
were deliberately this since true to their field-
theory approach they regarded scientific theories
as descriptions at a high level of abstraction.

4 Parallelograms where the lengths of the diagonals
are compared form the one exception to this.

5 His development of the theory can be traced in
the various numbers of the 'Recherches sur le
Développement des Perceptions'. The first number
in 1942 which dealt with the Delboeuf illusion and
advanced an explanation in terms of centration and
decentration aimed at being deductive in its
approach, setting out more formally than in his
book a numbered set of postulates and of definitions. The fourth number (1945) applied this to
the divided line illusion and gave the first form
of the Law of Relative Centrations. The sixteenth
number revised the Law, bringing it near its final
form with the purpose of applying it to all primary illusions. Most of the other studies up to
that time had been on secondary effects, particularly on size constancy and related phenomena.
However the twentieth to the twenty-seventh
numbers (from 1954 to 1956) dealt with the primary
illusions and the question of centration. The
twenty-second number gave the final form of the
Law of Relative Centrations, and three others
were addressed to the task of assimilating the
'angle' illusions to the Law and thus greatly
extending its attempted range of prediction.
Application of the Law to the trapezia and then to
the Müller-Lyer illusions is first reported in the
book itself.

6 Piaget wrote that 'it was not our aim to make a
contribution to the psycho-physiological theory
of vision' and added that he hoped to achieve 'a
model whose basic constructs ... are of such a
general nature that they will fit into any physiological explanation' (p. 83). However I think
it will be obvious from what follows that Piaget's
was in fact a physiological theory, however general.

7 What is inconsistent with this however is the dis-
appearance of the Zehender illusion, mentioned
above, when the variable is a dot rather than a
line (Curthoys, Wenderoth and Harriss, 1975).

8 Wundt like Watson rejected imagery on grounds of

ideological purism but in fact, again like Watson,
merely named what others called images, 'sensations'.
9 In Army selection during the war when copious
statistical data had to be dealt with by human
brain rather than machine power we speedily found
that all work had to be double-checked because of
the frequency of errors of addition and multipli-
cation.

REFERENCES

BOUMA, H. and ANDRIESSEN, J.J. (1968), Perceived Orien-
tation of Isolated Line Segments, 'Vision Res.', vol.
8, 493-507.
BOUMA, H. and ANDRIESSEN, J.J. (1970), Induced Changes
in the Perceived Orientation of Line Segments, 'Vision
Res.', vol. 10, 333-49.
BRENTANO, F. (1894), Zur Lehre von den optischen
Täuschungen, 'Z. Psychol.', vol. 6, 1-7.
CHIANG, C. (1968), A New Theory to Explain Geometrical
Illusions Produced by Crossing Lines, 'Percept.
Psychophys.', vol. 3, 174-6.
CURTHOYS, I., WENDEROTH, P. and HARRIS, J. (1975), The
Effects of the Motion Path and the Length of the
Variable Segment in the Poggendorff Illusion without
Parallels, 'Percept. Psychophys.', vol. 17, 358-62.
DAY, R.H. (1973), The Oblique Line Illusion: the
Poggendorff effect without parallels, 'Q. J. exp.
Psychol.', vol. 25, 535-41.
DAY, R.H. (1974), The Poggendorff Illusion: apparent
displacement of the oblique lines, 'Aust. J. Psychol.',
vol. 26, 49-59.
DAY, R.H. and DICKINSON, R.G. (1976), The Components
of the Poggendorff Illusion, 'Br. J. Psychol.' (in
press).
GILLAM, B. (1971), A Depth Processing Theory of the
Poggendorff Illusion, 'Percept. Psychophys.', vol. 10,
211-16.
GLASS, L. (1970), Effect of Blurring on Perception of
a Simple Geometric Pattern, 'Nature', vol. 228, 1341-2.
GOLDSTEIN, M.B. and WEINTRAUB, D.J. (1972), The
Parallel-less Poggendorff: virtual contours put the
illusion down but not out, 'Percept. Psychophys.',
vol. 11, 353-5.
GOUGH, H. and DELCOURT, M.-J. (1969), Developmental
Increments in Perceptual Acuity among Swiss and Ameri-
can School Children, 'Devel. Psychol', vol. 1, 260-4.
GOUGH, H. and McGURK, E. (1967), A Group Test of

Perceptual Acuity, 'Percept. mot. Skills', vol. 24,
1107-15.

GOUGH, H. and OLTON, R.M. (1972), Field Independence
as Related to Nonverbal Measures of Perceptual Performance and Cognitive Ability, 'J. consult. clin.
Psychol.', vol. 38, 338-42.

GREEN, R.T. and HOYLE, E.M. (1964), The Influence of
Spatial Orientation on the Poggendorff Illusion, 'Acta
psychol.', vol. 22, 348-66.

HOTOPF, W.H.N. and OLLEREARNSHAW, C. (1972a), The
Regression to Right Angles Tendency and the Poggendorff Illusion: I, 'Br. J. Psychol.', vol. 63, 359-67.

HOTOPF, W.H.N. and OLLEREARNSHAW, C. (1972b), The
Regression to Right Angles Tendency and the Poggendorff Illusion: II, 'Br. J. Psychol.', vol. 63, 369-79.

HOTOPF, W.H.N., OLLEREARNSHAW, C. and BROWN, S. (1974),
The Regression to Right Angles Tendency and the Poggendorff Illusion: III, 'Br. J. Psychol.', vol. 65, 213-31.

HOTOPF, W.H.N. and ROBERTSON, S. (1975), The Regression
to Right-Angle Tendency, Lateral Inhibition and the
Transversals in the Zöllner-Poggendorff Illusions,
'Percept. Psychophysic.', vol. 18, 453-9.

KANIZSA, G. (1974), Contours without Gradients or
Cognitive Contours?, 'Ital. J. Psychol.', vol. 1, 93-
113.

KRANTZ, D.H. and WEINTRAUB, D.J. (1973), Factors
Affecting Perceived Orientation of the Poggendorff
Transversal, 'Percept. Psychophys.', vol. 14, 511-17.

KÜNNAPAS, T.M. (1955), An Analysis of the 'Vertical
Horizontal Illusion', 'J. exp. Psychol.', vol. 49,
134-40.

OBONAI, T. (1931), Experimentelle Undersuchungen über
den Aufbau des Sehraumes, 'Arch. ges. Psychol.', vol.
82, 308-28.

PIAGET, J. (1969), 'The Mechanisms of Perception',
London: Routledge & Kegan Paul.

PIAGET, J. and STETTLER-von ALBERTINI, B. (1954),
Observations sur la perception des bonnes formes chez
l'enfant par actualisation des lignes virtuelles,
'Archives de Psychologie', vol. 34, 203-42.

PIAGET, J. and LAMBERCIER, M. (1956), Les comparaisons
verticales à intervalles croissants, 'Archives de
Psychologie', vol. 35, 321-67.

PIAGET, J. and MORF, A. (1956a), Note sur la comparaison
de lignes perpendiculaires égales, 'Archives de
Psychologie', vol. 35, 233-55.

PIAGET, J. and MORF, A. (1956b), Les comparaisons
verticales à faible intervalle, 'Archives de Psychologie',
vol. 35, 289-319.

PIAGET, J. and MORF, A. (1961), La comparaison des
verticales et des horizontales dans la figure en
équerre, 'Archives de Psychologie', vol. 38, 69-88.
RESTLE, F. (1969), Illusions of Bent Line, 'Percept.
Psychophys.', vol. 5, 273-4.
ROBINSON, J.O. (1972), 'The Psychology of Visual
Illusion', London: Hutchinson.
TONG, L. and WEINTRAUB, D.J. (1974), Contour Displace-
ments and Tracking Errors. Probing 'twixt Poggendorff
parallels, 'Percept. Psychophys.', vol. 15, 258-68.
VIRSU, V. (1971), Underestimation of Curvature and
Task Dependence in Visual Perception of Form, 'Percept.
Psychophys.', vol. 9, 339-42.
VIRSU, V. and WEINTRAUB, D.J. (1971), Perceived Curva-
ture of Arcs and Dot Patterns as a Function of Curva-
ture, Arc Length, and Instructions, 'Q. J. exp.
Psychol.', vol. 23, 373-80.
WEINTRAUB, D.J. and KRANTZ, D.H. (1971), The Poggen-
dorff Illusion: amputations, rotations and other
perturbations, 'Percept. Psychophys.', vol. 10, 257-64.
WEINTRAUB, D.J. and TONG, L. (1974), 'Percept. Psycho-
phys.', vol. 16, 213-21.
WUNDT, W. (1886), 'Grundzüge der physiologischen
Psychologie', Leipzig: Engelmann.
ZEHENDER (1899), Uber geometrisch-optische Täuschung,
'Z. Psychol.', vol. 20, 65-117.

Part four

INTERACTION IN THE
DEVELOPMENT OF COGNITIONS

While the papers in part two dealt with the child's construction of the physical properties and relations of objects the two papers in this final section are concerned with the social and interactional context within which development occurs.

It can be argued that Piaget's theory demands an interactional perspective for understanding all cognitive development. However, in examining the physical world and learning to understand its properties the nature of the necessary interaction may well differ from the interaction involved in learning to understand and predict the behaviour and intentions, the abilities and the rules which govern the social world. The acquisition of language is an area of discourse which relates three theoretical strands: theories of language, theories of cognition and theories of communication. Although Piaget wrote about language in 1926 the main impact of his theory on developmental psycholinguistics has been through the work of his colleague, H. Sinclair-de-Swart; his contribution must be seen in the context of the seminal works of Vygotsky, the linguistic determinism of Sapir and Whorf and the critical impact on linguistic theory of Chomsky's transformational grammar. All of these strands are connected in Gisela Szagun's paper on the development of tense forms in young children. What she has done is to examine the role of cognition - that is of understanding and knowing - in language acquisition and use, and she shows, with considerable force, how cognitive development interacts with and informs the development of grammar.

The final paper emphasises the social and interactional basis of knowing, focusing on the way in which the child understands his social world. It is

an attempt to relate developmental psychology to
social psychology, not by drawing parallels or
analogies between the concepts used by each sub-
discipline but by utilising a developmental perspective and examining some of the research into the way
the child cognises and relates to others in his
world.   The critical concept around which the paper
revolves is that of decentration.   The process of
decentration refers to the growth of the capacity to
take account of features which could balance and
compensate for the distorting effects of single
centrations.   In social behaviour the process is
translated into the gradual loss of egocentricity,
a process which is based on the interactions of the
child and others in his world.

Chapter 7

TIME CONCEPTS AND TENSE FORMS IN CHILDREN'S SPEECH

Gisela Szagun

During the past two decades the question of how children acquire language has been the focus of much
research by psychologists and by linguists. It
seemed, for some time, that theories of language
acquisition which were based on the linguistic theory
of transformation grammar gave quite an adequate account
of the development of language in children. More
recently, however, it has become clear that a satisfactory theory of language acquisition must relate the
acquisition of language to cognitive development in
general. In this paper I want to look at some of
the reasons for this claim, and I want to look at
what can be said about the relationship between
language development and cognitive development.

DISTRIBUTIONAL AND EARLY TRANSFORMATIONAL ACCOUNTS OF
THE ACQUISITION OF GRAMMAR

The studies by Brown and Fraser (1963), Braine (1963),
Miller and Ervin (1964) can be regarded as the starting
point of 'modern' studies on language acquisition.
These studies looked at samples of early child speech in
terms of distributional analysis. Independently, the
three studies classified the words occurring in children's
two-word utterances as belonging to two classes, called
by Braine a 'pivot'-class and an 'open'-word class.
'Pivot' words, derived from adult function words, are frequently used. 'Open' words, derived from lexical words,
are not so frequently used. The relation of pivot grammar
to adult grammar is not always made explicit. One
suggestion is that from the initial pivot/open word
distinction all the form classes of adult grammar
develop by a process of differentiation. McNeill (1966)

proposed that the pivot/open distinction is a generic
classification which potentially admits all the distinctions of adult grammar.   The process of differentiation renders at various stages the hierarchy of
distinctions postulated by Chomsky (1965) in his
notion of degrees of grammaticalness. (1)
     However, it was the search for innate linguistic
universals which provided the main inspiration for
work on language acquisition in the 1960s.   Chomsky
(1965) postulates a Language Acquisition Device (LAD)
with which the child is endowed.   The input to LAD
is the 'primary linguistic data', that is, the actual
utterances heard by the child, and its output is the
child's grammatical competence (i.e. internalised
rules (Chomsky, 1965)).   LAD enables the child to
acquire any language.   It contains linguistic information of a universal kind, which leads the child to
make the right type of hypotheses about the rules
underlying the primary linguistic data.   It also
contains an evaluation procedure which helps him to
choose between possible grammars.   This innate linguistic knowledge includes a realisation that all
languages have an abstract deep structure underlying
the surface structure.   Psycholinguists such as
McNeill (1970) attempted to elaborate and refine this
picture.   McNeill proposed that part of a child's
innate inheritance is a knowledge of the basic
grammatical relations, which constitute the deep
structure.   In the acquisition process children work
from deep structure to surface structure (McNeill,
1970):   starting with deep structure they gradually
acquire the transformations of their language.   In
short, transformationalist accounts of the acquisition of language have given a description of how
grammatical structures are built onto an innate knowledge of linguistic universals.
     According to transformationalist theories of
language acquisition, language unfolds lawfully, and
one aspect of this lawfulness is that the order of
acquisition of linguistic structures is stable.
This view is confirmed by Brown's findings (Brown and
Fraser, 1963;   Brown and Hanlon, 1970;   Brown, 1973)
and by C. Chomsky (1969).   Brown found that the
order of acquisition of the   same fourteen morphemes
was stable across three different children.   These
fourteen morphemes are: present progressive, 'in',
'on', plural, past irregular, possessive, uncontractible copula, articles, past regular, third person
regular, third person irregular, uncontractible

auxiliary, contractible copula, contractible auxiliary. Brown and Hanlon (1970) found a stable order in the emergence of 'yes' - 'no' questions, negatives, truncated predicates, truncated questions, negative questions, truncated negatives and truncated negative questions.   C. Chomsky (1969) studied the acquisition of sentence constructions following the verbs 'ask', 'tell', 'promise', the acquisition of structures like 'John is easy to see', and also of pronominalisation. In her sample of forty children aged between five and ten years, she found that although the rate of acquisition of these structures varied, the order of their acquisition was stable.

This stable order of acquisition of linguistic structures can be naturally accounted for if it can be shown that a child's knowledge of the structure of his language grows from a derivationally less complex grammar to a derivationally more complex grammar. This prediction was confirmed by Brown and Hanlon's (1970) results: the simple, active, affirmative, declarative sentence type, which is derivationally the simplest, was acquired first, and the truncated negative question sentence type, which is derivationally the most complex, was acquired last.   Although the order of emergence of the sentence types in between the two extreme points was not quite so orderly, Brown and Hanlon's results indicate that, on the whole, a principle of cumulative derivational complexity operates in the order of acquisition of grammatical forms.

Menyuk (1964), studying several hundred children between three and seven years, indicates that the number of transformational rules and the type of transformational rules affect the order of acquisition of linguistic structures.   Structures requiring fewer transformational rules are acquired first, and deletion, addition, substitution are acquired before permutation.   Brown and Hanlon's and Menyuk's findings support the theory that derivational complexity determines the order of acquisition of grammatical structures.

They do not, however, suggest that it is the *only* factor.   In their analysis of derivational complexity, neither Brown nor Menyuk succeed in separating the derivational complexity of a structure from the semantic complexity of a structure.   What is derivationally more complex is often also semantically more complex, and as long as the two factors are confounded, the conclusion that derivational complexity is the

determinant of order of acquisition is not justified.
This early phase in psycholinguistic research, in
which it was tacitly assumed that distributional
analyses were adequate, that derivational complexity
was all important, and that linguistic universals
were independent of cognitive ones, gradually came to
an end, as psychologists and linguists realised the
importance of cognitive development and the need for
a semantically based grammar.

SEMANTIC MOTIVATION OF GRAMMAR

Is pivot grammar an adequate description of child
speech?   Some observers question the usefulness of a
distributional analysis of child language and point
to the fact that semantic and cognitive factors are
of crucial importance in the development of grammar.
Miller and Ervin (1964) point out, for instance, that
an utterance like 'Mummy sweater on' may mean:
'Mummy has her sweater on' or 'Mummy, put my sweater
on.'   An analysis in terms of privileges of occurrence of the morphemes of the utterance does not distinguish between the two meanings, and the utterance
is therefore ambiguously characterised.   Bowerman
(1973) too shows the inadequacy of pivot grammar,
which is not able to distinguish reliably between
semantically different utterances.
A more satisfactory way of analysing an utterance
is to analyse it in terms of the context in which it
occurs and the meaning it conveys.   Bloom (1970)
has carried out such a description of child speech.
In a longitudinal study of three children she carefully noted the contexts in which the children's
utterances occurred and she performed an inten-
sive analysis of semantic intent in early child
speech.   From her analysis it is quite clear that
formally identical two-word utterances occur in varying contexts, expressing a variety of meanings.   For
example, 'Mummy sock' can be described as expressing
the agent-object relation when mother is putting on
the child's sock, or the possessive relation when the
sock belongs to the mother.   'No sock' can express
various types of negation;   it can mean non-existence
(when there is no sock), rejection (when there is a
sock and the child does not want to wear it), or
denial (when there is a sock, but the child states
that there is none).   For noun-noun combinations
Bloom notes five different underlying relations:

conjunction, attribution, genetive, subject-locative, subject-object.   She demonstrates that two-word sur- face structures have rich underlying semantic struc- tures.   This characterisation of two-word utterances is more satisfactory than pivot grammar, since it dis- tinguishes utterances with different meanings which would be ambiguous in pivot grammar.

In their two-word utterances children intend mean- ings for which they have not yet acquired the appro- priate linguistic way of expression, and evidence of the child's knowledge of these semantic relations can be obtained by careful analysis of the context of the utterance.   Bloom points out that the acquisition of language is crucially related to the child's cognitive- perceptual growth and his interaction in an environ- ment of objects, events and relations.   In an analysis of the one-word stage Bloom (1973) shows that the child's syntax at the beginning of language derives from cognitive categories, and *not* syntactic ones. Relationships among persons, objects and events become represented as cognitive categories, and these cogni- tive categories form the basis for the child's learning of syntax.   Learning syntax is a matter of encoding these relationships in terms of the struc- tural relationships between categories of words in utterances.   'The child learns language as a linguis- tic coding of certain cognitive representations of his experience' (Bloom, 1973, p. 31).

Brown (1973) also reports findings which can be interpreted as indicating that the child expresses particular semantic intentions with simpler, familiar linguistic forms prior to the acquisition of the appropriate linguistic forms which adults use to express these same meanings.   In his analysis of the spontaneous speech of three children he noted that, at first, verbs were used in their uninflected form. Parents' responses to these forms, and occasional expansions, made it possible to isolate four kinds of meanings of these uninflected forms: (i) naming an action of temporary duration and true at the time of the utterance, (ii) referring to the immediate past, (iii) stating the child's current wish or intention, (iv) imperative.   Examining the emergence of verb inflections he noticed that the first formal inflec- tions marked exactly these four functions: (i) the progressive '-ing' in reference to an ongoing action, (ii) the simple past tense in reference to the imme- diate past, (iii) 'catenative' verbs ('gonna', 'hafta', 'wanna') referring to the child's wish, intention,

(iv) imperative, which is, of course, unmarked in
English.   The emergence of the verb markings in children's speech corresponds exactly to those functions
which were implicit in the use of the verb during the
unmarked stage.

   Cazden (1968), in examining the emergence of inflection in verbs and nouns in three children, found
that tense markers were acquired before the use of
the auxiliary, and that the present progressive
marker '-ing' was used before the 3rd person singular
present marker /z/.   All three children used the
present progressive marker before any others, next
the past marker, and lastly the 3rd person singular
present marker, which was only used by two children
up to criterion (using a criterion of 90 per cent
correctness).   This late use of the 3rd person
singular present cannot be due to phonological complexity, since the equally complex plural markers on
nouns were being used at the stage when the 3rd person
singular present was not.   The order of acquisition
of inflections follows a semantically motivated
principle: those inflections which are necessary to
signal a semantic distinction, '-ing' for indicating
process, '-ed' for indicating past, were acquired
first, while those inflections which have purely
formal value and carry no meaning element, 3rd person
singular present, are acquired later.   In the acquisition of verb modifications the child appears to be
following the principle that semantic relations must
be marked clearly, whereas formal linguistic complexities may be temporarily ignored.

   Brown (1973) also found that the English progressive inflection never overgeneralises.   There is a
semantic distinction between verbs which take a progressive inflection and those which do not.   Verbs
which can take a progressive form refer to processes,
whereas those which do not refer to states.   According to Brown, children never add the progressive
'-ing' to state verbs, e.g. they do not say 'wanting',
'needing'.   An inflection which is semantically
motivated is never used incorrectly.   However, inflections which are not semantically based but are
purely formal, like irregular past tenses, are often
overgeneralised.

   In this context, further evidence for the semantic
motivation of the acquisition of inflections comes
from the study of German children.   Park (1971)
studying the acquisition of German morphology in two
Swiss children found that the verbal prefix 'ge-' was

acquired later than other prefixes.   The prefix 'ge-'
has no specific semantic function;   its only grammatical
function is to indicate whether or not a past participle
is derived from an infinitive with an inseparable prefix or the suffix '-ieren'.   Separable prefixes, on
the other hand, occur early - they are semantically
differentiated, e.g. 'zu-' (to), 'aus-' (out), 'auf-'
(on).   Park found that the children used a number of
separable prefixes alone without the verbal component,
and that these represented the semantic function
corresponding to the component verb: e.g. the children
would say: 'Mama auf' meaning 'Mama aufstehen' (Mama
get up), or: 'Tür zu' meaning 'Tür zumachen' (shut the
door).   Such participle constructions are acceptable
because they cause no semantic ambiguity.   Separable
prefixes which are semantically differentiated occur
before the prefix 'ge-' which has no semantic function.
Park interprets this finding as evidence of the fact
that semantic functions of the morphemes influence the
acquisition of morphophonemic rules. (2)
    Slobin (1972b) shows the similarity in the kinds of
meanings expressed in simple two-word utterances by
children across languages, no matter what the grammatical means for encoding these meanings are.   In
highly inflected languages, such as the Slavonic
languages or Finnish and Hungarian, inflections are
acquired early.   These inflections encode the same
semantic intentions encoded in English by means of
word order and prepositions.   Slobin draws up a list
of semantic intentions typical of early child speech
for English, German, Russian, Finnish, Turkish,
Samoan, Luo (Slobin, 1972b, p. 199):

Identification	see doggie
Location	book there
Repetition	more milk
Non-existence	allgone thing
Negation	not wolf
Possession	my sweets
Attribution	big car
Agent-Action	mama walk
Action-Object	hit you
Action-Location	sit chair
Action-Recipient	give papa
Action-Instrument	cut knife
Question	where ball?

The findings discussed in this section suggest three
things: (i) semantic and cognitive factors influence
the order of acquisition of grammatical forms.   (ii)
The child has semantic intentions before he has the

structurally complete linguistic means of expressing
them.   Cognitive development precedes linguistic
development: children develop certain meanings and
then find the appropriate linguistic expressions for
these meanings.   (iii) The meanings which children
have are universal across languages. (3)

RELATION OF LANGUAGE DEVELOPMENT AND COGNITIVE
DEVELOPMENT

We have shown that there is a relation between cognition
and language in the sense that a particular cognition
precedes its appropriate linguistic expression.   Can
we find any other relation between cognitive development
and language development?   Can we, for instance, claim
that the development of language in general has its
root in preceding cognitive development?

     While a transformationalist account of the develop-
ment of language regards language development as largely
independent of general cognitive development and postulates some innate linguistic structures, Piaget (1926,
1970) has argued that language is dependent entirely on
cognitive development.   The formation of representational thought and the acquisition of language belong
to the general process of the constitution of the
symbolic function.   The sources of intellectual operations, and also of language, are to be found in the
preverbal sensori-motor period.   There is a progressive development from sensori-motor schemata to thought
and language.   The child's discoveries become knowledge of objects rather than reactions to objects and
events.

     What does the child know about objects at this
stage?

     By the end of the sensori-motor period the child
understands that objects have an independent existence
separate from himself.   He realises that objects
have a permanence when removed in space and time,
knows that they exist, can be removed and recur.   The
separation of objects and self, one of the major
achievements of sensori-motor intelligence, implies a
distinction between subject and object, objects and
actions.   We find that the categories of nouns and
verbs, and of subject and object are exactly the first
ones to occur in the child's development of language.
As Bloom's and Slobin's analyses of early child speech
seem to indicate, the first meanings express exactly
these achievements of sensori-motor intelligence:

existence, non-existence, recurrence, location and
immediate times, agent-object relations.   Sinclair
(1971) also draws an analogy between some sensori-
motor schemes and linguistic abilities: the ability
to classify an action, to apply a whole category of
action schemes to one object, has its linguistic
equivalent in grammatical categorisation into the
main categories of noun phrase and verb phrase.   She
suggests that the ability to use categories of
objects and actions correctly has its linguistic
equivalent in the correct use of grammatical functions,
i.e. subject, object;   the ability to order things is
reflected linguistically in concatenation.   Finally,
the ability to embed action schemes into one another
has its linguistic counterpart in the recursive
properties of phrase markers.   Thus, the first grammatical structures have their precursors in sensori-
motor schemata.   The child translates his experience
on the level of practical intelligence to the level
of representational, or verbal, intelligence.   Here,
the views of Sinclair and Bloom converge.

Cromer (1971), in an analysis of the development
of temporal reference in Brown's longitudinal data,
noted that certain cognitive abilities have to develop
first before the child acquires the appropriate linguistic forms.   He found that the present perfect
does not develop until about the age of four.   The
frequency of parental use of the present perfect
remains constant, the child hears the present perfect
frequently, he also commands the relevant formal
components of the grammatical structure, since he has
used past participles and the auxiliary 'have' since
the age of 2:6.   However, he does not use the present
perfect until a certain level of cognitive development
is attained.   The present perfect in English is
employed to refer to a past time with present relevance, and, in order to use this tense properly, the
child must have the ability to relate a point in time
in the past to the present point in time.   This
relating of two points in time may be seen as a complex intellectual operation which children have to be
able to perform before they can use the present perfect
properly.   Cognitive factors can therefore be said
to place limitations on the forms children use.
Cromer describes this cognitive constraint in terms
of Piagetian notions of initial egocentrism and the
inability to decentre in time.

While the relationship between language development
and cognitive development has been examined in the

first stages of language acquisition, there is little
research on the relationship between language development and cognitive development at a later stage of
childhood, once language has been established.
Sinclair-de-Zwart and Inhelder tested experimentally
the relation between language development and cognitive development (Sinclair-de-Zwart, 1969).   Using a
Piagetian conservation task, children were divided
into three groups: (i) those who had conservation,
(ii) those who did not yet have conservation, (iii)
those who were in the intermediate stage.   The children were then given verbal tasks in which they were
asked to describe simple situations, involving comparative judgments and statements.   The results
showed that of the children in group (i)(conservation
group) 100 per cent used comparatives for the description of different numbers of marbles, whereas of the
children in group (ii) (non-conservation) only 20 per
cent did so.   In the case of discontinuous quantity
(marbles) children who had conservation also had the
use of the appropriate relational linguistic expressions, comparatives, whereas non-conservers used
fewer comparatives.   In the case of continuous
quantity, of the conservation children (group (i))
70 per cent used comparatives for the description of
different quantities of plasticine, whereas the non-
conservation children (group (ii)) used only absolute
terms for the description of continuous quantity.
    These experiments show that higher levels of cog-
nitive development go with higher (4) levels of
linguistic development.   Furthermore, there seems
to be a parallel between cognitive development and
linguistic development: the conservation of discrete
units is acquired before that of continuous quantities,
and this principle was also reflected in the children's use of language: both, conservation and non-
conservation groups used more comparatives for describing discontinuous quantities than for describing
continuous quantities.   In the same series of experiments children were also asked to describe an object
differing in two dimensions.   The conservation group
described the object in two clauses, co-ordinating the
two dimensions, whereas the non-conservation group
described it in one dimension, or used separate
sentences.
    While these experiments suggest a very close rela-
tionship between cognitive development and linguistic
development, they do not tell us which of the two is
primary.   Sinclair-de-Zwart (1969) carried out other

experiments to test whether the use of linguistic
structures influences cognition.   Children of the non-
conservation group were taught expressions used by
children with conservation, and they were then retested in a conservation task.   While they were now
able to describe appropriately the level of water,
this linguistic ability did not lead to conservation.
Verbal training may well lead to directing attention
to the relevant aspects of the problem, but it does
not bring about the acquisition of operations of
reversibility.   Sinclair concludes that cognitive
development is primary to linguistic development and
that language abilities when taught to the child do
not affect cognition.   The appropriate cognition has
to be there before linguistic structures can be used
truly spontaneously and meaningfully.   However,
Fodor et al. (1974) points out that Sinclair's results
do not prove that cognitive development determines
linguistic development, but only that linguistic
development does not determine general cognitive
development.   Sinclair's conclusion *may* be justified,
but the evidence is inconclusive.

While Sinclair may not have demonstrated a causal
relationship between cognitive development and language development, in the sense that cognitive development is a necessary condition for language development,
she has shown that there is a relationship between the
two.   If we generalise from the relationship which
Sinclair found between comparatives and reversibility,
we can say that by looking at how children use linguistic structures we can gain insight into the
child's stage of cognitive development.   Previous
analyses of child language have only looked at whether
a particular structure is acquired or not, but have
not concerned themselves with the subsequent use of
the structure.   For instance, does the child use
particular linguistic structures with the same frequency as adults?   And, what meanings does the child
express when he uses particular linguistic structures?
These questions are crucial if we want to know more
about the relationship between language development
and cognitive development.   Frequencies have to be
studied against a background of stable, known adult
frequencies, if they are to be studied meaningfully
(see also Brown et al., 1969).   If we were to find
that child frequencies differed from adult frequencies,
we would have to account for the difference in frequency of use of linguistic structures.   One hypothesis would be that the child's frequency of use of

linguistic structures is a reflection of his cognitive
stage, in other words, the child's use of language is
a reflection of the cognitive representations of his
experience.   We may also look at the contexts in
which linguistic structures are used after they have
been acquired.   When the child uses a particular
linguistic structure, does he express the same meanings as an adult who uses the particular linguistic
structure?   These questions, which are of great
importance when studying the relationship between
language development and cognitive development, have
not yet been considered and examined by the research.

COGNITIVE AND LINGUISTIC COMPLEXITY

The argument has led me to the view that language
acquisition is intimately related to cognitive development.   The data from studies of the acquisition of
various languages suggest that the child's cognitions
at the time of the beginnings of grammar concern themselves with existence, non-existence and recurrence.
The child then progresses to an understanding of the
location of an object in space and time, and he
expresses these meanings linguistically.   Having a
particular cognition in his repertoire the child goes
about finding the linguistic means of expressing it.
One might be tempted to say that linguistic development follows universal cognitive development, and
that the course of grammatical development follows a
course of increasing cognitive complexity of the
linguistic forms which are acquired.   In other words,
the order of acquisition of linguistic structures
could be said to be determined by the cognitive complexity of the linguistic structures.

The influence of cognitive complexity on the order
of acquisition of linguistic structures has not been
tested in detail.   There seems to be a difficulty in
distinguishing cognitive complexity from semantic
complexity.   Semantic development refers to the
learning of the meanings of words and the meaning
relations between words.   Cognition, on the other
hand, is more than that and implies the capacity to
operate on meanings and on the environment.   Cognitive development concerns itself with the mental representation of one's experience.   Research has focused
mainly on semantic complexity.

Brown (1973) tested the hypothesis that the degree
of semantic complexity of linguistic structures deter-

mines their order of acquisition.   In his analysis of
the acquisition of fourteen morphemes, he concludes
that semantic complexity is a determinant of the
order of acquisition of these morphemes.   However,
Brown is unable to separate semantic complexity from
the grammatical complexity of linguistic structures.
He interprets his data to show equally that grammatical
complexity is a determinant of the order of acquisition of the fourteen morphemes.

While increasing cognitive complexity of the
notions grammatical forms express is one principle in
the order of acquisition of grammatical forms, there
comes a point where formal complexity plays a part as
well.   Slobin (1972a) cites Bowerman (1970) in a
study on the acquisition of Finnish in Finnish children, who points out that Finnish yes-no questions
are formed by attaching a question particle to the
word questioned and moving that word to the front of
the sentence - a fairly complex formal arrangement.
In her research she found that young Finnish children
do not ask 'yes - no' questions in a formally marked
way.   Slobin (1972a) also cites an example of the
role of formal complexity by referring to a study of
Serbo-Croatian - Hungarian bilingual children by Mikes
and Vlahović (1966).   The two girls studied were able
to use a variety of Hungarian case inflections on
nouns, expressing such locative and directional
notions as those expressed by the English prepositions
'into', 'out of', 'onto', 'on top of'.   In Serbo-
Croatian, however, they were not expressing these
notions, the reason for this presumably being the
greater formal complexity of the same locative notions
in Serbo-Croatian, where they require not only case
inflections on the end of the noun, but also locative
prepositions before the noun.   As Slobin points out,
if the same bilingual child gives linguistic expression to a semantic domain in one language but not in
the other, it is reasonable to conclude that the
child has mastered the particular semantic relation
or cognition, but formal complexities put a restraint
on his linguistic achievements.

What do we mean by 'formal' or 'linguistic' complexity?   Brown and Hanlon (1970) talk in terms of
'derivational' complexity and show that this factor
influences the order of acquisition of truncations.
Brown (1973) talks in terms of 'grammatical' complexity
and finds that grammatical complexity, while it cannot
be separated from semantic complexity, is a determinant
of the order of acquisition of the fourteen morphemes

which he studied.   When defining grammatical complexity,
Brown follows the representation of Jacobs and Rosenbaum, and Brown's detailed analysis of the grammatical
complexity of each of the fourteen morphemes is, in
essence, an analysis of their transformational complexity.   The analysis of linguistic complexity has not
moved away from an analysis in terms of transformational grammar, and therefore has all the disadvantages
this entails - these deriving from the assumption that
what is complex for the child is identical to what is
complex in terms of a formal linguistic theory.

In order to find a new approach to defining
linguistic complexity, it is useful to consider
Slobin's (1972a) analysis of the processes of language
acquisition.   Slobin looks at the strategies which
the child adopts in perceiving and producing speech.
These strategies allow us to see what the child can
or cannot master.   Those aspects of grammatical
structure which these strategies focus on will be less
complex for the child and easy to learn.   An example
of such a strategy is one of Slobin's operating
principles (Slobin, 1972a) which states that children
pay attention to the ends of words, or, at least, the
end of nouns.   Realisations of semantic intentions
by means of suffixes should therefore be easier to
learn and acquired earlier than realisations of the
same semantic intentions by means of prefixes or
prepositions.   Data from inflected languages like
Russian, Finnish, Polish show, for instance, that
genetive, dative, accusative inflections on nouns are
acquired early.   But when these same inflections are
realised in the form of prenominal articles, like in
German, they are acquired later.   English children
have problems with acquiring prepositions - in
English, of course, these semantic relations of
genetive and dative are expressed by means of
prepositions, that is, they are marked prenominally
and therefore less attention is paid to them.

Another operating principle which is related to the
first one, is that underlying semantic relations should
be marked overtly and be perceptually salient.   Formal
modifications which are not perceptually salient, for
example, the German prenominal article inflections,
are linguistically more complex for the child because
of their lack of perceptual salience.   C. Chomsky's
work (1969) has shown that sentences of the kind
'John is easy to see' and 'John is eager to see', sentences in which the underlying semantic relations are
not marked overtly and clearly, are not understood
until an age of about six to eight years.

Slobin enumerates a further strategy which children use in acquiring language: they pay attention to word order and tend to keep it unchanged. Sentence structures which keep standard word order should therefore be easier to learn and acquired earlier than those which do not. Support for this principle comes from Bever's (1970) work who found that young children interpreted any Noun-Verb-Noun sequence as Actor-Action-Object. This strategy would make passive sentences more difficult to understand and to produce.

Another operating principle children bring to the task of language acquisition is a tendency to preserve the underlying structure in the surface structure. Brown, Cazden and Bellugi (1969) noted that the inversion of subject and auxiliary is absent in English 'yes-no' questions and wh-questions when these first appear. Slobin also points out that children have a tendency to simplify discontinuous constituents into continuous morphemes. Brown (1973) found that, at first, the English present progressive is used without auxiliary and only '-ing' attached to the verb. Structures which require the rearrangement and interruption of linguistic units are complex for children.

Slobin points out that his operating principles are essentially language processing variables. The young child can only master what his speech perception and production strategies allow him to master, and what is within the storage capacity of his long-term and short-term memory. Memory constraints on young children are considerable. We find then, that what constitutes linguistic complexity for the child is best described not in terms of derivational complexity, but in terms of operating principles like those outlined by Slobin, which take into consideration the language processing abilities and storage capacities of young children. Looked at in this way, linguistic complexity turns out to be a *psycho*linguistic complexity.

Our discussion has shown that the development of semantic intentions reflects the child's general cognitive development, and that it precedes the acquisition of the appropriate adult linguistic forms which express these intentions. The evidence from various languages suggests that the kinds of semantic intentions and their order of acquisition are universal across languages - as is the case for cognitive structures generally. The formal means of expressing semantic intentions may vary considerably across languages, and the more linguistically complex a

particular grammatical structure is, the longer should
be the period of time between its occurrence in an unmarked form and its occurrence in the appropriately
marked grammatical form.   In summary then, the order
of acquisition of grammatical structures would depend
on (i) the order of acquisition of semantic intentions, (ii) the particular formal complexities of the
linguistic structures of a particular language, and
(iii) the level of development of the cognitive-
perceptual strategies and the storage capacities of
the child.   Factors (i) and (iii) are universal
cognitive factors, whereas factor (ii) is particular
to each individual language.

THE ACQUISITION OF TENSE (5) IN ENGLISH AND GERMAN CHILDREN

My own research (1976) investigates the acquisition of
tense in English and German children between the ages
of 2:3(0) and 4:10(0), and the relationship between
the children's use of tenses and their level of cognitive development.   I have examined whether processes
in the acquisition of language can be interpreted in
terms of Piagetian concepts, and whether, at any
particular stage in development, language development
is a reflection of cognitive development.
    Firstly, let us look at processes in the acquisi-
tion of linguistic structures.   The transformationalist approach pays no attention to the gradual
acquisition of grammatical structures, but simply
looks at whether a structure is acquired or not.
It cannot account for the fact that children acquire
only part of a grammatical structure, such as '-ing',
instead of both components 'be' + '-ing', which
together form one unit in deep structure.   However,
as Brown (1973) notices, the present progressive is
first used without auxiliary (he calls this form the
'primitive' progressive).   Only after the 'primitive'
progressive has been used for several months, the progressive 'proper' (progressive with auxiliary) is
acquired.   This is an indication that the acquisition
of grammatical forms is, or can be in some cases, a
gradual process, and this slow development of a grammatical form is rather similar to the gradual development of cognitive structures in general.   Piaget
points out that cognitive structures are at first
unstable, but gradually get established.   For
instance, in the attainment of conservation, the

child first achieves conservation on a few occasions,
then more often, then fluctuates between conservation
and non-conservation, and finally attains conservation.   These initial, unstable structures are *prestructures*.

Regarding grammatical structures as cognitive
structures, we can apply the notion of prestructures
to the development of linguistic structures.
Sinclair (1969) defines a grammatical prestructure as
an isolated instance of a certain syntactic structure,
strongly content- and context-bound, but not yet
fully established.   I would like to suggest that
there are three kinds of linguistic prestructures:

1   Prestructures which indicate that there is an
    understanding of the meaning of a particular
    grammatical form, but this meaning is expressed
    by a grammatical form which is simpler, in terms
    of linguistic complexity, than the appropriate
    adult form,
2   Prestructures which indicate that, in addition
    to an understanding of the meaning of a particu-
    lar grammatical structure, its appropriate
    linguistic expression has been acquired, but this
    is formed only partially correctly,
3   Prestructures which indicate that the under-
    standing of the meaning of a particular grammati-
    cal structure is there, and the grammatical
    structure is correctly imitated, but does not yet
    occur in spontaneous speech.

In studying the acquisition of tenses in English
and German I found that children in both languages
had considerable difficulties in acquiring some tense
forms which involve discontinuous constituents.
These were the English present progressive (e.g.
'I am laughing'), the present perfect ('I have
laughed'), 'going to' + infinitive ('I am going to
laugh') and the German Perfekt, which is grammatically
equivalent to the English present perfect ('ich habe
gelacht').   At first, the meanings of these grammatical structures were correctly understood by the
children, and this was expressed by the use of the
unmarked form in the appropriate linguistic and
extra-linguistic context.   Then the appropriate
grammatical forms were acquired, but difficulties
with the correct arrangement of their formal components
remained for several months.   Usually, the auxiliary
was left out.

Let me now discuss the gradual development of
these linguistic structures in terms of prestructures 1

and prestructures 2 (prestructures 3 will not concern us here).

Examples of prestructures 1 are expressions of semantic intent by verb forms as yet unmarked for tense. The semantic intent of the unmarked verb-forms in the speech of the youngest children were analysed from the situational and linguistic context. For English, examples of the use of the unmarked verbforms at 2:3(0) by Anna show that these forms expressed the three basic temporal meanings which are later expressed by present progressive, present perfect/simple past, 'going to' + infinitive/will + infinitive. The unmarked forms are used to express:

1 *immediate present, action going on now:* the un-marked form is used to describe an action which is going on at the time of the utterance. In adult English the present progressive would be used in such a context. E.g.

Anna 2:3(0): 'I swing'
                situational context: she is swinging
                at the time of the utterance.
                'I stroke cat'
                situational context: she is stroking
                the cat at the time of the utterance

2 *past, before-present:* the unmarked form is used to describe an action which has just happened. In adult English the simple past or present perfect would be used in such a context. E.g.

Anna 2:3(0): 'I crash'
                'I prick finger'
                situational context: both actions have
                just happened and they are completed,
                she is not crashing any more or prick-
                ing her finger.

3 *immediate future:* the unmarked form is used to describe an action which is about to happen. In adult English a future form with 'going to' or 'will' would be used. E.g.

Anna 2:3(0): 'I turn it on'
                situational context: she is looking at
                the investigator while she is making
                the statement and then proceeds to turn
                on the tap

For German the discussion of grammatical prestruc-tures is limited to the prestructures for Perfekt and Präteritum (present perfect and past) since there is no progressive aspect in German, and future is usually expressed by Präsens (present). Examples of pre-structures 1 are given by an analysis of some verbforms

which were marked as present tense but intended a
meaning of 'past, before-present'.   E.g.

Meike 2:6(0):   'Jan hingehe?' - (Jan go?)
                       situational context: Jan, her
                       brother, has just left through the
                       door.

Christine 2:6(0):   'so eine lange Blume nehmen' - (such
                       a long flower take)
                       situational context: Christine has
                       just picked a flower with a long
                       stem and she is showing it to her
                       mother.

Anna, Meike and Christine intend temporal meanings
which exceed their grammatical competence, and they
express these meanings by using a prestructure of the
grammatical structure which they will acquire eventually.

   In the case of the English progressive, present
perfect, 'going to' + infinitive, prestructures 2
occurred; that is, the grammatical structure has been
acquired but not with all its formal components, and
the auxiliary is left out.   E.g.

Anna 2:5(0):
present progressive: 'Louise feeding herself'
                           'Man talking like that'

present perfect: 'I done hoovering'
                           'He gone in back door'

'going to' + infinitive: 'I going to drink coffee'
                           'I going to climb up there'

In German, too, prestructures 2 occurred.   The auxiliary is left out when the Perfekt is used.   E.g.

Meike 2:6(0):   'Papa Krach gemacht' - (Papa made
                       a noise)
                       'hier abgereisst' (6) - (here torn)

Finally, in English and German, the correct grammatical
forms with auxiliary were acquired.

   In the acquisition of the English present perfect,
and possibly also the present progressive, 'going to'
+ infinitive, and the German Perfekt the same developmental sequence occurred: first, the particular
temporal meaning was expressed by prestructures 1, the
unmarked form; secondly, it was expressed by prestructures 2, the appropriate grammatical structure
but not with all its formal components; and thirdly,
the meaning was expressed by the appropriate and
correctly formed grammatical structure.   In the case
of English simple past, 'will' + infinitive and the
German Präteritum (grammatically equivalent to the
English simple past) prestructures 1 occur, followed

by the correct grammatical structure.   After the
correct form has been acquired, children still use
prestructures 1 and 2.   They fluctuate for several
months between the use of these two types (or one
type) of prestructures and the correct grammatical
form.   This developmental sequence of prestructures
1, and (where applicable) prestructures 2, and the
correct form, and also the fluctuation between the
use of these forms, show that the acquisition of a
grammatical structure is a gradual process.   This
process can be usefully analysed in terms of grammatical prestructures.   At each stage in the
development of a particular tense there is an increased mastery of the formal complexities of the
grammatical structure.

Regarding the order of acquisition of tenses, our
results showed that this order was, on the whole,
similar in both languages and across children.   This
confirms the view which is generally held (Brown, 1973,
C. Chomsky, 1969, McNeill, 1970) that order of acquisition of linguistic structures is stable.   We
tested three variables which could possibly account
for this stable order of acquisition of tenses: (i)
linguistic complexity, (ii) cognitive complexity,
(iii) frequency of parental use.

In determining what constitutes the linguistic
complexity of tense forms, we chose a surface structure analysis which made use of three criteria.   The
first was 'length', that is, the number of morphemes
which a particular tense contains.   The second
criterion was 'discontinuity'.   This refers to
whether a tense contains discontinuous constituents
or not, and if so, how many.   The third criterion
was 'marking preceding the verb stem'.   This refers
to the number of grammatical markers which precede
the verb stem and are therefore perceptually less
salient.   Our analysis of linguistic complexity has
moved away from a transformational analysis as presented by Brown and Hanlon (1970) and Brown (1973),
but makes use of the operating principles outlined by
Slobin.   These criteria of linguistic complexity
are sensitive to memory constraints and perceptual
salience, and are therefore more likely to be a
reflection of the psychological processes of how the
child discovers syntactic relations.

Three criteria were used to determine the cognitive
complexity of the tenses.   The first measure referred
to the number of time differentiations which the concept of time expressed by a particular tense presupposes.

The second measure referred to the degree of remoteness from the present which is expressed by a particular tense.   A third measure encoded the special difficulty of future tenses.   Fraisse (1963) argues that an understanding of future presupposes an understanding of past - and therefore future is more complex than past.   Our criteria of cognitive complexity define the cognitive complexity of tenses on the basis of what is known about the development of concepts of time in young children.

All three factors, linguistic complexity, cognitive complexity and frequency of parental use, were found to affect the order of acquisition of tenses signifi- cantly in English and in German (see rank correlations in Table 7.1).   Cognitive complexity was found to be

TABLE 7.1 Spearman rank correlations between order of acquisition and linguistic, cognitive complexities, frequency

	r_S		sig. level	
	English	German	English (N=17) %	German (N=8) %
linguistic complexity	0.75	0.76	1	5
frequency	0.75	0.81	1	5
cognitive complexity	0.96	0.95	1	1

the most important variable in determining order of acquisition of tenses in English and in German.   In English it affected the order of acquisition signifi- cantly more than any of the other two variables (the difference between 0.75 and 0.95, is significant).

With cognitive complexity being the most crucial variable which determines the order of acquisition of tenses in both languages, our results show that tenses are acquired according to a principle of in- creasingly finer time discrimination in the concepts of time which they express.   At first, children acquire tenses which express a meaning of present time.   Next, they acquire tenses which express the meaning of immediate past, followed by tenses which

express the meaning of immediate future.   Then, they
acquire tenses expressing more elaborate concepts of
past, and lastly, the tenses expressing more elaborate
concepts of future.   We are justified in concluding
that the order of acquisition of tenses follows a
cognitive pattern of the development of the understanding of notions of time.

Next, we examined how linguistic development and
cognitive development relate, after children have
acquired the necessary tenses.   We studied the frequency of use of the various tenses by the children
at different age levels.   Is the children's frequency
of use of tenses a reflection of adult frequency of
use, or is it a reflection of their understanding of
concepts of time?   Our results showed that the
younger children in both languages used mainly present
tenses and that, as age increased the use of present
tenses decreased significantly ($r = -0.97$ for English
children, and $r = -0.91$ for German children).   The
frequency of use of past and future tenses therefore
increased significantly over age.   At the higher age
levels, the children's frequency pattern of use of
tenses approached the adult frequency pattern.   But
this was not the case at the lower age levels.   Here,
the children's frequency of use of tenses reflected
their stage of cognitive development: young children
live in the 'here and now', they are concerned with
immediate, rather than temporally remote situations.
The frequency pattern of use of tenses were identical
in English and German, and this fact gives further
support to the view that it is a reflection of a cognitive pattern, and not a language-specific one.

The relationship between language development and
cognitive development was further examined by corre-
lating the frequency of use of tenses with the children's performance in cognitive tasks testing their
ability to decenter in time.   The children's performance in the cognitive tasks showed that the
younger children were not able to decentre temporally,
but focused on the dimension of immediacy and on a
spatial dimension of proximity.   With increasing
age, children were able to see the temporal relationships between events.   The children's performance in
the cognitive tasks correlated significantly with
their frequency of use of present tenses in spontaneous speech, and this was the case in both languages
(English: $r = -0.80$, $r = -0.82$, German: $r = -0.87$,
$r = -0.74$;   performance in cognitive tasks is inversely related to frequency of use of present tenses).

The children's increasing ability to decenter in
time, as manifested by their performance in cognitive
tasks, is paralleled by their increasing frequency of
use of past and future tenses in spontaneous speech,
manifestations of decentering on the linguistic level.
While we have found manifestations of increasing
decentering on the linguistic level and on the cognitive level, we have no direct evidence to conclude
that cognition determines linguistic behaviour, or
vice versa.   Our evidence agrees with Sinclair's in
showing that there is a very close relationship
between language development and cognitive development.
   What temporal meanings do children express when
they use past and future tenses?   The analysis of the
meanings which children express showed that, while
children in both languages may use adult linguistic
forms, they do not always express adult meanings.
The younger children were found to have a preference
(in terms of significantly higher frequency of use)
for the meanings of immediate past and immediate
future.   With increasing age children expressed the
meanings of distant past and distant future significantly more frequently, although reference to distant
future remained relatively infrequent and not well
understood.   The analysis of the meanings expressed
by some individual tenses, such as the English present
progressive and present perfect, provided further
support for the fact that children have only a limited
understanding of all the temporal meanings which a
tense can have.   Our results therefore bring evidence
counter to Bloom's (1970) 'rich interpretation':
children's surface structure does *not* always have a
rich underlying semantic structure, but it may exceed
the underlying semantic structure.   In other words,
children use tense forms without understanding all
the meanings which these forms can have, or they have
preferences for certain meanings which they understand
better.   Their semantic competence may not yet be
equivalent to that of adults.
   From our analysis of the acquisition of tenses
and temporal adverbs in two languages and children's
performances in cognitive tasks involving decentering
in time, we can distinguish three stages in the
acquisition of tense and concepts of time:
   1   Concepts of present time are understood and
present tenses are acquired.   There is a basic understanding of past and of future.   The concepts of past
and of future are vague and undifferentiated, or refer
to only immediate past and immediate future.   This

basic understanding has not yet been further differentiated on either the level of meaning or the level of
form.   This first stage precedes the acquisition of
the first syntactic forms to express the notions of
past and of future.

2   The tenses are acquired (with the exception of
some very complex ones).   But the child does not yet
have an understanding of temporal relations which is
equivalent to that of adults.   His use of temporal
adverbs indicates that reference to specific points
in past and future are not understood well, or not at
all.   His use of tenses indicates that he has a
preference for expressing meanings of present, immediate past and immediate future.   Some tenses are
used only with some of the meanings which they can
have in adult language.   We find, therefore, that,
while the child uses tenses correctly, the temporal
meanings expressed by these tenses can be limited.
The child uses grammar with his own meaning system.
Temporal concepts, in the sense of the calendar, are
not understood well.   Temporal decentering, in the
sense that the temporal order between a sequence of
events is seen, is not well developed yet either.
But there is an understanding of temporal relations,
in the sense that the basic meanings of individual
tenses are understood.

3   The tenses are used to express meanings like those
expressed by adults.   The adult categorisation of
time in terms of the calendar is largely understood,
although there are still difficulties in understanding
reference to distant future.   The child has achieved
a certain level of temporal decentering and can see
the ordering relation between a short sequence of
events in time.

In short, our results show that there is an inter-
dependence of form and meaning: cognition precedes
grammar, but grammar also precedes cognition.   It
looks as if language cannot develop without cognition,
and cognition cannot develop without language.

CONCLUDING REMARKS

In the light of the evidence, it is clear that language
development and cognitive development are crucially
related.   Three observations suggest that language
development and cognitive development are so crucially
related that cognitive development is a pre-condition
to language development.

1   A semantic intention exists before the acquisition
of the appropriate linguistic means to express this
semantic intention.   This has been demonstrated by
many researchers (Bloom, Slobin and others), and was
again observed in our study on the acquisition of
tenses in English and German.   We showed that the
acquisition of tenses is a gradual process which makes
use of prestructures.   We may term the state of
semantic intent a state of 'readiness' for the
acquisition of a grammatical structure.   Piaget (1970)
has stressed that a new structure has to be assimilated
into already existing structures.   Applying this
principle to language development, we may say that a
child is not sensitive to a grammatical structure
and cannot attend to it, until he understands the
meaning of such a structure.   When the child has
reached a stage in which the semantic intent of a
grammatical form is in his system of meanings, he can
be said to have been sensitised to the particular
grammatical structure, to be 'ready' for it.   In this
sense, cognition precedes grammar and is a pre-condition to it.

2   In our research, the cognitive complexity of
tenses was the most crucial determinant of their order
of acquisition.   We can therefore say that, in the
case of English and German tenses, language development follows cognitive development.

3   So far, cognition has been used with reference to
how the child operates on meaning.   But there are
more general cognitive faculties, such as memory.
The cognitive factor of memory constraints puts a
limitation on the type of linguistic structures which
the child can acquire at a particular age.   In our
research we found that children used prestructures
only until the age of about three years.   They used
prestructures of present perfect, present progressive,
but not later, when they acquired past perfect and
past progressive.   Why is it that children only
struggle with certain linguistic complexities at an
early age and not at a later age, when these same
(and more) linguistic complexities present themselves?
The reason for this may be that young children operate
under considerable constraints on memory.   Their
memory and processing span and their perceptual
strategies are limited.   It only makes sense therefore to talk of linguistic complexity in child
language acquisition, if we define linguistic complexity
by means of criteria which are sensitive to the child's
speech perception and production strategies and to his

memory capacity, but not in terms of derivational complexity (this latter may, or may not, overlap with speech perception strategies).   Constraints on memory may well be the reason why we find expressions of semantic intent in early child speech.   Expressions of semantic intent may not be so much an indication that meaning precedes grammar, but more an indication that the child's memory and processing span is too limited to cope with certain formal complexities.

Our analysis of the use of tenses subsequent to their acquisition showed that the younger children did not use tenses with the same frequencies as adults, but that the child frequencies were in accordance with the children's understanding of temporal relations, that is, in accordance with their level of cognitive development.   The cognitive constraint of the inability to decenter temporally manifested itself on the linguistic level and on the level of performance in cognitive tasks testing the ability to decenter in time.   These findings further support the view that cognitive development and processing capacity may be a precondition to language development.   However, we also found evidence that children use adult grammar with their own meaning system, that is, they used tenses correctly and appropriately, but did not yet have an adult understanding of temporal relations.   In this sense, language development precedes cognitive development.

The evidence of recent research suggests very strongly that language development is part of general cognitive development, a view which has been held by Piaget (1926, 1970).   I hope I have shown that the acquisition of language can only be studied meaningfully if we see it in relation to the development of general cognitive abilities.   My approach to analysing the acquisition of linguistic structures stresses process and the gradual development of form and of meaning.   It views language acquisition as it is influenced by such psychological factors as memory, speech perception and production strategies, and cognition.   It represents an attempt at finding a *psychological* theory of language acquisition.

NOTES

1 McNeill (1970) abandons the idea of the pivot/open distinction representing a generic classification in favour of a distinction whereby pivot words

constitute a class of words occurring with nouns,
and open words a class of words that occur in any
context.

2   It is also possible that the separableness of the
prefix contributes to its early acquisition, since
the prefix can be placed in final position of the
sentence, and it has been found that children pay
more attention to ends of words and phrases.

3   The evidence also suggests that children translate
cognitive, and not syntactic categories into surface structure.   This finding does, of course,
throw doubt on the usefulness of the concept of
syntactic deep structure altogether.   But this
question will not be discussed here.   The concepts of semantic and syntactic deep structure
have been discussed by McCawley (1968);   Lakoff
(1968) and Fillmore (1968).

4   By 'higher' we imply more mature and structurally
more complex.

5   For the sake of simplicity of expression, all verb
modifications whether tense or aspect, are referred to as 'tense' here.   This is justifiable
in view of the fact that tense and aspect overlap
and intersect (see Lyons, 1969, p. 316-17).

6   In this example morphophonemic rules are not
observed either.   Park (1971) reports similar
findings.

REFERENCES

BELLUGI, U. and BROWN, R. (eds) (1964), 'The Acquisi-
tion of Language', 'Monogr. Soc. Res. Child Dev.', vol.
29.
BEVER, T.G. (1970), The Cognitive Basis for Linguistic
Structures, in J.R. Hayes (ed.), 'Cognition and the
Development of Language', New York: Wiley, pp. 279-362.
BLOOM, L. (1970), 'Language Development: form and
function in emerging grammars', Cambridge, Mass: MIT
Press.
BLOOM, L. (1973), 'One Word at a Time', The Hague:
Mouton.
BOWERMAN, M.F. (1970), Learning to Talk: a cross-
linguistic study of early syntactic development, with
special reference to Finnish, unpublished doctoral
thesis, Harvard University.
BOWERMAN, M.F. (1973), 'Early Syntactic Development: a
cross-linguistic study with special reference to
Finnish', Cambridge University Press.

BRAINE, M. (1963), On Learning the Grammatical Order
of Words, 'Psych. Review', vol. 70, pp. 323-48.
BROWN, R. (1973), 'A First Language', London: George
Allen & Unwin.
BROWN, R. and FRASER, C. (1963), The Acquisition of
Syntax, in N. Cofer and B. Musgrave (eds), 'Verbal
Behaviour and Learning', New York: McGraw-Hill, pp.
158-201.
BROWN, R., CAZDEN, C. and BELLUGI, U. (1969), The
Child's Grammar from I to III, in J.P. Hill (ed.),
'Minnesota Symposia on Child Psychology', vol. 2,
Minneapolis: University of Minnesota Press, pp. 28-73.
BROWN, R. and HANLON, C. (1970), Derivational Complexity
and Order of Acquisition in Child Speech, in J.R.
Hayes, 'Cognition and the Development of Language',
New York: Wiley, pp. 11-53.
CAZDEN, C. (1968), The Acquisition of Verb and Noun
Inflections, 'Child Dev.', vol. 39, pp. 433-48.
CHOMSKY, C. (1969), 'The Acquisition of Syntax in
Children from 5 to 10', Cambridge, Mass: MIT Press.
CHOMSKY, N. (1965), 'Aspects of the Theory of Syntax',
Cambridge, Mass: MIT Press.
CROMER, R.F. (1971), The Development of Temporal Ref-
erence during the Acquisition of Language, in T.G.
Bever and W. Weksel (eds), 'The Structure and Psycho-
logy of Language', vol. 2, New York: Holt, Rinehart
& Winston.
CROMER, R.F. (1974), The Development of Language and
Cognition: The Cognition Hypothesis, in B. Foss (ed.),
'New Perspectives in Child Development', Penguin Books.
FILLMORE, C. (1968), The Case for Case, in E. Bach and
R.T. Harms (eds), 'Universals in Linguistic Theory',
New York: Holt, Rinehart & Winston.
FLAVELL, J.H. (1963), 'The Developmental Psychology of
Jean Piaget', London: Van Nostrand.
FODOR, J.A., BEVER, T.G., GARRETT, M.F. (1974), 'The
Psychology of Language', New York: McGraw-Hill.
FRAISSE, P. (1963), 'The Psychology of Time', New
York: Harper & Row.
HAYES, J.R. (ed.) (1970), 'Cognition and the Develop-
ment of Language', New York: Wiley.
LAKOFF, G. (1968), Instrumental Adverbs and the Concept
of Deep Structure, 'Foundations of Language', vol. 4,
pp. 4-29.
LYONS, J. (1969), 'Introduction to Theoretical Lin-
guistics', Cambridge University Press.
McCAWLEY, J.D. (1968), The Role of Semantics in a
Grammar, in E. Bach and R.T. Harms, 'Universals in
Linguistic Theory', New York: Holt, Rinehart.

McNEILL, D. (1966), Developmental Psycholinguistic, in
F. Smith and G. Miller, 'The Genesis of Language',
Cambridge, Mass.: MIT Press, pp. 15-84.
McNEILL, D. (1970), 'The Acquisition of Language', New
York: Harper & Row.
MIKES, M. and VLAHOVIĆ, P. (1966), Razvoy gramatickih
kategorija u decjem govoru (The Development of Gramma-
tical Categories in Child Speech), 'Prilozi
Proučavanju Jezika', vol. 2, Novi, Sad, Yugoslavia.
MILLER, W.R. and ERVIN, S. (1964), The Development of
Grammar in Child Language, in U. Bellugi and R. Brown,
'The Acuisition of Language','Monogr. Soc. Res. Child
Dev.', vol. 29, pp. 9-33.
PARK, T.Z. (1971a), The Acquisition of German Morpho-
logy; working paper, Psychological Institute, Univer-
sity of Bern, Switzerland.
PARK, T.Z. (1971b), The Acquisition of German Verbal
Auxiliary; working paper, Psychological Institute,
University of Bern, Switzerland.
PIAGET, J. (1926), 'The Language and Thought of the
Child', New York: Harcourt, Brace.
PIAGET, J. (1970), Piaget's Theory, in P.H. Mussen
(ed.), 'Carmichael's Manual of Child Psychology', vol.
1, New York: Wiley.
PIAGET, J. (1971), 'Biology and Knowledge', University
of Chicago Press.
PIAGET, J. and INHELDER, B. (1966), 'The Psychology of
the Child', London: Routledge & Kegan Paul.
SINCLAIR, DE ZWART H. (1969), Developmental Psycho-
linguistics, in D. Elkind and J.H. Flavell (eds),
'Studies in Cognitive Development', Oxford University
Press, pp. 315-36.
SINCLAIR, H. (1971), Sensorimotor Action Patterns as
a Condition for the Acquisition of Syntax, in R. Huxley
and E. Ingram (eds), 'Language Acquisition: modes and
methods', Longon: Academic Press.
SLOBIN, D.I. (1972a), Cognitive Prerequisites for the
Development of Grammar, in D.I. Slobin and C.A.
Ferguson (eds), 'Studies of Child Language Develop-
ment', New York: Holt, Rinehart & Winston.
SLOBIN, D.I. (1972b), Seven Questions about Language
Development, in P.C. Dodwell (ed.), 'New Horizons in
Psychology', Harmondsworth: Penguin Books.
SZAGUN, G. (1976), The Acquisition of Tense and Aspect
in Young English and German Children, Ph.D. thesis,
University of London.

Chapter 8

TOWARDS A DEVELOPMENTAL SOCIAL PSYCHOLOGY

Beryl A. Geber

INTRODUCTION

This paper is an exploratory one: it aims to bring
into contact related developments in social and developmental psychology by focusing specifically on the
question: how does the developing child construe his
social and personal world? While we will not present
a definite solution to this, a number of strands of
research can be woven together to provide the canvas
on which a picture can be sketched.

It is in the field of developmental psychology that
the major explosion of theory and research has occurred
over the past decade. The exploration of the child's
visual and arousal systems, understanding neonatal
capacities, detailing the relationship between mother
and child, documenting linguistic skills and particularly analysing the processes of intellectual growth
have all contributed to bring about a new appreciation
of the process of development. But it is not only
developmental psychology which has been the beneficiary
of this growth: the divisions within psychology are
traditional and expedient rather than substantive.
The problems examined by developmentalists: cognition,
concept formation, language, thinking and reasoning,
are increasingly of importance in the field of psychology as a whole. And so too is another change in
emphasis - the interest in the interactive framework
within which development occurs.

To a social psychologist this changing emphasis is
particularly welcome. It offers the opportunity for
forging links with developmental psychology which, I
believe, will be more rewarding than those previously
forged under the anvil of studies of socialisation.
This does not mean that socialisation studies are

anachronisms, but rather that the new bias allows the
integration with developmental psychology of fruitful
areas of social psychological research, specifically
the fields of attitudes and of symbolic interaction.

The concept of attitude has for many years held a
core position in social psychology, both theory and
research.   Given its widest interpretation attitudes
refer to the evaluative structures which organise the
concepts and classes relevant to the individual's
world.   Attitudes encompass what the individual
knows, what he feels as well as a readiness to behave
in a particular way (although research has shown that
the movement from 'readiness' to action is a complex
one), and they are organised into articulated structures varying in complexity and in centrality.

These structures may be similar to the schemes of
which Piaget writes.   This similarity is enhanced
when one realises that like schemes attitudes
assimilate to themselves experiences and input, and
that the structures can change or be accommodated to
experiences in the external world.

Piaget's theory posits changing equilibrations as
the basis of growth and suggests that schema are
accommodated to new or discrepant experiences - a
constantly shifting balance being achieved between
assimilation and accommodation;   studies in attitude
change specify the type of inputs and conditions necessary to achieve changes.   Indeed when one considers Feather's (1971) concept of a cognitive structure the similarity with Piaget's is immediately
clear.   Feather writes of simple schemas:

> over time the abstract structure and elements may
> come to exert a directive influence on the way in
> which the actual situation is perceived, permitting
> a simplified view of present reality in terms of
> the basic elements involved in the abstract struc-
> ture.   Also over time the abstract structure may
> be enlarged as more common elements are abstracted
> on the basis of experience.

For Piaget 'a schema is a cognitive structure which
has reference to a class of similar action sequences,
these sequences of necessity being strong, bounded
totalities in which the constituent behavioural elements are tightly interrelated' (Flavell, 1963).
Whereas attitude structures are labelled mainly by
their object (religious, political etc.) while schema
are labelled by the behavioural sequences to which
they refer (schema of sucking, schema of qualitative
correspondence, operational schema), there are never-

theless many similarities in the two concepts.   And
since for cognitive developmental theory it is the
development   of the schema and their operation that
is critical there is much of value in the research
for the social psychologist.

The second link between social and developmental
psychology goes back to two seminal works of the
1930s - Piaget's 'Moral Judgment of the Child' (1932)
and George Herbert Mead's 'Mind, Self and Society'
(1934).   Both these in their own context suggested
that the separation of the self from others was a
critical development for the individual, and that
this separation was a slow process rooted in social
interaction.   For Mead, self is a social concept,
dependent on the reflections received from others;
for Piaget social interaction produces conflicts
which demanded for their resolution the acceptance of
the relativity of evaluations, of the social and con-
sensual nature of mores and rules.   The writings of
Mead have had a wide influence in social psychology,
especially in analyses of the nature of social interaction and the types of self-other concepts that
particular experiences foster (Goffman, 1969; Harré,
1974).   These studies have emphasised two factors,
first the detail of the interaction and second the
meaning that particular experiences have for the
individual.   When the personality theory of Kelly
and the recent studies of attribution processes are
also considered then these theories of symbolic interaction can be seen to be a major current in present-
day social psychology.   They offer to a developmental
social psychology the challenge of describing and of
explaining changing behaviours, changing patterns of
social interaction and the cognitions which interpret
or give meaning and stability to the discrete and
changing experiences.   While the enormity of this
challenge is acknowledged there is one area of
research which might serve as a prototype for subsequent investigations: an area of research traditionally of interest to developmental personality
and social psychologists.   That area is that of
mother-child interaction.

MOTHER-CHILD INTERACTION

Recent years have seen a considerable change in the
way in which the bonding process between mother and
child is conceptualised.   The process reflects not

only the intellectual skills demanded in realising that
mother is a separate being from oneself, but also
reflects the social psychological nature of the relationship that is forged.   The publication by Bowlby
(1969) of his major work on attachment signified a
confluence of streams of theory and research springing
from many sources: the psychoanalytic writings of
Freud, Spitz and Klein, the social learning theories
of Miller and Dollard, Sears and Gewirtz and the
observational research writers such as Ainsworth,
Ambrose, Schaffer and Scott; Bowlby was further
stimulated by the writings of Piaget (1932) concerning
the process by which the infant, through interaction
with his environment and the feedback this produces,
develops the ability to construct or conserve objects.

The detailed analysis provided by Piaget of the
early sensori-motor stage of development focused
attention on the problem of how the child learns to
discriminate objects and how he understands them as
a being separate from himself with an independent
existence in space and time.   Bowlby (1969) and
Schaffer (1971) suggest that the social development
of the child relates to this intellectual development:
not only therefore is object constancy reflected in
the separation of the mother as an independent being,
but the major achievement of the early stage of
development, that of developing means-end relationships,
may also be reflected in the type of social manipulations the child employs.   And yet, as Schaffer (1971)
writes:

> considering both the importance of the development
> and the amount of work that has been done on the
> growth of the ability to differentiate inanimate
> stimuli in terms of previous experience it is sur-
> prising that we are still unable to supply answers
> to such fundamental problems as the age ... and
> the conditions under which social differentiation
> takes place. (pp. 81-2).

Recent studies by Ainsworth (1967, 1973) and others
begin to indicate possible answers to these questions.
What Ainsworth's observations have shown is that a
social development, such as that of attachment, is
influenced by the complex interaction of the behaviour
and attitudes of the mother, the characteristics of
the child, and the social system within which the
interaction occurs.   Ganda mothers and infants experience each other within socio-economic situations which
facilitate slightly different elements of the interaction from that of American mothers, although the

final result may be similar.   Other studies of mother-
child interaction support a multi-factor approach in
showing that the observed dynamic interaction is contributed to by both mother and child, and also by
environment.   Hospital policy about rooming-in,
about breast feeding, about the use of drugs during
delivery could well affect the nature of early mother-
child interaction as much as the mother's personality
or the baby's reactivity.   Recent trends in child
abuse research reflects the movement from an adult-
oriented explanatory system and from a 'social problem'
approach to one which gives weight to personal, interpersonal and environmental sources of tension, and is
prepared to concede that the characteristics of the
infant himself may be of importance.

The emphasis on both individual and social conditions in the development of behaviours reflects a
major trend in the way the developmental process is
conceived - no longer the passive outside stimulus
triggering a response, but an active construction of
the world in a framework of existing schemata, which
themselves alter as a result of what is done.
Behaviour is not seen as an inevitable unfolding of
potential, but a process influenced by both the nature
of the infant and the conditions under which he lives.
The model is of a goal-seeking, purposive and self-
regulating control system; an open system, which
becomes progressively patterned, differentiated and
articulated.

If an open-system model is to be accepted then an
understanding of human development will depend on
emphasising equally the external environment, the
internal environment and the articulation of these.
Therefore, a solid grasp of the way the child con-
serves the physical attributes of number, volume and
mass, or seriates or forms arithmetical groupings
must be balanced by an understanding of the child's
development of constancy in his perception of people,
how he begins to understand the nature of influence,
reciprocity and symmetry in human relationships, and
how he can go beyond the immediate observable present
to an understanding of motivation and purpose.   The
sophisticated cognitive structures which develop in
interaction with the material and physical world are
surely paralleled by structures, or even linked by
structures, developed by social interaction.

The research done on the relationship between
mother-child interaction and language and problem-
solving skills has indicated the close connection

between the nature of the child's social environment and the types of skills he develops.   If the heart of problem solving is a matching of means to ends, as Wood, Bruner and Ross (1974) have suggested then the nature of the constituent skill units that the child learns through interaction with his social and material environment will be crucial to his problem-solving ability.   If the appropriate skill lexicon is not provided then the means to any particular end may simply not be available to the child.

There are a number of approaches to this problem. One, following the work of Piaget, is mainly concerned with the development of *structures* involved in the achieving of means-end relationships;   it focuses on stages of development.   The other line of attack has been to focus on the *content* of the actions of the child, the detail both of what he does and the environment in which his actions occur;   not only to account for the universals of the process but also to establish some basis for understanding individual differences within the norm.   Bruner's studies of the infant's developing skills in manipulation and in language provides one example of the 'detail' investigation: the work on the mother-as-teacher, with its multiple origins reflecting the attempt to understand individual variations is another.

The research on the tutoring role of the mother has been based on the theses 'that the process of human development is essentially a social and interactive one' (Wood and Middleton, 1975).   For some theorists the focus of attention has been on the social-structural influences on the nature of the interaction. The work of Bernstein and Henderson (1969) has emphasised social class variations in control techniques and language use in mother-child interaction, as has the much-mentioned Chicago study of Hess and Shipman (1967).   Others have preferred to look at linguistic interactions, as in the handling of the child's curiosity and questioning (Robinson and Rackstraw, 1967).   These studies make certain assumptions about the generality of parental control techniques appearing to suggest that mothers use a particular, unvarying, method of interaction with the child, especially in what can be called 'cognitive' or problem-solving tasks.   More recent research has questioned this, examining whether task variations will provoke variations in mother's responses and style of teaching.   Wood and Middleton (op. cit.) have not only examined in detail how mothers assist their children and what happens if their help is unsuccessful but also whether mothers use similar techniques with their own and other children.   This latter research seems to suggest that the role of mother as tutor is built up gradually in conjunction with other mother-child interactions and therefore does not necessarily reflect a specific attribute.

We (1) have carried out a study in this area to examine how the interaction between mother and child alters under varying environmental constraints.   We hypothesised that tasks would differ in their demand characteristics and that the skill of the mother would be found in the way she was able to comply with these demands and vary her behaviour to her child accordingly.   The 'mother-as-teacher' role is one which, in the normal family routine, is constrained by a number of factors outside the mother-task-child triad. Help with homework has often to be given while cooking the dinner;   toddlers have to be encouraged and guided while the house is cleaned and the laundry done; even a quiet story is interrupted by the telephone, by the doorbell or by a half completed chore.   And where there is more than one child to make demands on the mother the situation is greatly complicated.   (Well do I recall a nasty toothless bite from my infant son when my attention drifted from him to his three sisters who were having difficulties with a construction toy in the corner of the nursery during feeding time!)

Thus the pure mother-as-teacher role is an ideal and we were concerned to show how constraints beyond the nature of the task affected mother-child interaction.   We employed a relatively primitive constraint - time limitation - and compared for each of twenty pairs of middle-class mothers and their three-year-old children the nature of their interaction in timed and untimed conditions on a divergent and a convergent task, randomised in order of presentation across the sample.   Each mother-child pair was brought separately to the laboratory and the entire interaction (with their knowledge) was videotaped. The two tasks we used were copying simple designs on an Etch-a-sketch toy and building anything out of Lego building bricks.

The Etch-a-sketch task is one used also by Hess and Shipman.   It consists of a small portable screen, rather like a television screen, and two knobs.   By varying the direction each knob is turned, lines of different orientations are etched onto the screen.

One knob controls vertical lines, the other horizontal
and by simultaneous movement diagonals may be drawn.
Very simple designs utilising only vertical and horizontal lines were presented to the mother-child pair
after a practice period.   They had to copy each
design, taking either as long as necessary (untimed
condition) or completing it within a very short time
(timed condition: thirty seconds per design).

The Lego task was a much less structured one: the
mother and child were told to build whatever they
liked out of the bricks provided taking however long
they wanted (untimed) or completing the constructions
within a three-minute period (timed).   We explained
to the mothers that we were interested in seeing how
mothers and children 'do things together', that we
wanted joint effort.   In the Etch-a-sketch the
instruction was for each to take control of one knob,
in the Lego to build something together.   The
'togetherness' of the action was what was stressed in
the instruction, rather than the quality of the final
product.

In our analysis, which will not be given in detail
here, we have paid particular attention to the sequenc-
ing of behaviour, to the feedback to the mother of
information about the success of her assistance
through what the child actually does in response to
help of various sorts.   We have looked at the way
the mother structures the task for the child, the
nature of her interventions, the sorts of suggestions
and initiatives taken by the child and the child's
success in gaining support and compliance from the
mother.   We have looked at the nature of both the
cognitive and emotional feedback each partner seeks
and gives through the four task conditions.   In other
words we are concerned to see how the child's problem-
solving skills are built up and utilised in particular
types of situations, how the environment helps or
hinders him in selecting the appropriate units from
his range of skills and then in assembling them to
reach an agreed goal.   These skills may be manipulative but equally well they may be negotiation skills.
Much insight has been gained in seeing how (or whether)
the mother and her child reach agreement on what to
build.   Not very much attention has been paid to the
child's skill in social manipulation, in developing
means-ends relationships or a set of 'plans' that
refer to his interpersonal world.   And yet it is
obviously as important a skill for the child as is
getting a cup to his lips successfully, or learning

how to embed one action in another in order to achieve
higher-order integration, as in moving an object into
the crook of the arm to free both hands for action.
Structuring the social world is an important skill and
we shall return to its discussion later.

A number of interesting findings have emerged from
our study.   If one examines looking behaviour certain
things become clear: firstly, across the sample as a
whole, there is far greater variability in the responses
of the mothers than of the children.   With one
exception, namely the Etch-a-sketch timed condition,
children look almost entirely at the task rather than
at their mother.   The exceptional condition is one
where particular specific mothers respond to the time
condition by taking over the copying task entirely,
not permitting the child to participate.   Under that
condition the child will look at the mother, or away
from the activity area altogether.   Mothers however
show far greater variability both across the sample
and across the tasks.   While they still spend more than
half the time looking at the task, they do spend a fair

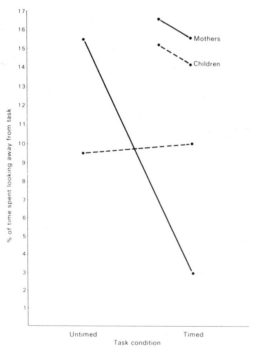

FIGURE 8.1 Percentage time spent looking away from task
in timed and untimed Etch-a-sketch

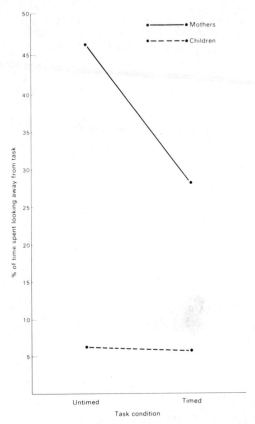

FIGURE 8.2 Percentage time spent looking away from task
in timed and untimed 'Lego' building

portion of the rest looking at the child.   Secondly,
their looking behaviour is more task-related than is
the child's.   Mothers look at the child more during
the construction task than during the copying task,
and look less during the timed conditions than during
the untimed.   If we take looking behaviour as our
index, mothers seem to be 'locked in' to the child's
behaviour correcting and altering their own responses
in the light of what the child does.
   Comparing the behaviour of the mother-child pairs
across the timed and the untimed conditions is also
interesting.   Again, despite careful selection of the
sample for social class and educational similarity
there were differences between the individual mothers.
At the one extreme was one mother who in the timed condition completely 'blocked out' the child;   single-

handed, with great determination and despite initial
attempts by her daughter to interfere, she completed
all tasks perfectly within the alotted time! At the
other end of the scale was the phlegmatic, non-
interfering mother who seemed to be happy to remain
passively watching, not actually doing any of the
tasks with the child.

However, in the sample as a whole certain changes
became clear when the time condition was introduced,
regardless of the nature of the task. Imposing a
time constraint leads to a change in the type of
assistance that the mother gives the child. Where
there is no limitation mothers generally use a
variety of techniques to motivate and direct the
child. They make orienting responses, non-specific-
ally directing the child, e.g.

'Now, what shall we make?' (Lego)
'Let's move the knobs and see what happens.'
(Etch-a-sketch)

They also structure the situation in such a way as to
suggest or hint at appropriate or possible action,
without specifically instructing the child as to what
to do. The child therefore participates with the
mother in solving the problem - the action is truly a
joint one. E.g.

'Remember the pilot needs to be able to see where
he's going.' (Lego)
'Look at these see-through bricks. What do you
think they're for?' (Lego)
'Which way do you think I should turn the knob
now?' (Etch-a-sketch)

In addition to these two non-directive techniques the
mothers do give the child specific directed instructions:

'Put the window on top of those bricks.' (Lego)
'Turn the knob to the right.' (Etch-a-sketch)
'We have to draw lines so that our picture looks
like the one Judy gave us.' (Etch-a-sketch)

Here the mother's intervention is precise and allows
the child only to comply or not, not to participate in
solving the problem.

In the timed condition the proportion of directed
instructions given to the child increases at the
expense of the non-directed. Not only is far less
assistance available as a whole (this applies even if
one simply compares the first three minutes of the
untimed Lego with the three minutes of the timed, and
takes 1½ minutes from the untimed Etch-a-sketch as
the unit of comparison with the timed condition), but

the structuring of the assistance is different: it is
an instruction or direction from mother to child, not
a joint activity, not a situation where the child is
encouraged to exercise his own skill in finding a
means to the stated end.

Another difference is also noticeable - the timed
conditions is associated with attenuated interaction
sequences. In the limitless situation there may well
be a number of interactions before any particular
action brings the sequence to the close:

Child suggests that they build a block of flats.
Mother hesitates, slightly alters child's suggestion to a house. Child starts to build, then
stops and adopts Mother's suggestion which Mother
then shifts in a new direction. They both stay
silent. Child makes new suggestion (car) which
starts new sequence. (Lego)
Child moves knob too far for particular design.
Mother stops him, laughs and they turn the sequence
into a game before erasing the design. (Etch-a-
sketch)

However, in the timed situation the interaction pattern
becomes very much shorter and sharper, a type of in-
struction-response sequence, with the mother cutting
short any playful or irrelevant responses. As a
result there is more negative feedback to the child
than in the untimed condition.

Finally, the amount of compliance the child shows
decreases in the timed tasks. Mothers giving direct
instructions to their children are not necessarily
more successful at eliciting the desired reaction
from the child than when using a less specific directive. The timed condition seems to discourage the
mother from pitching her response at a level or producing it in a form that the child can easily
assimilate: she becomes less sensitive to the child's
perspective and more likely when he does not comply
simply to repeat her directive or do it herself
rather than change the instruction to make it clearer
to the child.

I have described this study and our findings at
some length because they clearly illustrate the
points made earlier. The child acts, learns and
constructs his world in a personal environment, through
interaction with others as much as, if not more than,
in interaction with objects. The nature of the
interaction and the structural features of the environment which influence it, are crucially part of what
the child is assimilating, and to which he has to

accommodate.   And yet how minimal is our understanding
of how the child construes this reality and how it
specifically influences him.
  We have a growing body of information about mother-
child interaction in particular types of problem-
solving situation: we are still very far from having
a comprehensive picture of the child's social world.

THE WORLD OF CHILDHOOD

There are perspectives from the study of children's
games, rhymes, folklore and fantasies which can be
used to gain insight into the child's social world.
The verses and folklore collected by the Opies (1959)
present us with an understanding of the way children
regulate the world of childhood, a world outside the
control of adults.   Taking an historical view one
has a means of understanding the relationship between
political change and its representation in the life
of childhood.   As the Opies have discovered 'in their
self-contained community their basic lore and language
seems scarcely to alter from generation to generation',
nor from country to country.   Indeed my young children chant verses I chanted a childhood 6,000 miles
away!   And the sort of situations the rhymes regulate
have an astounding uniformity: there is 'an armoury
of ready responses' (Opies, 1959) which children use
in making rapid retort, in sorting out their personal
relations.   Phrases which allow the child to have
the last say and therefore assume dominance, which
ward off awkward questions, which rebuke the socially
unacceptable child are used extensively.   The shame
of having someone shout -
    You liar, You liar
    Your pants are on fire
    Your tongue is as long
    as a telephone wire
acts as a deterrent and as a form of establishing
social identities.   When a child calls out to another -
    I made you look
    I made you stare
    I made you change
    Your underwear
a particular form of superior influence is implied.
But this complex regulation of the child's social relationships is all but ignored by psychologists.   As
Harré (1974) has pointed out 'the skills and capacities
that go into the construction and maintenance of a

social world by ceremonial means are connected with
forms of symbolic action and so are deployed in
linguistic and paralinguistic interaction.' These
skills and capacities, social cognitions and social
behaviours are important items in the child's cognitive and social growth and should be relevant to both
developmental and social psychologists.

The Opies catalogue, with delightful scholarship,
the use of lore and language in the regulation of the
child's world: 'His affidavits, promisory notes,
claims, deeds of conveyance, receipts, and notices of
resignation, are verbal and are sealed by the utterance
of ancient words which are recognized and considered
binding by the whole community.' The code is
absorbed, is practised and is transmitted by each
generation as the problems of social life, of main-
taining the community, becomes relevant. As the all-
controlling role of the adult is eased out of the
schoolchild's world so his own cultural forms of control, regulation and ritual assume paramountcy.
Honour, truthfulness and affirmation, the bare bones
of trust; are expressed by gesture and oath, calling
for dreadful punishment if one should lie. The
issues expressed in many moral dilemma questionnaires
are real, and the notion of immanent justice not hard
to find: blistered tongues signify lies told. The
commerce of the child is regulated, with ideas of
reciprocity and of fairness, by oath, by custom and
by scathing epithets cast at transgressors of the
code. Even mild aggression can be stopped on the
production of the appropriate cue word. And behaviour
regarded as proper by the community is publicly recognised - spoil sports, trouble makers, boasters and
crybabies, tell-tales and teachers pets are castigated
by the apt verse, and the pithy epithet. If the
transgression continues punishment and torment are
available from the same tradition.

Piaget (1932) asked children to explain to him the
rules of their game of marbles and he used the information with his usual brilliance in his studies of
moral judgment. The folklore, the street games, the
community life of children present the opportunity of
discerning the way that the world of childhood is
constructed and understood. Despite the claim of
the Opies that this is a primitive or savage world, as
with ethnographic descriptions of simpler societies
one is amazed by the richness of the structures, the
complexities of the social relationships and the
sophistication of the transactions that are regulated

by traditions.   One cannot conçeive of these children
as a series of habit-hierarchies, or interpret their
behaviour simply in terms of intra-familial processes.
The problems and predicaments which they confront must
surely demand for their resolution a complex set of
constructs about people and social processes as well
as the understanding of the meta-processes that are
immediately implied in social interaction.

The making of plans of action in the animate world
involves less certainty about the relationship between
means and ends than in the inanimate.   Once the concept of 'ball' has been developed implying round and
bouncing, then all that interferes with achieving the
desired end, be it bouncing off a wall or knocking
over nine-pins, is the appropriate physical skill.
However, despite the capacity to discriminate 'mother'
from other people, or developing a concept of 'best
friend' the ability to get them to do any particular
thing is not simply related to one's own skills -
there is the other person's will to account for as
well.   The planning of a social action therefore
involves both oneself and the other as both agent and
as actor.   It is on this that research attention has
focused, in the guise of egocentricity.

EGOCENTRICITY IN CHILDREN

The notion of decentration, as students of cognitive-
development are aware, is a critical one in the
Piagetian system.   One of the most predominant
characteristics of preoperational thought is the
tendency towards centration, that is to focus attention on one dimension, either perceptually or intellectually.   'The child is unable to decenter, i.e. to
take into account features which could balance and
compensate for the distorting, biasing effects of the
single centration' (Flavell, 1963).   In similar
fashion the developing child is egocentric, (2) during
the sensori-motor stage with respect to actions,
during the preoperational stage with respect to representations and later according to Piaget this egocentricity is manifest in adolescence in the form of
the 'omnipotence of thought', a naive belief that if
he thinks it, it can be.

The importance that the concept of egocentricity
has assumed in the explanations of development, particularly social development, is reflected in the
large body of research directed to establishing the

nature of egocentricity, the stages during which it diminishes and the consequences of change.   Piaget focuses on this as an important development in his studies on moral judgment, where peer interaction is seen to demand taking account of the other's view. This decentration leads to a more relativistic basis for judgment and finally to mature social evaluations. More generally: 'One of the fundamental processes of cognition is that decentration relative to subjective illusion, and this process has dimensions that are social or interpersonal as well as rational' (Piaget, 1970).

The basic idea is that the child, until sometime during middle childhood, is unable to understand the perspective of others.   This, it is believed, is a rather generalised inability reflected in communica- tion skills (such as telling a story to another, or adjusting one's speech appropriately), in moral judg- ment, in judging perspective, and in taking the role of the other.   Each of these separate abilities is believed to be dependent on the eventual decentration, on moving away from a self-dominated schema to a socio-centric or allocentric perspective.   Until this occurs the child will make immature judgments in moral dilemma stories, will be ineffective in taking into account what others want and/or will do, and will not be able to communicate adequately his own views to others.

Flavell et al. (1968) in an important work stimu- lating considerable interest in the development of 'thinking about the social environment', relates clearly the dual aspects of role-taking and communicat- ing: the child's capacity to assess the capabilities and tendencies of the other in a particular situation is related to the specific ability to use this under- standing of the other person's role as a tool in communicating effectively with him.   If the speaker is to inform, persuade, send meaningful messages to the listener, the speaker must have some notion of how to phrase his thoughts to be congruent with the way he cognises the other.   Flavell posits a three-stage process: firstly, the subject cognises the topic or event and codes it for himself; secondly, the subject decides what the relevant attributes are of the listener which are pertinent to his receipt and decod- ing of the message; thirdly, the subject recodes the event as a message for the listener.   This third stage may well involve recoding if the listener is seen not to comprehend.   Successful social interaction therefore involves sophisticated cognitive skills, which demand decentration and which presumably follow the developmental sequence established on the basis of the child's knowledge of the physical world.

Using very ingenious tasks Flavell and his colleagues investigated the development of communication and role-taking skills in early and middle childhood. The studies suggested that the preschool child does not even understand that there could be a problem of varying perspectives. Though this understanding may well have developed when the child gets to school he is still not very skilled in analysing the particular requirements called for in a specific communication task, nor in assessing the relevant role attributes, although he manages an elementary inference of understanding what the other perceives. During middle childhood and adolescence the child becomes aware of the need to pay careful attention to the characteristics of his audience when communicating with it and increasingly skilled in understanding people.

Flavell's assumptions are supported by a number of studies examining the importance of role-taking skills in developing social cognitions. Selman (1971) showed that the development of reciprocal role-taking skills is related to the development of Kohlberg's (1963) conventional moral judgment. The study indicated that the reciprocal nature of interpersonal relations is a necessary (but not sufficient) condition for this development. Similarly Kohlberg and others have shown that early and intense peer interaction, which might be associated with role-taking skill (we shall return to this later) is also associated with precocity in moral development.

Support for the interactional origin of cognitive development comes from a Norwegian study. Hollos and Cowan (1973) examined children in three social settings in rural Norway - a farm community, a village and a town. These three situations differ mainly in the amount of verbal and social interaction the children have with parents and peers. The results showed that this had little influence on the development of logical operations (classification and conservation tasks) but had considerable impact on role-taking skills. The socially isolated farm children were low scorers on role-taking tasks.

The picture therefore emerges as follows: the young child, because of the general lack of sophistication in his intellectual operations, most specifically in his inability to take a perspective and view other than his own, lives in a world which is an extension of himself. His perceptions and understanding of his social world are therefore inadequate to allow him to plan, evaluate, judge and even empathise with others. This egocentricity is the basis for the child's 'distorted concepts of causality, relational concepts, moral judgements, spatial conceptualizations and communication difficulties' (Looft, 1972).

The asocial or egocentric nature of early development which these studies admit has not gone unchallenged. Shatz and Gelman (1973) have shown that four-year-old children are able to adjust their speech to a variety of listeners, a skill which Flavell's work would not really allow. If one adjusts speech then the needs of the listener must be accounted for - a move away from egocentricity. Shatz and Gelman suggest that the earlier studies which had demonstrated the absence of decentring had used tasks which were themselves beyond the capacities of the child. Previous studies therefore were not testing simply the child's ability to communicate effectively but also to understand a task of too great a complexity for his level of development. The Shatz and Gelman study showed not only that four-year-old children could communicate a task, but that they adjusted their speech to the status of the listener.

When talking to two year olds as opposed to peers or adults, four year olds produced shorter utterances; they were less inclined to use co-ordinate constructions, subordinate constructions, and certain forms of predicate complements; and they were more inclined to use words which attracted or sustained attention (Shatz and Gelman, 1973). There is some further insight about the communicative content of children's speech from a study by Schachter et al. (1974) which supports the idea of early egocentricism giving way to an allocentric perspective - but much earlier than Piaget and Flavell allow. The study showed that before age three the speech of children reflects the adualism of egocentrism: it is primarily directed to implementing desires and is particularly suitable for fostering child-adult bonds. After age three, speech to peers increases with joining and collaborative statements achieving importance. By age five speech patterns are adapted to the needs of the listener.

This adaptation may, according to Garvey and Hogan

(1973) occur as early as $3\frac{1}{2}$ years of age.   Videotapes
of dyadic play showed that there was a high level of
mutual responsiveness in both speech and behaviour, of
children of this age, and social speech shows a high
level of interpersonal understanding.

None of the speech studies deny the young child's
egocentricism.   What they suggest is that, at least
in verbal communication, the child loses his adualism,
or separates self from other, far earlier than had
previously been thought possible.   The child may, if
this is a general finding, be truly social in his constructs and action before the kindergarten stage.
It is therefore worth examining whether other types
of egocentric thought also can decentre before middle
childhood.

The study by Chandler et al. (1973) comparing the
judgment of intentionality on verbally and visually
presented moral dilemmas supports the view that the
task is critical in the assessment of the stage of
development during which egocentricity diminishes.
They showed that the children focused on outcome or
consequences as the basis for their moral evaluation
only with verbally presented material.   Where visually
presented, on a videotape, the children were able to
base their judgment on intention, and therefore gave
judgments more mature than had been previously indicated.   The isolation of cognitive developmental theory
from theories about memory processes etc., which
Lunzer speaks of in his paper in this volume, has
perhaps discouraged clear assessment of task demands,
and it may well be that the length of the verbally
presented task is too great for the young child's
short-term acoustic memory, permitting only the final
sequence to be clearly coded, whereas the visual
material may well be easier for the child to encode
as a whole.

One important element in the concept of egocentricity is the inability of the child to move from
his own perceptual perspective to that of the other.
What the child sees or feels is, for him, what any
observer regardless of position would experience.
Fishbein et al. (1972) report research wherein the
children of $3\frac{1}{2}$ are able, on the simplest tasks, to
co-ordinate perspectives.   This ability is the function of the complexity of the stimuli presented to
the child and the type of response the task demands.
In other words, the essential capacities of the child
will only be manifest if the task is actually suited
to him.   This assumption is given further support by

the work of Borke (1975) who replicated Piaget and
Inhelder's basic mountain perspective experimental
design but substituted a more age-appropriate task.
She found that three-year-old children could accurately
reflect another's perspective 80 per cent of the time.

De Villiers and de Villiers (1974), using as their
index the comprehension and production of spatial
deitic terms (this, that, the other), also have evidence of the capacity of the three-year-old to translate the speaker's perspective to their own if this
was necessary for understanding.   However, the three-
year-old could not easily do what four-year-olds can,
namely translate into the listener's perspective when
giving instructions.   This linguistic decentration is
quite clear in four- and five-year-old children.

Fishbein analyses what is required of the child in
perspective taking task into three stages.   During
the first stage the rule 'You see what I see' applies.
There is only one perspective - the child's.   The
second stage (or 'rule' as Fishbein prefers to call it)
accepts that 'if you are not in my place you don't see
what I see.'   The child can accept the difference,
but cannot necessarily identify it.   This only occurs
during rule 3 which states 'If I were in your place I
would see what you see.'   However the resolution of
the problem of establishing what the other sees would
depend on the complexity of the task.   (For support
for this see Masangkay et al., 1974.)

It would therefore appear that at least in two
types of tasks - communicative skill and visual or
spatial relativity - children younger than school age
are able to perform non-egocentrically.   It remains
to ask whether this implies either that the concept
of egocentric thought is imprecise and not useful in
explaining social development, or that at least it
may not be a unitary concept.

There is an impressive body of thought supporting
the idea that the ability to decentre is a single
factor which would subsume various types of egocentricism.   Feffer (1970) writes that 'the structuring
of the physical world and the ability to assume
different social perspectives are cognitive activities
which are related to each other and which reflect a
development trend.'   He supports this by showing
that a role-taking task and various impersonal cognitive tasks were both positively related to chronolo-
gical age and also to each other.   Looft (1972) uses
egocentricism as a unifying concept to account for a
variety of behaviours across the individual's lifespan,

extending the age range normally studied in decentration, but bringing in the issue of cultural variations
in egocentricity relating to the nature of the social
interactions fostered by the society.   (We have made
a similar point earlier in discussing moral judgment
and peer interaction.)   Then, of course, there is
the work of Flavell and of Piaget which would encour-
age a unitary view of egocentricity.

Rubin (1973) systematically examined the various
cognitive skills which are assumed to be influenced
by the child's egocentricity: communicative skill,
role taking, spatial egocentricism and private speech.
In addition four possibly related variables were
added to the study - age, mental age as examined by
the Picture Vocabulary Test, conservation (of number,
space, continuous quantity, substance and weight) and
finally popularity.   The data were submitted to a
factor analysis, which produced two factors with
eigen values greater than 1.00.   The first factor,
accounting for 56 per cent of the total variance was
defined by all measures of egocentricism and conservation, with the private speech measure loading least
on the factor, and the second factor was defined by
popularity.   This study by Rubin confirms the decentration hypothesis previously discussed, and lends
some credence to the view that egocentricity is a
unitary concept.   It would appear that the shift in
perspective allowing more than one dimension to be
considered at a time, which encourages conservation
responses, has its parallel in the social field in
the shift in perspective from self to other, which
permits the child to make allowances for other's needs
and viewpoints.

However, the youngest children in Rubin's sample
were already five years old ($\bar{x}$ = 67.35 months) and,
as the studies of Borke, Fishbein and de Villiers
have shown, the child learns to decentre earlier than
this.   What Rubin does not show is whether all forms
of decentration develop together, or whether there are
forms of décalage.   A later study (Rubin, 1974)
supports the concept of a more gradual development of
the relevant cognitive operation and the necessary
structural grouping which underlies the non-egocentric
performances, and therefore allows for décalage.
This later study used two measures of egocentricism
(spatial and communicative) across the life-span, and
found that at the age of seven years the correlation
between the two tasks was non-significant.

Selman and Byrne (1974) have provided a structural

developmental analysis of role taking which serves as
a framework for some of the matters we have discussed
in this section.   They have derived, from the literature and their own research, a sequence of age-
related logical structures which the individual
'displays in his understanding of other's point of
view'.   Four levels are apparent:
   Level 0: Egocentric Role Taking.   During this
early stage the child can differentiate himself
from others as entities (as in constituting the
mother as object) but cannot differentiate their
point of view.   And he cannot relate perspectives.
   Level 1: Subjective Role Taking.   The child now
can understand that people, because of different
situations or information, will feel and think
differently, but he is unable to maintain his own
perspective while putting himself in the position
of others, nor judge himself from their viewpoint.
As yet the position of persons as subjects is
unclear.
   Level 2: Self-selective Role-Taking: The child
can now accept and understand that people have
their 'own, uniquely ordered' set of values or
purposes which will make them think and feel differently and he will be able to reflect on his
own behaviour from another's point of view.   He
can also anticipate the others reactions to his
purposes, but these two reflections cannot occur
simultaneously.
   Level 3: Mutual Role-Taking: The child can now
differentiate self's from generalised other's
perspective, he can understand his own dyadic
interaction from a third person's perspective.
He can also understand that both self and other
can understand each party's point of view simultaneously and mutually.
   The picture therefore emerges of a slow process of
decentring, first manifest in speech adjusted to the
needs of the listener (Shatz and Gelman, de Villiers
and de Villiers, Schachter et al.), and in the
simplest forms the ability to understand another's
perspective (Fishbein, Borke).   Chandler and Greenspan
(1972) have in fact queried whether Borke really was
testing egocentricism, although they replicated her
findings.   In an early study Borke (1971) demonstrated
empathetic responses in children.   Young children
under six were able to anticipate the emotional responses in other people.   The obvious problem, so ably
documented by Gage and Cronbach (1955) is of stereotypy

and of establishing a criterion for accuracy in social
judgment.   Are the children truly empathetic or
simply making socially stereotyped responses?   According to Chandler and Greenspan this latter possibility
would disallow the one Borke study being counted as
non-egocentric thought since empathy is not 'simply
a synonym for accurate social judgment but implies
the ability to anticipate what someone else might
think or feel or feel precisely when those thoughts
and feelings are different from one's own' (Chandler
and Greenspan, 1972).   The problem of anticipating
the feelings of others may not yet be developed.
This would be illuminated by studies of guessing games.
    Guessing games are an interesting part of inter-
active play.   Which hand? hiding objects behind simple
obstacles is part of the play experience of most
Western children.   The cognitive demands of the task
are complex in that the child has to take account of
meta-perceptions.   'He hid it there last time, he
thinks I think he won't do that again, and I will
choose the other hand, so he will trick me and leave
it where it is.'   Not only does this reasoning encompass a very difficult double-cross strategy, but it
also assumes that the child understands that the game
is competitive and that it needs secrecy and decep-
tion, and that both players will be using the strategies available.   Devries (1970) reports some studies
in which children of various ability levels and three
age levels (three years to six) took part in a game
of guessing in which hand a penny was hidden, both as
'hiders' and as 'guessers'.   Her results show that
children find it easier to act as hiders than as
guessers - the meta-perceptions of guessing demand
greater skill than the children have.   The specific
lack may well be role-taking skill, but this was not
tested.   What Devries did show was that psychometric
ability was more crucial than age in developing
guessing skills at the lower end of the psychometric
range: at the higher end age is the more crucial
variable.   Therefore, once the pertinent capacity is
present, age brings greater sophistication in one's
role as hider.   This role demands that the child
understands the need to 'keep his own strategy plan
distinct from his function in the role of the hider'
and also encourages the development of the role-taking
skills necessary to understand the other person taking
into account one's own perspective.
    However, at the early stages of development of
social cognitions these skills are not present.   What

sorts of information has the child structured in order
to cope with his interactions with others?   We have
seen that children of four years assume that younger
children are less competent (Shatz and Gelman, 1973)
but beyond this the literature is very sparse on the
preschool child's cognitions of others.

PERSON PERCEPTION IN YOUNG CHILDREN

There are a number of severe difficulties involved in
getting a very young child to tell one about his
social world, not the least of these being the limited
linguistic skills which he possesses.   Asking a child
to describe people in order to elicit his constructs
does not permit the experimenter to be certain whether
he is delving into the child's conceptual capacities
or simply tapping his verbal fluency.   It is perhaps
for this reason that most of the cognitive studies of
the child's percepts of others have started with
school-age children.   Livesley and Bromley (1973)
have provided an excellent summary of the relevant
literature so that there is no need to detail it here.
What it is pertinent to report is that the general
trend of the research supports the sequence detailed
by Bruner (1966) and by Werner (1957):   concepts move
from being global, action-based, unintegrated and
egocentric to being concerned with psychological and
abstract qualities, integrated and articulated into
an hierarchical structure.
   A study (3) we carried out employed a variety of
techniques to elicit the constructs used in descriptions of others given by children aged seven and
eleven.   The children were asked to describe a number
of target people (mother, father, teacher, best friend
and a disliked school mate).   The analysis of the
responses showed a number of trends.   The first
links with the decentration process we have described
earlier.   The younger children when talking about
others do so with reference to themselves.   The
best friend 'gives me things', 'I beat him in running';
the disliked boy is called Nicho - 'we put his head
under a tap and he cried.'   Mothers, fathers and
teachers 'help me, teach me, spank me.'   Only at the
older age are attributes or activities described
without (constant) reference to self.
   Secondly, the nature of the descriptions follows
the sequence Bruner posits for representation: enac-
tive, iconic and symbolic.   The younger children give

responses which are predominantly action-based: what
the other actually *does* is apparently what defines
them.   This may indeed be not only because of the
cognitive limitations of the child, but may be in a
functional sense, the most necessary schema for the
child to develop.   Direct here and now interactions
between people demand that one concentrates on
behaviour, even if momentary, rather than on less
immediate factors.

   Indeed, in analysing the type of perceptual cues
which would be selected in particular sorts of interpersonal situations, Jones and Thibaut (1958) suggest
that in an instrumental interaction directed towards
achieving personal goals the perceiver would have to
make frequent, episodic judgments of the behaviour of
the others involved in the situation to gain information about the success of the venture.

   The older children give mainly descriptive statements, emphasising physical attributes and less often
but quite substantially still, role demands.   There
are an increasing number of attribute-statements,
statements referring to enduring psychological states,
but even by the age of eleven these are not the predominant responses.

   The inaccuracy of judgment and the nature of the
errors children make is documented by Looft (1971) in
a study looking at children's age judgments.   The
age-physical size relationship is evident even to two-
or three-year-old children, but leads them to make
inaccurate judgments when drawings of human figures
of varying size-age relationships are presented,
errors attributable to a figure-size response set.
This is one of the few studies available using pre-
school subjects.

   The classic study of Scarlett, Press and Crockett
(1972) based on a sample of school-aged boys, suggested that the developmental sequence in person perception followed Werner's orthogenetic principle -
namely change occurs by moving from a state of relative globality to a state of differentiation, then to
a state of articulation of the differentiated elements
and to a hierarchical integration of the whole domain.
Bigner (1974) followed with a study of younger children's perception of older siblings, which gives some
insight into the interactive basis on which judgment
might be based.

   In line with cognitive development theory, as described independently by Piaget, Bruner and Werner we
would expect change to occur because of the interaction

between the individual and his world, physical or
social.   Interaction demands the assimilation of
input into existing schema and the accommodation of
schema to discrepant input.   If this operates also
in construing the social world, then the greater the
interaction the more articulated and differentiated
the relevant schema should be.   In studies of cognitive complexity in adults there is some support for
this in that the more familiar domains which are
more articulated and integrated.   Bigner's sibling
study confirms this -

> One would expect, in this regard, that more abstract
> and non-egocentric constructs would be used by
> children who were close in age to their siblings....
> Egocentric-concrete constructs, as used more
> commonly by closely spaced children to describe the
> liked qualities of the older sibling, were dynamic
> in action and positive in content (Bigner, 1974).

The age-related changes that occur, and are well documented, are stimulated both by maturation and by the
nature of the interactions the child experiences.
Shifts in the nature of moral evaluation, of judgments
of kindness (Baldwin and Baldwin, 1970) of understanding the distinction between accident and intention
(King, 1971) are part of the general shift in centration; but the nature of the impetus to change, the
characteristics of the social interactions which
'trouble' the schema and stimulate equilibration
needs yet to be considered.

Earlier I referred to the emphasis given by Piaget
to peer interactions as an agent in encouraging the
development of mature moral judgment.   This interpersonal influence was independently stressed by
G.H. Mead in his analysis of the social origins of
the concept of self.   Research into the role of peer
interaction has examined mainly the role of this
factor in moral development, looking at precocious
development of mature judgment in relation to co-
operative or individual living situations.

What these mainly correlational studies do not show
is what it is in 'social interaction' that is the
critical element, or elements, in stimulating development.   Social interaction involves a great number of
separate skills and inputs, as well as a number of
choices about what are the essential variables demanding attention.   It may well be that the general
maturation of the child's information-processing
abilities, including memory and attention span, are
the prime substrate on which social interaction is

etched, but beyond this, understanding of the nature
of the interaction process is limited.

ROLE PLAYING

One major variable that has been singled out is that
of role playing.   Role-taking ability, which we have
discussed earlier, refers to the cognitive process of
taking into account the needs and demands of others.
Role playing is said to be the adoption, for a short
period, of the duties and behaviours associated with
a social position other than one's own.   Playing at
being someone or something else can obviously be an
individual activity, not demanding the interphasing
of one's own actions with those of others, but under
such circumstances it might be best to refer to
fantasy play rather than role playing.
     Playing roles, learning the duties and responsibil-
ities attaching to particular status and occupational
positions in the society is a traditional vehicle for
the socialisation of the child.   Sex-appropriate
behaviours, economic roles, potentially threatening
situations can all be made familiar to the child
through role play.   In some Eastern European coun-
tries role play is deliberately encouraged and organised in early education in order to ensure smooth
transition of values from one generation to another
and to foster the maintenance of the group.   In our
own society, with its emphasis on individualism, the
playing of roles is less used as a manipulative
technique.
     In 1968 Smilansky observed the behaviour of advan-
taged and disadvantaged Israeli children and concluded
that the disadvantaged lacked the ability to integrate their experiences, to 'articulate' the discrete
elements into a meaningful whole.   Watching free play
she found that a major difference between the two
groups lay in the poor quality and amount of role
play and socio-dramatic play of the disadvantaged
group, which seemed to relate not to the amount of
play material but to the lack of verbal, cognitive
and social skills.   She therefore introduced systematic training in socio-dramatic play, and found that
it produced significant changes in the behaviour of
the disadvantaged children.   Rosen (1974) replicated
the study with disadvantaged North American children.
Using various toys to stimulate role play, and
directly involving herself with play and productive

behaviour, she encouraged and suggested, by deliberate intervention, shifts in the level of free play. The intervention lasted forty days.

The results that Rosen reports lend support to the effectiveness of her interventions in improving the amount of role play and socio-dramatic play in her experimental groups. The experimental groups also showed more effective group productivity on a team-building task, and more efficient problem solving in a task demanding maximum co-operation. Perhaps most interesting for our purposes was the finding that the experimental group increased their role-taking skills as measured on a perspective task and an object preference selection task. In the latter task children are asked to select gifts for another person, or be another person selecting a gift for himself. The changes in role-taking skills are less dramatic than changes in the other skills, though significant at $p < 0.05$.

The problem with both the Smilansky and Rosen studies is that it is difficult to discern exactly which element in the intervention is the critical one. Is the child practising role play and is this the mediating variable producing change, or is it the production of new ideas by the experimenter in the intervention which is crucial - or could one suggest an affective basis for change?

Some answers may be found in the research done at LSE by Ursula Cornish (1975). Using samples of advantaged play-group children, pre-test observations were made of the childrens' free play behaviour. Three manipulations were introduced, each lasting for two weeks, for an hour a day. For one group the play-leader each day introduced a role-play situation. A particular theme was selected each day - hair-dressers, restaurant, doctors, buses - and the children would each take a particular role. The play leader's job was to introduce the theme, ensure that each child was involved and when necessary offer help. In order to ensure that it was not simply the intro-duction of the theme and the encouragement of imagi-native play which could be the stimulus for any change a second manipulation was used. In this children, again for the same time period, sat in a circle while one at a time they talked about a picture representing a scene such as was used in the role-playing manipula-tion. This manipulation differed from the first in leaving out the interphasing of behaviour and the action, but controlled for the stimulation of ideas

and for the encouragement of verbal production.   The
third manipulation was a copying one, movement without
speech, where the leader presented a theme - for
example, cleaning the house - and the children mimed
the appropriate actions (sweeping, dusting) on their
own.   This provided for the action component of the
role-playing manipulation but excluded verbal activity.
The post-test observations showed that both the role-
playing and the story-telling manipulation produced
positive changes in the children's behaviour: more
verbal interaction, more creative play, less random
behaviour.   The role play however had one major advantage - it produced more co-operative behaviour.   The
manipulation of miming had few of these advantages.

Staub (1971) supports the use of role playing in
the induction of social co-operative (pro-social)
behaviour.   He used role playing of both victim and
helper in five situations as one training procedure,
and contrasted it with an induction group, a role
playing plus induction group and a control group
simply enacting scenes without help or role exchange.
He examined kindergarten children in post-test situations - helping a child, helping the experimenter,
candy sharing.   The results showed that girls who
had experienced role playing helped a distressed child
significantly more and boys who had done so shared
candy significantly more than did control subjects.
The effect of role playing is therefore seen to be
non-specific since the scenes played did not include
sharing situations.   These effects appeared to be
relatively persistent.   The induction treatment had
a negligible effect.   What appears to be critical is
the acquisition of some understanding of the role or
perspective of the other from having experienced a
similar role, or the capacity to generalise from one
interactive learning situation to another.

Certainly all of these behavioural studies support
strongly the opinion that preschool children can
understand the process of role playing, of filling a
social role other than their normal one, and that
this seems to act as a catalyst in developing the
skills necessary for cognitive role-taking tasks.
The interactionist approach, seeing behaviour with and
in the world as the foundation for cognitive growth,
gains support.

PRO-SOCIAL BEHAVIOUR

And yet all developmental social psychology is not
simply a hymn of praise to the cognitive theorists.
The tradition of social learning theory as the foundation on which a sound study of socialisation is
based, has not shrivelled and wilted before the in-
vading forces of genetic epistemology.   Indeed, one
of the major problems confronting the developmental
social psychologist, as with social psychology as a
whole, is that of accurately predicting behaviour.
Can we, once we know how the child classifies, constructs and cognises the social world, really predict
how he will behave?   The answer does not ring out
clearly as an affirmation.   Just as attitude
measures do not of and by themselves enable one to
predict behaviour so we are unable to anticipate
social behaviour from social cognitions.   We may be
examining two distinct domains, neither of which is
truly explicable in terms of the others.   Cognitions
may predict other types of cognitive response (role-
taking tasks relate to moral evaluation;   conserving
volume suggests the conservation of number) and
behaviours relate to other behaviour, but do relationships across domains remain chance and unpredictable?
If this is really the case then more than one theory
may well be necessary to explain social development.

Cognitive developmental theory, with its concern
for epistemological issues, for understanding internal (mental) structures with its interactionist
emphasis, may be exactly the approach for studying
social concepts, but not at all relevant to social
behaviours - from attachment, through social control,
influence, co-operation, conflict, helping, sharing
or fighting.   (And where is our taxonomy of
behaviour?)   For these a theoretical approach relying
on observable behaviour, on the formation of habits,
of specifying cueing conditions and antecedent associations (such as is encompassed in social learning
theory) may well be more appropriate.   Although per-
sonally not welcoming the theoretical split, there
are some grounds for questioning the fit between the
behavioural and the cognitive domains and the general
applicability of cognitive developmental theory.

The area of helping, sharing and generosity,
stimulated by the studies of Latané and Darley with
adults is one of considerable interest both to social
and to developmental psychologists.   What makes it
interesting is that it is possible to examine, through

studies of pro-social behaviour, the relative contribution of social learning and cognitive developmental theories to the understanding of social behaviours. Similar, well-documented tests can be found in attachment theory where psychoanalytic and social learning theories both offered explanations, and in the field of conscience development, where three theoretical orientations each offer explanations of separate, perhaps related aspects of the total problem.   Psychoanalytic theory can account for feelings on transgression of rules, social learning theory focuses on what the child actually does in particular critical situations, and cognitive developmentalists are interested in the judgments, the evaluations, of action.   One is reminded of the three aspects of attitude: conative, affective and behavioural.

Studies at LSE by Rushton and Wiener (1975) and Emler and Rushton (1974) examined in some detail the relationship between cognitive factors and pro-social behaviour in middle-childhood.   Emler and Rushton tested the relationship of role taking, moral judgment and generosity on a sample of seven- to thirteen-year-olds.   They based their study on the hypothesis that generosity is based on sympathy, which requires the capacity to take the role of the other.   They found age-related trends in all tasks, but whereas the two role-taking tasks were significantly related to each other, only one was related to moral judgment, that being a guessing task similar to but more complex than that used by Devries and described earlier.   A task based on telling a story to another on the basis of pictures the other cannot see, did not relate to moral judgment.   However, moral judgment was related to generosity.   This latter was tested as follows: the children individually played at a bowling game and could win tokens.   Alongside the tokens was a bowl and a 'Save the Children Fund' poster of a hungry child.   The experimenter told the child that he could donate tokens for charity if he so wished.   What the Emler and Rushton study could not show, was a relationship between role-taking skills and generosity: in this experiment how much the child gave to charity could not be determined by knowing how well he could take the role of the other.

Rushton and Emler's result is in contradiction to that of Rubin and Schneider (1973) who specifically tested for the relationship between egocentricity, moral judgment and altruistic behaviour.   They argue that the ability to decentre is necessary for the

recognition of the need for help, and that helping
others would relate to the understanding of reciprocal
relationships.   Their results are consistent with
this.   They found a positive and significant correlation between decentration skills, moral judgment
and altruism: but when mental age was partialled out
(all the children were seven years old) the correlation between decentration and helping behaviour was
significantly greater than decentration and generosity.   Although Rubin and Schneider suggest that it
is the ability to decentre which is critical to both
the moral judgment and to the pro-social behaviour, a
correlational study really cannot give one this information.   All one can say is that the relationship
exists, one cannot determine its direction.

A second study by Rushton and Wiener suggests that
the relationship which Rubin found may not be a
direct one, but one mediated by general development
rather than by the specific force of decentration
which enables the child to take the role of the
other.   Using a sample of seven- and eleven-year-olds,
the children were given two role-taking tasks adapted
from Flavell et al. (1968), a conservation task, two
tests of person perception (photo-grouping;   repertory
grid test) and three social behaviour measures (generosity to a charity, to a friend and a test of compet-
itiveness).   The results show significant relationships between the behavioural measures;   to a lesser
extent the cognitive measures bear some relationship
to each other.   But there is very little interaction
between the two sorts of measures.   Rushton believes
that this throws doubt on the idea of a stage process
of development, particularly as an explanation of
social behaviour.

There is evidence to suggest that principles of
social learning may be a better basis for predicting
pro-social behaviour than cognitive development alone.
Modelling cues, with the experimenter or confederate
donating money, or helping, appear to be more powerful
determinants of generosity than cognitively directed
verbal exhortation (Bryan and Welbeck, 1970) and
Yarrow et al. (1973) showed that preschool children
could be taught altruistic behaviour (both helping
and verbal sympathy) by modelling.   The stimulus-
response thesis receives greater support in a study
showing that subjects pull a lever resulting in
delivery of money to a 'charity' box more frequently
than to a neutral one.   Other studies bear witness to
the fact that children can be encouraged in generous

and helpful behaviour by imitation rather than by preaching.   That imitation is a powerful source of source of social responses is not under debate. There is much research in all fields of self-control, aggression, fear reduction, to ensure the role of imitation as an important process in social learning. What is worth considering however is whether social learning or imitation explanations, linked as they are to learning theories and to socialisation, are alternative to cognitive explanations, or whether they can be integrated to give a more comprehensive view of social development.

Piaget in his discussion of functional invariants in cognition refers to two major activities - assimilation and accommodation.   These have been referred to earlier and need no further exposition here.   The relevance at the moment is in the way which Piaget views imitation - as a pure case of accommodation. This implies that before any action can be copied there should be available a schema which is sufficiently close to the model's responses to allow the child to adjust to it.   Observation of speech imitation shows that until the child has at least the pre-structure necessary for a particular grammatical form he will not produce an accurate copy (see Szagun, 1976).   Nor does the child playing at roles produce an exact replica of the adult activity: his level of physical maturity and skill and the level of his cognitive operations are too immature to permit identity of product.   But the imitation is there. The model in studies of pro-social behaviour makes particular responses and environmental cues salient, enables the child to adjust to them and accommodate relevant schema where possible: unless however the child has the cognitive skills to integrate the experience into his conceptual system they may well remain situation specific.

Some support for this view can be drawn from the combination of two sources: firstly, the work by Piaget and Inhelder on memory supported by later studies by Furth et al. (1974) and by Liben (in press). These researches showed that contrary to expectation, children's memory as tested by reproduction of a previously performed drawing task, actually improved over time.   The explanation was related to the general improvement through the development of relevant operations, of the skills involved in the reproductive task between the original exposure and later retest.

The second element is to be found in a result reported by Rushton on the effect of model's preaching on pro-social responses.   To suggest that the effectiveness of modelling denies the importance of cognition, demands more than a test immediately following exposure.   This indicates no more than conformity, not operativity.   Rushton therefore tested for delayed effect (two-month retest) and for generality. The results of his study showed no immediate effect of preaching on generosity, but after two months preaching had a highly significant overall effect on the number of tokens donated to a charity.

This effect is similar to the 'sleeper effect' in attitude change;   the impact of new information is not immediate but almost seems to need time to be 'filtered' through the cognitive structure;   the structure needs to be accommodated to the input. Some sort of assessment process may need to take place which demands a fairly long time to make itself evident.   Or alternatively, relating back to the memory studies, the general process of development which occurs between the test and retest allows the manipulation to be assimilated to new structures and thereby achieve meaning and impact.

There is, in infant research at least, a growing body of evidence allowing one to doubt the unfettered power of learning.   Simple conditioned responses seem to need a 'ready' modality for effectiveness and there is evidence of the need for cerebral integration and organisation before conditioning can occur (Millar, 1974).   Sameroff (1971) has implied the need for cognitive schema corresponding to the conditioned stimulus before successful conditioning can occur. The dichotomy between cognitive-developmental theories and social learning theories is brought into doubt. It is tempting to argue by extension that the more complex social situations examined in studies of pro-social behaviour, would also benefit from an explanatory system utilising the insights from a variety of theories.   The behaviour observed would therefore be seen to be the result of the child's interpretation of the demands of the situation and the behaviours which he is able to exhibit.   The interpretation would depend on the stage of cognitive development reached; on the environmental events, both physical and social, that can be assimilated to the schema;   on the cues employed to establish the salience of events, be these cues repetition (as in memory), or adult action (as in modelling), or the observation of consequences of

action; on the behaviours actually within the repertoire of the child.   This would demand a more comprehensive view of child behaviour: one which would
without hesitation imply the involvement of social
psychological insights and analyses.

RETROSPECT AND PROSPECT

This paper has ranged widely over the recent approaches
to the child's social development, reporting on a
number of related researches which seem to reflect in
varying ways concern for the factors which underlie
the child's increasing skill and sophistication in
social interaction and judgment.   Possibly because
of the ebullience and enthusiasm marking developmental
research these studies have not drawn much on traditional social psychological theory and data, except
in the recognition of the seminal influence of Mead
which has a ritual mention in most introductory para-
graphs to research reports.
      There is one exception to this, a paper which
marries the two fields of psychology through the work
of Piaget and Asch.   Feffer (1970) finds a comple-
mentarity between Piaget's 'genetic emphasis on
impersonal content' and Asch's genetic concern for
the interpersonal.   As a Gestaltist Asch shares with
Piaget a belief in the organised and structured nature
of knowing the world, although they part in Piaget's
espousal of a dialectic view of the relationship
between the organism and the environment in which
the relationship between subject and object changes
as a function of interchange from one equilibrium to
another.   These varying equilibria are the basis of
the stages of cognitive development.   For the
Gestalt school however, the nature of organisation
would be the same across time and across contents:
for Piaget

> The object is known, that is has meaning, only by
> virtue of being organised by a particular schema
> and if at the same time this schema changes as a
> function of the peculiar nature of the object
> being assimilated, then the meaning also changes
> by virtue of the fact that the basis for knowing
> the object has changed (Feffer, 1970).

The equilibration model accounts for change in terms
of the resolution of contradictions inherent in
primitive or unstable forms of organisation.
      Feffer characterises the approach of Asch as

essentially differing from Piaget in that Asch structures the relationship of individual to group as a
part-whole relationship isomorphic to Piaget's advanced
cognitive operation.   Asch suggests

a reciprocal relationship exists between individual
and group namely that on the one hand there is a
unique quality of individual cognition that gives
rise to groups at the human level, and on the
other, that group conditions transform the cognitive nature of the individual into that which is
truly human (Feffer, 1970).

The problem to be answered becomes how do the thoughts
and motives of one become known to another so that
social interaction can occur.   For Asch, the answer
lies in Gestalt principles: isomorphism of experience
and action, organisation of percepts in terms of
similarity and proximity and in terms of a part-whole
relationship in which one has more than simply the
addition of elements.   It draws him to the conclusion
that the individual is the seat of social events: the
transcendence of one's own viewpoint to bring it into
line with the other occurs in the individual.   Feffer
quotes Asch:

The paramount fact about social interaction is that
the participants ... turn towards each other, that
their acts interpenetrate and therefore regulate
each other.

If this analysis is correct then the problems posed
by both Piaget and Asch are surprisingly similar and
the answers found would resolve some major problems
in social psychology.   The conflict between the
individual and the mutual experience as foci for explanation goes back to the early days of psychology,
to ideas of the transcendental Group Mind as opposed
to the observable individual group members.   For
Feffer there are three points of correspondence
between Asch and Piaget.   Firstly, they share the
idea of structuring reality in the form of complemen-
tary polarities.   Secondly, for both the stability
of cognitive organisation lies in the reciprocal
balance between the polarities, and finally for both
reciprocal modification or conservation is achieved
in terms of a particular part-whole organisation in
which the whole is represented in part.   The task,
then, of a developmental social psychology would be
the elucidation of these structures by charting change
and relating this to the nature of the polarities
which balance each other.

We have reported attempts to illuminate these

issues, attempts which have conceived of the process as one of achieving a balance between self and other, the interphasing of behaviour and the development of mutuality of perspective finally manifest in empathic responses.   Much progress has been made in that direction in understanding the process of decentration as reflected in speech, perception of the other, role taking, moral judgment and pro-social behaviour. Only in morality and person perception have the studies focused as assiduously on content as they have on structure and it is perhaps for this reason that these two areas are most easily integrated into the main body of social psychology.   Without the content to fill out the structure the relationship between early and mature behaviour and cognition is impossible to elucidate.

One is still left, however, with a feeling that only a small part of the world of childhood is being scrutinised.   Even referring to the growing number of observational studies of preschool play behaviour does not dissipate a sense of narrowness in our perspectives.   Childhood is a time of intense social living not explicable in the bloodless studies of the influence of the peer group.   These studies oppose the individual and the group;   they do not reflect the mutuality and equilibrium at which both Asch and Piaget hint.   Social living is itself structured;   its parts are co-ordinated in complex relationships which give meaning and form to the whole. There are polarities in the systems and these need to be reconciled in order to achieve a cognitively stable view of the self in society.   Without this our understanding of social psychology will for ever remain at the level of the individual *and* the group. We will not achieve the understanding which will enable us to represent and examine the fact that the individual is the group as it is he.   Perhaps it is through a developmental social psychology that we will be able to focus on what Tajfel (1972) has suggested as the main point of departure for social psychology:

> The social setting of intergroup relations contributes to making the individuals what they are and they in turn produce this social setting: they and it develop and change symbiotically (Tajfel, 1972, p. 90).

Piaget's theories, if they do nothing else, emphasise this symbiosis and provide a framework for examining it within the individual, within the group, now and over time.

NOTES

1 The research was carried out with Judy Cooper and
   the coding of behaviour is being done together
   with Aubrey Baillie.
2 That is 'the cognizer sees the world from a simple
   point of view only - his own - but without knowledge of the existence of viewpoints or perspectives and, *a fortiori*, without awareness that he
   is the prisoner of his own' (Flavell, op. cit.).
3 The study was carried out in conjunction with
   Janet Wiener and Marie Blampied, as part of their
   Master's programme at the London School of
   Economics.

REFERENCES

AINSWORTH, M.D.S. (1967), 'Infancy in Uganda: Infant
Care and the Growth of Love', Baltimore: Johns Hopkins
University Press.
AINSWORTH, M.D.S. (1973), The Development of Infant-
mother Attachment, in B.M. Caldwell and H.N. Ricciuti
(eds), 'Review of Child Development Research', vol. 3,
Chicago: University of Chicago Press.
BALDWIN, C.P. and BALDWIN, A.L. (1970), Children's
Judgements of Kindness, 'Child Development', vol. 41,
pp. 29-48.
BERNSTEIN, B.B. and HENDERSON, D. (1969), Social Class
Differences in the Relevance of Language to Socialisa-
tion, 'Sociol.', vol. 3, pp. 1-20.
BIGNER, J.J. (1974), A Wernerian Developmental Analy-
sis of Children's Descriptions of Siblings, 'Child
Devel.', vol. 45, pp. 317-23.
BORKE, H. (1971), Interpersonal Perception of Young
Children: Egocentrism or Empathy, 'Devel. Psychol.',
vol. 5, pp. 263-9.
BORKE, H. (1972). Chandler and Greenspan's 'Ersatz
Egocentrism': a rejoinder, 'Devel. Psychol.',vol. 7,
pp. 107-9.
BORKE, H. (1975), Piaget's Mountains Revisited: changes
in the egocentric landscape, 'Devel. Psychol.', vol. 11,
pp. 240-3.
BOWLBY, J. (1969), 'Attachment and Loss', vol. 1
'Attachment', London: Hogarth Press.
BRUNER, J. (1966), On Cognitive Growth: I & II, in J.
Bruner, R.R. Olver and P.M. Greenfield, 'Studies in
Cognitive Growth', New York: John Wiley.
BRYAN, J.H. and WELBECK, N.H. (1973), The Relationship

between Moral Judgement, Egocentricism and Altruistic Behaviour, 'Child Devel.', vol. 44, pp. 661-5.

CHANDLER, M.J. and GREENSPAN, M. (1972), Ersatz Egocentricism: a reply to H. Borke, 'Devel. Psychol.', vol. 7, pp. 104-6.

CHANDLER, J.J., GREENSPAN, M. and BARENBOIM, C. (1973), Judgements of Intentionality in Response to Video-taped and Verbally Presented Moral Dilemmas, 'Child Devel.', vol. 44, pp. 315-20.

CORNISH, U. (1975), The Influence of Role-Play on the Social Behaviour of Pre-school Children, unpublished research, London School of Economics.

DEVRIES, R. (1970), The Development of Role-taking as Reflected by Behaviour of Bright, Average and Retarded Children in a Social Guessing Game, 'Child Devel.', vol. 41, pp. 759-70.

EMLER, N. and RUSHTON, J.P. (1974), Cognitive Developmental Factors in Children's Generosity, 'Brit. J. Soc. Clin. Psychol.', vol. 13, pp. 277-81.

FEATHER, N.T. (1971), Organisation and Discrepancy in Cognitive Structures, 'Psychol. Rev.', vol. 78, pp. 355-79.

FEFFER, M.H. (1970), Developmental Analysis of Interpersonal Behaviour, 'Psychol. Rev.', vol. 77, pp. 197-214.

FEFFER, M.H. and GOUREVITCH, V. (1960), Cognitive Aspects of Role-taking in Children, 'J. of Pers.', vol. 28, pp. 383-96.

FISHBEIN, H., LEWIS, S. and KEIFFER, K. (1972), Children's Understanding of Spatial Relations: co-ordination of perspectives, 'Devel. Psychol.', vol. 7, pp. 21-33.

FLAVELL, J. (1963), 'The Developmental Theory of Jean Piaget', D. van Nostrand.

FLAVELL, J.H., BOTKIN, R.T., FRY, C.L., WRIGHT, J.W. and JARVIS, P.E. (1968), 'The Development of Role-Taking and Communication Skills in Children', New York: Wiley.

FOUTS, G.T. (1972), Charity in Children: the influence of 'charity' stimuli and an audience, 'J. of Exp. Child Psychol.', vol. 13, pp. 303-9.

FURTH, H., ROSS, B. and YOUNISS, J. (1974), Operative Understanding in Reproductions of Drawings, 'Child Devel.', vol. 45, pp. 63-70.

GAGE, N.L. and CRONBACH, L.J. (1955), Conceptual and Methodological Problems in Interpersonal Perception, 'Psychol. Rev.', vol. 62, pp. 411-22.

GARVEY, C. and HOGAN, R. (1973), Social Speech and Social Interaction: egocentricism revisited, 'Child Devel.', vol. 44, pp. 562-8.

GOFFMAN, E. (1969), 'The Presentation of Self in Everyday
Life', London: Allen Lane.
HARRÉ, R. (1974), The Conditions for a Social Psychology
of Childhood, in M. Richards (ed.), 'The Integration of
the Child into a Social World', Cambridge University
Press.
HESS, R.D. and SHIPMAN, V.C. (1967), Cognitive Elements
in Maternal Behaviour, in J.P. Hill (ed.), 'Minnesota
Symposium on Child Psychology', vol. 1, University of
Minnesota Press.
HOLLOS, M. and COWAN, P.A. (1973), Social Isolation and
Cognitive Development Logical Operations and Role-
taking Abilities in Three Norwegian Social Settings,
'Child Devel.', vol. 44, pp. 630-41.
KING, M. (1971), The Development of Some Intentional
Concepts in Young Children, 'Child Devel.', vol. 42,
pp. 1145-52.
KOHLBERG, L. (1963), Moral Development and Identifi-
cation, in H.W. Stevenson (ed.), 'Child Psychology',
62nd Year Book of the National Society for the Study
of Education, University of Chicago Press.
LIBEN, L.S., Evidence for Developmental Differences in
Spontaneous Seriation and its Implications for Past
Research on Long-term Memory Improvement, 'Devel.
Psychol.' (in press).
LIVESLEY, W.J. and BROMLEY, D. (1973), 'Person Percep-
tion in Childhood and Adolescence', New York: Wiley.
LOOFT, W.R. (1971), Children's Judgements of Age,
'Child Devel.', vol. 42, pp. 1282-4.
LOOFT, W.R. (1972), Egocentricism and Social Inter-
action across the Life-Span, 'Psychol. Bulletin', vol.
78, pp. 73-92.
MASANGKAY, Z.S., McCLUSKEY, K.A., McINTYRE, C.W.,
SIMS-KNIGHT, J., VAUGHAN, B. and FLAVELL, J.H. (1974),
The Early Development of Inferences about the Visual
Percepts of Others, 'Child Devel.', vol. 45, pp. 357-66.
MEAD, G.H. (1934), 'Mind, Self and Society', Univer-
sity of Chicago Press.
MILLAR, W. Stuart (1974), Conditioning and Learning in
Early Infancy, in B. Foss (ed.), 'New Perspectives in
Child Development', Harmondsworth: Penguin Books.
OPIE, P. and OPIE, I. (1959), 'The Lore and Language
of Childhood', Oxford University Press.
PIAGET, J. (1932), 'The Moral Judgement of the Child',
London: Kegan Paul.
PIAGET, J. (1952), 'Origins of Intelligence in Chil-
dren', International Universities.
PIAGET, J. (1970), Piaget's Theory, in P. Mussen (ed.),
'Carmichael's Manual of Child Psychology', vol. 1, New
York: Wiley.

PIAGET, J. and INHELDER, B. (1968), 'Memoire et
Intelligence', Paris: Presses Universitaires de France.
ROBINSON, W.P. and RACKSTRAW, S.J. (1967), Variations
in Mother's Answers to Children's Questions, 'Sociol.',
vol. 1, pp. 259-79.
ROSEN, C.E. (1974), The Effects of Sociodramatic Play
on Problem-solving Behaviour among Culturally Disadvantaged Pre-school Children, 'Child Devel.', vol. 45,
pp. 920-7.
RUBIN, K. (1973), Egocentricism in Children: a unitary
concept?, 'Child Devel.', vol. 44, pp. 102-10.
RUBIN, K. (1974), The Relationship between Spatial and
Communicative Egocentricism in Children and Young and
Old Adults, 'J. of Genetic Psychol.', vol. 125, pp.
295-301.
RUBIN, K. and MAIONI, T.L. (1975), Play Preference and
its Relationship to Egocentricism, Popularity and Class-
ification Skills in Pre-schoolers, 'Merrill-Palmer
Quarterly', vol. 21, pp. 171-9.
RUBIN, K. and SCHNEIDER, S.W. (1972), The Relationships
between Moral Judgment Egocentrism and Altruistic
Behaviour, 'Child Dev.', vol. 44, pp. 661-6.
RUSHTON, J.P. (1973), Social Learning and Cognitive
Development: Alternative approaches to an understanding
of generosity in 7 to 11 year olds, unpublished Ph.D.
thesis, University of London.
RUSHTON, J.P. and WIENER, J. (1975), Altruism and Cog-
nitive Development in Children, 'Brit. J. Soc. Clin.
Psychol.', vol. 14, pp. 341-50.
SAMEROFF, A.J. (1971), Can Conditioned Responses be
Established in the New-born Infant?, 'Devel. Psychol.',
vol. 5, pp. 1-12.
SCARLETT, H.H., PRESS, A.N. and CROCKETT, W.H. (1971),
Children's Descriptions of Peers: a Wernerian develop-
mental analysis, 'Child Devel.', vol. 42, pp. 439-54.
SCHACHTER, F.F., SCHACHTER, J.S., KIRSCHNER, K.,
KLIPS, B., FREDERICKS, M. and SANDERS, K. (1974),
'Everyday Pre-school Interpersonal Speech Usage: meth-
odological, developmental and sociolinguistic studies',
'Monogr. Soc. Res. Child Devel.', vol. 39, no. 3.
SCHAFFER, H.R. (1971), 'The Growth of Sociability',
Harmondsworth: Penguin Books.
SCHAFFER, H.R. and EMERSON, P.E. (1964), 'The Develop-
ment of Social Attachments in Infancy', 'Monogr. Soc.
Res. Child Devel.', vol. 29, no. 3.
SELMAN, R. (1971), The Relation of Role-taking to the
Development of Moral Judgement in Children, 'Child
Devel.', vol. 42, pp. 79-91.
SELMAN, R. and BYRNE, D.F. (1974), A Structural Develop-

mental Analysis of Levels of Role-taking in Middle Child-
hood, 'Child Devel.', vol. 45, pp. 803-6.
SHATZ, M. and GELMAN, R. (1973), 'The Development of
Communication Skills: modification in the speech of
young children as a function of listener', 'Monogr.
Soc. Res. Child Devel.', vol. 38, no. 5.
SMILANSKY, S. (1968), 'The Effects of Sociodramatic
Play on Disadvantaged Pre-school Children', New York:
Wiley.
STAUB, E. (1971), The Use of Role Playing and Induction
in Children's Learning of Helping and Sharing Behaviour,
'Child Devel.', vol. 42, pp. 805-16.
SZAGUN, G. (1976), The Development of Tense and Aspect
in Young English and German Children, unpublished PhD
thesis, University of London.
TAJFEL, H. (1972), Experiments in a Vacuum, in J.
Israel and H. Tajfel, 'The Context of Social Psychology:
A Critical Assessment', Academic Press.
VILLIERS, P.A. de and VILLIERS, J.S. de (1974), On This,
That and the Other: non-egocentricism in very young
children, 'J. Exp. Child Psychol.', vol. 18, pp. 438-47.
WERNER, H. (1957), The Concept of Development from a
Comparative and Organismic Point of View, in D.B.
Harris (ed.), 'The Concept of Development', University
of Minnesota Press.
WOOD, D., BRUNER, J.S. and ROSS, G. (1974), The Role of
Tutoring in Problem Solving, in J. Mehler (ed.), 'Hand-
book of Developmental Cognitive Psychology', forth-
coming.
WOOD, D. and MIDDLETON, D. (1975), A Study of Assisted
Problem Solving, 'Brit. J. of Psychol.', vol. 66, pp.
181-91.
YARROW, M.R., SCOTT, P.M. and WAXLER, C.Z. (1973),
Learning Concern for Others, 'Devel. Psychol.', vol. 8,
pp. 240-60.

INDEX

accommodation, 5-6, 27, 29-
31, 33-5, 69-70, 209, 240
adaptation, 29-33, 39, 42,
168, 225
adolescence, 121-3, 132,
222, 224
Ainsworth, M.D.S., 211
alignment displacement
effect, 164-5
altruism, 236, 238-9, 241
Ambrose, A., 211
Ames, L.B., 87
Andriessen, J.J., 159, 162
anticipation, 27-8, 31, 39,
140, 141, 144
Apostel, L., 134
'Archives de Psychologie',
136, 148
Ariès, Philippe, 10
Asch, S.E., 242-3
assimilation, 5-6, 27, 30-1,
68-9, 209
association, 58, 80, 147,
168
Atkinson, J.W., 8
attachment, 211, 237
attitude, 209, 237, 241
attribution, 210

Baldwin, C.P. and A.L., 233
behaviourism, 55
Bellugi, U., 86, 189, 193
Bernstein, Basil B. and
Henderson, D., 213

Bertalanffy, L. von, 3
Bever, T.G., 193
Bigner, J.J., 232-3
biological aspects, 3, 22,
25, 27-8, 31-2, 42, 45,
55-6, 71
Bloom, L., 182-3, 186-7,
201, 203
Boesch, E., 136
Borke, H., 227-30
Bouma, H. and Andriessen,
J.J., 159, 162
Bovet, M., 94
Bowerman, M.F., 182, 191
Bowlby, John, 211
Bracewell, R.J. and Hidi,
S.E., 131
Braine, M., 179
Brentano, F., 165
Brimer, M.A. and Dunn, L.M.,
86
Bromley, D., 231
Brown, R., 86, 180, 183-4,
187, 190-2, 193, 194,
198; and Fraser, C.,
179, 180; and Hanlon,
C., 180-1, 191, 198; et
al., 189, 193
Brown, S., 162, 166
Bruner, J.S., 10, 122, 213,
231-2
Brunswik, E., 143
Bryan, J.H. and Wellbeck,
N.H., 239

Bryant, P.E. and Trabasso, T., 61, 77-8
Burt, Cyril, 54, 121-2, 132
Byrne, D.F., 228

Carmichael, L., 82
causality, 17-18, 20, 21, 32-4, 45-7, 140, 144
Cazden, C., 184, 189, 193
centration/decentration, 51, 137-40, 142, 143-4, 146, 148, 152-4, 156-8, 160, 168-9, 178, 187, 200-2, 204, 222-9, 231, 238-9, 244
Chandler, M.J. and Greenspan, M., 229-30; et al., 226
Chiang, C., 166
children: games and rhymes, 220-1; perception of others, 178, 212, 222-32, 234, 236, 238-9, 244; social environment, 211-13, 219-21, 223, 244
Chomsky, C., 180-1, 192, 198
Chomsky, Noam, 170, 177, 180
Clarke, Anne, 119
class-inclusion, 85, 94, 120
classification, 24-6, 51, 66, 85, 106, 109, 224, 237
cognition, 1-2, 4-6, 10, 27-32, 99, 177; development, 68, 94, 177, 208, 210, 222, 224, 226, 232, 237-8, 241-2; and language acquisition, 7, 177, 179, 183, 186-94, 198-204
Cole, M., et al., 56
combinatorial analysis, 121-2, 125
combiners, 65-6
communication, 177, 223-8
commutativity, 70-1
conservation, 32, 33, 43, 45, 51, 70, 85, 94, 106,

143, 146, 188, 194-5, 211, 212, 224, 228, 237, 239, 243
'content', 23-6, 41
Cornish, Ursula, 235
Cowan, P.A., 224
Crichton Vocabulary Scale, 86, 104, 109
'criterion', 23-8, 41
Crockett, W.H., 232
Cromer, R.F., 86, 187
Cronbach, L.J., 229
Curthoys, I., 159, 162

Darley, F.L., 237
Davey, M., 130-1
Day, R.H., 164; and Dickinson, R.G., 159, 161, 162, 166
De Boysson-Bardies, B. and O'Regan, K., 61
décalage, 134, 228
deep structure (transformational grammar), 86, 109, 128, 180, 193, 194, 201
definitions, 21, 40, 46-7
Delboeuf illusion, 136-7, 148-9, 153, 155
Delcourt, M.-J., 166
development, 7-10, 25, 178, 213, 222; mental, see intelligence, development
Devries, R., 230
Dickinson, R.G., 159, 161, 162, 166
Dolan, T., 85
Dollard, J., 211
Dunn, L.M., 86

educational implications, 4, 83, 104, 106, 112, 119
egocentricity, 42, 138-9, 144-5, 178, 187, 222-3, 225-9, 238
Emler, N. and Rushton, J.P., 238

empathy, 225, 229-30, 244
empiricism, 15, 16-20, 26,
    28, 31-2, 34-5, 37, 39,
    41-2, 45, 70, 147, 167
'encounters', 138, 156-8
English Picture Vocabulary
    Test (EPVT), 86, 109, 228
environment, 4, 29-30, 36-7,
    51; social, 7, 211-13,
    219-21, 223, 244
environmentalism, 8-9
epistemology, 2, 6, 15, 147-
    8, 167; genetic, 22, 28,
    119, 237
equilibration, 5, 22-7, 30,
    32-4, 37, 39-43, 45-6,
    102, 119, 122, 209, 233,
    242, 244
error of the standard, 138,
    158
Ervin, W.R., 179, 182
Evans, Jonathan, 124
experiments described
    Bryant and Martin: col-
    oured sticks (inference
    without recourse to end-
    points), 62
    Bryant and Trabasso:
    coloured sticks (infer-
    ence), 61-2, 77
    Cole et al.: Kendlers'
    test replicated on Lib-
    erian adults, 56-7
    Cornish: role playing
    (effect on pro-social
    behaviour), 235-6
    Furth and Milgram:
    labelled pictures (mem-
    ory with labelling), 76-7
    Furth et al.: stick fig-
    ures (apparent inference
    really figurative), 78-80
    Furth et al.: tilted
    half-filled glasses (mem-
    ory), 72-6
    Geber et al.: Etch-a-
    sketch, Lego (mother-
    child interaction), 214-
    19

Hewson: objects in
    drawers (inference), 57
Johnson-Laird et al.:
    sealed/unsealed enve-
    lopes with 4d/5d stamps
    (inference), 130-1
Kendlers: steel marble
    selection (inference),
    55-6, 57
Lunzer: measures of cog-
    nitive performance (sys-
    tematisation of think-
    ing), 82-112
Piaget: tilted half-
    filled glasses (memory),
    72
Piaget: towers of
    bricks (inference), 59-60
Somerville: girl/boy/
    animals location (spa-
    tial inference), 58
Szagun: English/German
    verb forms (use of tenses
    and cognitive develop-
    ment), 194-205
Van Duyne: inscribed
    envelopes (inference with
    realistic guise), 131-2
Wason: blue/red circles/
    triangles (inference),
    125-7
Wason: four-card problem
    (inference), 123-5
Wason and Golding: N+L-
    cards (inference), 128-30
external world, see reality,
    external

facts, 19-20, 26-7, 33-4,
    37, 42, 45, 67-8
Falconer, W.A., 131
falsification/verification,
    124, 128-9, 132
Feather, N.T., 209
feedback/feed out (FB/FO),
    27-8, 31, 33-5, 37, 39,
    43, 45-6, 71
Feffer, M.H., 227, 242-3

field effects, 141-3, 145
figurative knowledge, 5-6,
    52, 65-72, 75-8, 80
Fishbein, H. et al., 226-9
Flavell, J.H., 209, 228;
    et al., 87, 112, 223-5,
    239
Fodor, J.A. et al., 189
Fraisse, P., 199
Fraser, C., 179, 180;   et
    al., 86
Freud, Anna, 211
Freud, Sigmund, 44, 119
Furth, H.G., 119;   and Mil-
    gram, N.A., 77;   et al.,
    72, 240

Gage, N.L. and Cronbach,
    L.J., 229
Galanter, E., 101
Galileo, 17, 28, 35, 46
Garvey, C. and Hogan, R.,
    225
Gay, J., 56
Gelman, R., 225, 229, 231
Gestalt psychology, 136,
    141-3, 147-8, 167, 242-3
Gewirtz, J.L., 211
Gilhooly, K.J. and Falconer,
    W.A., 131
Gillam, B., 166
Glass, L., 166
Glick, J.A., 56
Goffman, E., 210
Golding, E., 128-9;   et al.,
    130
Goldstein, M.B. and Wein-
    traub, D.J., 159, 166
'good' figures, 141, 143
Gough, H. et al., 166
grammar, 86, 109, 170, 177,
    179-81, 186, 187, 190-2,
    194, 202, 204
Green, R.T. and Hoyle, E.M.,
    165
Greenspan, M., 229-30
groups and individuals, 7,
    9, 26, 235, 243, 244

guessing games, 230, 238

Halford, G.S., 83, 132
Hanlon, C., 180-1, 191, 198
Harré, R., 210, 220
Harris, J., 159, 162
Harrison, C., 130-1
health, mental, 19-20, 27
Henderson, D., 213
Hess, R.D. and Shipman,
    V.C., 213, 214
Hewson, Simon, 57
Hidi, S.E., 131
Hobbes, Thomas, 10
Hogan, R., 225
Hollos, M. and Cowan, P.A.,
    224
Hotopf, W.H.N.:   and Oller-
    earnshaw, C., 161-2,
    164;   and Robertson, S.,
    162-3;   et al., 162, 166
Hoyle, E.M., 165
Hume, David, 147

identification, 23, 67-8
identity, 22, 35-7, 40-2
Ilg, F.L. and Ames, L.B.,
    87
illusions, visual, see
    visual illusions
images, 167-8;   labelling,
    77, 87;   mental, 70, 72,
    117
imitation, 68-70, 75, 239-
    41
induction, 155
inferences, 26, 54-8, 66-7,
    80, 130, 146;   spatial,
    58-9;   transitive, see
    transitivity
Inhelder, B., 6, 72, 85,
    87, 94, 120-3, 130, 227,
    240;   et al., 94
intelligence, 4-5, 45;
    development, 2, 15, 22-
    4, 30, 51, 187, 208, 211;
    and perception, 117-18,

138, 145-8, 166-70;
tests, 87-8
interaction, social, 177,
208-13, 219, 223-4, 232-
4, 236, 237, 242-3
intersection of classes, 85,
99-103

Jacobs, R.A. and Rosenbaum,
P.S., 192
Johnson-Laird, P.N., 124;
et al., 130
Jonckheere, A.B., 134
Jones, E.E. and Thibaut,
J.W., 232
judgments, 167; of age,
232, of intention, 233;
moral, 221, 223-6, 233,
237, 238-9, 244

Kanizsa, G., 141
Kelly, E.L., 210
Kelvin, P., 8-9
Kendler, T.S. and H.H.,
55-7
King, M., 233
Klein, Melanie, 211
knowing, see cognition
knowledge: theory of, see
epistemology; see also
figurative, operative
knowledge
knowledge-as-assimilation/
-as-copy, 5-6
Koffka, K., 167
Kofsky, E., 94
Kohlberg, L., 224
Köhler, W., 167, 168
Kohnstamm, G.A., 94
Krantz, D.H., 162, 165, 166;
and Weintraub, D.J., 166
Künnapas, T.M., 160

Laing, R.D., 35
Lambercier, M., 136, 160
language, 52; acquisition,

4, 82-3, 86, 88, 90, 94,
96, 103, 106, 112, 179-
82, 208, 212-13, acqui-
sition device (LAD), 170,
180; and cognitive
development, 7, 177,
179, 183
Latané, H.A. and Darley,
F.L., 237
Law of Relative Centrations,
137-8, 148, 152, 154,
156-7, 160
learning, 3, 4, 30-1, 34,
85-6, 88, 104, 106, 167-
8, 177, 240-1; social,
see social learning
Legrenzi, P., 130
Liben, L.S., 240
Livesley, W.J. and Bromley,
D., 231
Locke, John, 147
logic, 22, 24, 25, 27, 33,
34, 51, 65, 70, 80, 121-
2, 130, 160, 224;
development, 53-63, 66
Looft, W.R., 225, 227, 232
Lunzer, E.A., 106, 123,
226; et al., 130-1

McClelland, D.C., 8
McGurk, E., 166
McLaughlin, G.H., 83, 96
McNeill, D., 179-80, 198
Maier, N.R.F., 55, 57
Martin, Susan, 62
Masangkay, Z.S., 227
maturation, 6, 38, 44, 233
Mead, George Herbert, 210,
233, 242
measurement, 24-6, 60, 62-3
mechanistic model, 2-3, 8
memory, 4, 37, 39, 51, 52,
61-2, 71-8, 82-3, 86-8,
90, 94, 96, 104, 106,
109, 112, 167-8, 170,
193, 198, 203-4, 226,
233, 240-1
Menyuk, P., 181

Merriot, P., 96
Michotte, A.E., 140, 142
Middleton, D., 213
Mikes, M. and Vlahović, P.,
   191
Milgram, N.A., 77
Millar, W.S., 241
Miller, E., 211
Miller, G.A. et al., 101
Miller, W.R. and Ervin, S.,
   179, 182
modelling, see imitation
Modgil, S., 82
moral evaluation, see judg-
   ments, moral
Morf, A., 160
mother-child interaction,
   208, 210-20, 225
motive, see causality
Müller-Lyer illusion, 137,
   148, 150-3, 155, 160,
   163, 165
Munsterberg illusion, 148,
   155

Neale, M.D., 88, 104
number, 20, 22, 24, 25-6,
   33, 34, 37-41, 45-6, 70-
   1, 76, 85, 212, 228, 237

objectivity, 3, 18-19, 21,
   27, 32, 47, 52
Obonai, T., 159
observation, 2-3, 10, 18,
   19-20, 28, 37, 40, 41,
   46-7, 67-8, 70, 155
Ollerearnshaw, C., 161-2,
   166
Olton, R.M., 166
operations, 66, 145-6; concrete, 51, 120-3, 125,
   133; formal, 117, 119-
   34, 168
operative knowledge, 5-6,
   52, 65-8, 70-2, 75-8, 80,
   82-3, 85, 94, 103-4, 106,
   117; and language com-

petence, 88, 90, 96, 112;
   and learning, 90; and
   memory, 88
operators, 65-6
operatory stage, 68-9, 71
Opie, Peter and Iona, 220-1
Oppel-Kundt illusion, 155
O'Regan, K., 61

Park, T.Z., 184-5
pathology, 18-19, 20
peer interaction, 223-4,
   225, 233, 244
perception, 4, 68-70, 72,
   75; haptic, 85, 90; and
   intelligence, 117-18,
   138, 145-8, 166-70
person perception, see children: perception of
   others
phantasy, 27, 42-3
phenomenalism, 146, 147,
   167-8
Piaget, Jean (mentions of
   Piaget in connection with
   specific topics are too
   numerous to be usefully
   listed here, and reference should be made from
   the topic concerned): as
   child psychologist, 3,
   39, 41, 54, 66; compared
   with Asch, 243-4; compared with Freud, 119;
   criticism of, 117, 136-
   70; as genetic epistemologist, 2-3, 22, 28,
   65, 119; influence on
   Bowlby, 211; signifi-
   cance of work, 2-4, 10,
   16, 22, 82, 137;
   works
   'Child's Construction of
   Reality' (1954), 58
   'Genetic Epistemology'
   (1970), 58
   'How Children Form Mathematical Concepts' (1953),
   60

'Logique et Equilibre dans les Comportements du Sujet' (1957), 102
'Mécanismes Perceptifs' ('Mechanisms of Perception') (1961), 136-70
'Moral Judgment of the Child' (1932), 210, 211, 221
'Piaget's Theory' (1970), 2, 3, 4, 5, 82, 203
'Principles of Genetic Epistemology' (1972), 121
works with collaborators
and Inhelder, B., 'Child's Conception of Space' (1956), 85; 'Mémoire et Intelligence' (1968), 227, 240
'Mental Imagery in the Child' (1971), 5-6
and Lambercier, M., 'Comparaisons Verticales à Intervalles Croissants' (1956), 160
and Morf, A., 160
and Stettler-von Albertini, B., 'Observations sur la Perceptions des Bonnes Formes chez l'Enfant' (1954), 141
and Vurpillot, E., 159
works as collaborator
with Inhelder, B., 'Early Growth of Logic in the Child' (1964), 94, 120-1
'Growth of Logical Thinking from Childhood to Adolescence' (1958), 122-3, 130
Picture Vocabulary Test, see English Picture Vocabulary Test
pivot grammar, 179-80, 182-3
Plato, 25, 34, 36, 37, 41, 168

Poggendorff illusion, 137, 148, 160-3, 165
Popper, Karl, 119, 155
preaching, 241
pre-operational thought, 51, 120, 123, 127, 146, 222
pre-operatory stage, 66, 68, 71
Press, A.N., 232
prestructure, linguistic, 195-8, 203, 240
Pribram, K.H., 101
problem-solving, 53, 132 167-8, 212-13, 215
process, 28, 31-2, 34, 38, 43, 45
propositional calculus, 117, 170
pro-social behaviour, 236-41, 244
psychoanalysis, 15, 16-20, 28, 31, 41-5, 47, 119, 211, 238
psycholinguistics, 177
psychology, 2-4, 10, 15; developmental, 7, 178, 208-9; and psychoanalysis, 16-20, 28, 31, 41-5
Pythagoras, 25

Rackstraw, S.J., 213
Raven's Progressive Matrices, 87-8
reading ability, 88, 104, 106, 109
reality, external, 5, 15, 16-19, 23, 28, 32-3, 35, 67-8, 70, 209
Reich, S.S., 130
Restle, F., 165
reversibility/irreversibility, 36-9, 77, 117, 120-1, 127-8, 132, 145, 168, 170, 189
Roberts, R.G. and Lunzer, E.A., 106
Robertson, S., 162-3
Robinson, J.O., 172

Robinson, W.P. and Rack-
straw, S.J., 213
role-playing, 223-4, 227-30,
234-6, 237, 238-40, 244
Rosen, C.E., 234-5
Rosenbaum, P.S., 192
Ross, B.M., 72
Ross, G., 213
Rousseau,Jean-Jacques, 10
Rubin, K., 228;　and
Schneider, S.W., 238-9
Ruger, H.A., 168
Rushton, J.P., 238, 241;
and Wiener, J., 238-9
Russell, Bertrand, 122

Sameroff, A.J., 3, 241
Sander parallelogram, 148
Sapir, Edward, 177
Sartre, Jean-Paul, 35
Scarlett, H.H. et al., 232
Schachter, F.F. et al.,
225, 229
Schaffer, H.R., 211
schematisation, 68-9, 71,
76, 143, 146, 168, 209-
10, 212, 233, 242
Schneider, S.W., 238-9
Schonel, F.J., 88
Scott, P.M., 211
Sears, R.R., 211
self/not-self differentiation, 186, 210-11, 226,
229
Selman, R., 224;　and Byrne,
D.F., 228
semantic intention and
linguistic competence,
181-6, 190-4, 196-7,
203-4
semantics in problem-
solving, 132
sensori-motor activities,
68-9, 143, 146, 167, 186-
7, 211, 222
seriation, 51, 85, 106, 109,
120, 212
Shapiro, D., 130

Sharp, D.W., 56
Shatz, M. and Gelman, R.,
225, 229, 231
Shipman, V.C., 213, 214
Sinclair (-de-Zwart),
Hermina, 94, 177, 187,
188, 189, 195, 201
Slobin, D.I., 185-6, 191-3,
198, 203
Smilansky, S., 234-5
social class, 123, 213
social learning, 211, 237,
239-41
social psychology, 7-8;
developmental, 178, 208-
11, 243-4
socialisation, 8-9, 208,
234, 240
Somerville, Susan, 58
Sonino Legrenzi, M., 130
Spitz, R.A., 211
S-R behaviourist tradition,
55
Staub, E., 236
Stettler-von Albertini, B.,
136, 141
structures, 3-5, 33, 40-2,
44-6, 65-8, 76-7, 82,
87-8, 99, 117, 119, 121,
194-5, 203, 209, 211,
212, 241
subject-object interaction,
3-4, 6, 29, 67, 70-1,
146, 242
subjectivity, 18-19, 21-2,
27, 47
surface structure (trans-
formational grammar),
128, 180, 193, 201
symbols, 67, 69-70, 94, 96,
99, 145, 170, 186
systems theory, 3
Szagun, Gisela, 240

Tajfel, H., 244
tenses, verbal, 177, 183,
187, 194-204
theories, 20, 155

Thibaut, J.W., 232
Thorndike, E.L., 168
Tong, L., 166; and Wein-
    traub, D.J., 162, 166
Tuddenham, R.D., 94
Trabasso, T., 61, 77-8
transformational grammar,
    86, 170, 177, 179-81,
    186, 192, 194
transformations, 6, 65, 67,
    71-2, 85, 170
transitivity, 51, 58-63, 66,
    77-80
transports, 139-43

unconscious, 18, 45
universals, linguistic, 180,
    182, 193-4

Van Duyne, Petrus, 131-2
Veldman, D.J., 104
verification/falsification,
    124, 128-9
Villiers, P.A. de and J.G.
    de, 227
Virsu, V. and Weintraub,
    D.J., 159
virtual lines, 141, 151,
    153, 158
visual illusions, 117, 137-
    8, 141, 147-70; secon-
    dary, 139-40, 141-2, 149,
    155, 160
Vlahović, P., 191
Vurpillot, E., 159
Vygotsky, L.S., 177

Wason, P.C., 130, 168;   and
    Johnson-Laird, P.N., 124;
    and Evans, J., 124;   and
    Golding, E., 128-9;   and
    Shapiro, D., 130
Watts Language Scale, 86
Weintraub, D.J., 159, 162,
    166;   and Krantz, D.H.,
    162, 165, 166
Welbeck, N.H., 239
Wenderoth, P., 159, 162
Werner, H., 10, 231-2
Whorf, Benjamin, 177
Wiener, J., 231
will, 17, 20, 31-3, 35, 42,
    44-6
Wittgenstein, Ludwig, 119
Wood, D. et al., 213
Woodward, M., 101
Wundt, W., 147, 159, 161

Yarrow, M.R. et al., 239
Youniss, J., 72

Zehender illusion, 159,
    161-2, 164-5
Zöllner illusion, 137, 148,
    153, 160-1